THE BODY IMAGE BOOK FOR GIRLS

UPDATED EDITION

LOVE YOURSELF AND GROW UP FEARLESS

DR. CHARLOTTE MARKEY

ILLUSTRATIONS BY TIM OLIVER

Shaftesbury Road, Cambridge CB2 8EA, United Kingdom

One Liberty Plaza, 20th Floor, New York, NY 10006, USA

477 Williamstown Road, Port Melbourne, VIC 3207, Australia

314–321, 3rd Floor, Plot 3, Splendor Forum, Jasola District Centre, New Delhi – 110025, India

103 Penang Road, #05–06/07, Visioncrest Commercial, Singapore 238467

Cambridge University Press is part of Cambridge University Press & Assessment,
a department of the University of Cambridge.

We share the University's mission to contribute to society through the pursuit of
education, learning and research at the highest international levels of excellence.

www.cambridge.org
Information on this title: www.cambridge.org/9781009545075

DOI: 10.1017/9781009545082

First published 2021
Updated edition published 2026

Illustrations by Tim Oliver

Printed in Great Britain by Ashford Colour Limited

A catalogue record for this publication is available from the British Library

A Cataloging-in-Publication data record for this book is available from the Library of Congress

ISBN 978-1-009-54507-5 Paperback

♥ For Grace, always ♥

An empowering, practical guide to help girls navigate the challenges of growing up and the many appearance pressures that can bring, this is a comforting, reassuring book that will benefit young and old alike. This is not another book written by an adult telling kids how to deal with things. It includes the voices and experiences of real young people, reducing the stigma and shame that can come with body image insecurities. It's packed with easily digestible, evidence-based advice and information, making a vast and nuanced topic accessible for all.

Molly Forbes, Founder and Executive Director of The Body Happy Organisation

Charlotte Markey has given a great gift to the world: a trusted guide to help girls feel good in their own skin and take care of their bodies rather than be at war with them. And this new edition couldn't have come at a better time, as young women are being bombarded with appearance pressures and wellness misinformation like never before. I wish everyone with a daughter could hand her this book.

Oona Hanson, Educator and Parent Coach

This book gives girls powerful, evidence-based tools that they can use to feel more positively about their bodies, take good care of themselves, and be agents for positive change in the world. These are important skills that they will carry with them throughout their entire lives.

Dr. Jessica M. Alleva, Assistant Professor of Psychology, Maastricht University, the Netherlands

Dr. Markey clearly knows how to motivate girls to rebel against harmful ideals and be more conscious, critical media consumers. Within the pages of this book, girls will find all the information they need to live more healthfully and happily.

Lexie and Lindsay Kite, PhDs and co-founders of Beauty Redefined

Dr. Markey has created an evidence-based, fun, and engaging book for girls. Each chapter addresses a critical body image issue and contains beautiful illustrations and valuable information in a readable, fun format. Body image is on all girls' minds and they need information on how to process it. Dr. Markey discusses this issue in a positive, health-oriented, down-to-earth way that is appealing to girls. Finally we have an excellent resource to share with girls about their bodies. Every girl should read this book!

Dr. Meghan Gillen, Associate Professor of Psychology, Penn State Abington

If you have a body, which I suspect you do, then you stand to learn something from The Body Image Book for Girls. Dr. Charlotte Markey expertly translates a complex body of scientific research into this accessible and beautifully illustrated book, interweaving the science of body image with the lived experiences of real girls.

Jamie Dunaev, PhD. Rutgers University, Camden

I enthusiastically recommend Dr. Markey's body image book for girls. This research-based book teaches girls how and why to appreciate their bodies. Girls will learn to resist the potentially negative influences of cultural encouragement of body comparison, the diet industry, and image-based social media with an informed and positive mindset. Chapters on the enjoyment of healthy food, the benefits of exercise, and the value of mindfulness activities offer girls many ideas for creating a positive body image. Each chapter is written in a concise, focused manner with goals and summaries to make the points clear. The solid research base is enlivened with illustrations, stories from real girls, and the debunking of common body-related myths. Dr. Markey provides references for more information, and a helpful glossary of important terms. Girls should leave this book feeling empowered to "be the change," as Dr. Markey encourages in the last chapter.

Sarah Murnen, Professor of Psychology, Kenyon College

This book uses scientific research to educate girls about the changes they will experience through puberty and to make recommendations about how they can care for their body. It treats girls as smart and capable and addresses issues girls face every day, for example, social media and dieting. Girls will gain useful tools for developing a positive view of their body and establishing healthy habits around eating and exercise. They will also learn strategies for staying positive about their own body despite social pressures about appearance. This book is a highly valuable resource that will help girls appreciate their bodies.

Elizabeth A. Daniels, Ph.D., Associate Professor of Psychology, University of Colorado

Charlotte Markey offers a comprehensive, direct and supportive guide for girls to build positive relationships with their bodies. Her friendly, conversational style will engage tween girls and support them to resist the disruptions in embodiment that are so common in the adolescent years.

Elizabeth Scott, LCSW, CEDS-S, Director of Training, The Body Positive

DR. CHARLOTTE MARKEY

is a body image scientist, having studied all things body image and eating behavior for nearly three decades. She is passionate about understanding what makes us feel good about our bodies and helping people to develop a healthy body image. Charlotte loves to share her body image wisdom with others and is an experienced book author, speaker, researcher, clinician, and professor at Rutgers University, Camden. She currently lives in Pennsylvania with her husband, Dan, and their dogs, Lexi and Zoe. For fun, she likes to run, swim, read, and visit her daughter and son, who are away at college, living fearless lives.

Other titles by Dr. Markey:

TABLE OF CONTENTS

Negative thoughts

How to Read This Book

This is a book about body image, but it is about more than that. It is a book about mental and physical health, and some of the topics I bring up can be challenging to consider. Some of the issues I discuss, such as eating disorders, social media, and relationships, may not be things that you are experiencing now but may affect you in the future.

You may hear about many of these topics from friends, at school, or online. Unfortunately, a lot of what you hear may be people's opinions and not based on science. My goal is to share the most accurate information with you in this book.

It's a great idea to read this book with a parent, another trusted adult, or an older sibling. If you are reading it alone and want to talk about any of the issues discussed in this book, don't be afraid to talk to someone who you feel comfortable with. Growing up can feel hard, and there are a lot of people who want to support you, but they don't always know how to help or what questions you may have. Use *The Body Image Book for Girls* to start meaningful conversations with your friends and others who care about you.

It is my greatest hope that this book helps you be a girl who loves herself and is fearless.

CHAPTER 1

WHAT IS BODY IMAGE?

#BodyImageBasics

"You are a
wonderful creation."

Oscar Wilde, Irish Poet
and playwright

Sage Elizabeth, 14 years old, she/her, UK

I'm not sure I've ever really liked my body. On some level, I know there's nothing wrong with my body, but it's just hard to really embrace it.

I think when I was 6 or 7, I started to not be as fond of my body. Around that time, I was bullied by this girl at school. She called me fat. At the time, I was devastated. Now I understand that she was just trying to be hurtful. It's the most basic and upsetting thing that people think they can say when they want to make you feel bad. It's actually very unoriginal when it comes to insults!

At school, popularity is linked with appearance. Being friends with the popular people increases your status, and the prettier girls are often the most popular. People want to be friends with these prettier people. The same thing happens on social media.

Online, all the people you see are perfect. They have perfect hair, perfect make-up, and perfect, skinny bodies. Of course, this is all supposedly "natural" beauty, but these people don't seem to exist in real life. Most of us just don't look like people do on social media. We all look different — we aren't all supposed to look the same!

Every now and then I think I want to change parts of my appearance, but I realize that I can't really change how I look. I have to learn to accept how I look. Some days I feel like I can focus on what I like about myself, but I have to be in the right headspace for that.

I wish I could tell my younger self that it's important to talk to other people when you're feeling dissatisfied with your body. Talking about all of this is underrated. I wish schools and parents talked more with kids about body image. Talking about my insecurities out loud has helped me to realize how ridiculous some of them are. Keeping those concerns inside your head allows them to grow.

Do you ever feel like you're too short (or too tall)?

Do you ever wish that your hair was straight and not curly?

Have you ever looked in the mirror and wished for longer legs?

Do you wish your breasts were larger (or smaller)?

If you've ever had a negative thought about your appearance, you're not alone. Most girls and women would like to change at least one thing about how they look – if not many.

Even celebrities – the people we often think of as looking "perfect" – often struggle with concerns about their appearance. Taylor Swift said, "I definitely have body issues, but everyone does." Actress Amandla Stenberg admitted that she gives herself body image pep talks while looking at herself in the mirror, and actress Lili Reinhart said, "I felt this strange, constant struggle of having to live up to the expectation of the appearance that I had already established to the world."

It's not just average people who think about their appearance and wish they could look different; it's almost everyone. The goal of this book is to help you develop a positive view of yourself. A positive view of yourself doesn't mean that you think you're better or more beautiful than everyone else. Lili Reinhart has also confessed that she thinks it is ridiculous that so many of us feel like we need to explain anything about our body to other people.

Your life isn't a beauty pageant. A positive view of yourself means learning to treasure and care for your body. You can achieve this goal, and this book will guide you along the way.

IN THIS CHAPTER YOU'LL LEARN:

○ how body image is defined

○ why it's important to have a **positive body image**, and

○ why reading this book and working on developing a positive body image will improve your life in a variety of ways.

What is body image?

Body image is how you think and feel about your body. But it is also much more than this. It is a part of your identity, and how you view yourself. Your body image affects your mental health and it can affect your behaviors. For example, if you dislike your curly hair, you may spend a lot of time trying to straighten it. If you wish you were taller, you may wear shoes with platform soles or high heels. If you really want your nose to be smaller, you may consider getting surgery to change the size or shape of it.

But what if there is a better way to think about your body? Maybe changing how you look isn't the answer. Maybe there is an easier way. **This book is full of information and advice about body image that will help you understand your body and develop positive feelings about it.**

Most women I know (including myself) wish they'd had this sort of information when they were girls your age.

Why I wrote this book

I have a daughter, and when I worked on the first edition of this book, she was about 12 years old. She actually read some of the chapter drafts and provided me with feedback about them. I remember desperately wanting her and her friends to have this book and to read it either on their own or with their moms, dads, sisters, cousins, and friends. I wanted a book that was full of helpful, **evidence-based information** that my daughter and her friends – and you and your friends – could turn to for answers to questions about body image and re ated topics, such as **nutrition** and physical activity.

Even though, as I write this, my daughter is 17 and my son is 19 years old, I still worry about them. Most moms worry about their kids, but sometimes I think it's worse as a parent when you know too much. With almost 30 years of experience as a **research scientist** studying eating behaviors and body image, I know all about the mistakes people make, and I don't want my kids to make those mistakes. I don't want you to, either.

There is a lot of bad information available about the topics I cover in this book. This bad information is dangerous and can lead to risky decisions. In fact, adults often don't do a good job of making sense of what to eat, how much to exercise, and when to go to sleep. This book can help you develop good habits while you're young – good habits that I hope will stick with you as you get older.

My goal in writing this book is to create a resource that you will refer to again and again as you become a teenager and young adult. I hope that you'll read it from cover to cover, but also pick it up when you have a question about something and you want a factual answer. Sure, you can google all the topics I cover in this book, but you'll find a lot of misinformation and myths about body image on the Internet. My goal is to provide you with **scientific evidence** about the issues I discuss, not just my opinions.

EXPERT ADVICE

Tracy Tylka, PhD, *body image expert, Professor at Ohio State University*

"Having a positive body image means that you appreciate your body, which helps you respect and care for it. You don't focus on how your body looks as much as how it feels and all the cool things it is able to do. It's so important to build a positive body image because it can help you feel good about yourself and cope with stress in healthy ways. Overall, a positive body image can offer peace of mind."

In each chapter, you'll find:

- **Reliable information:** I summarize the latest science on the topics covered in each chapter. If you see a word you don't know, check the glossary in the back of this book. As you read, remember you're a member of a large community that cares about these issues. I don't know any women who haven't been concerned about these issues, and talking about them can be helpful and empowering.

- **Q&A:** During my career, I've talked with hundreds of girls. For this book, I've asked them what questions they have about their bodies, eating, exercising, and all the other topics in this book. I provide factual answers to their questions – which are probably the questions you have, too.

Q&A ?!?

- **Myths and misbeliefs:** In each chapter, I'll share "**myths** and **misbeliefs**" about body image and related topics and explain why they aren't true.

Telling people that they need to lose weight or look better — "body shaming" — will motivate them to do so.

There is no evidence that this is true! In fact, it seems that the opposite is true!

People come in different shapes and sizes, and not everyone is going to have big feet or be tall or slender. You may think that someone should lose weight, but this is not necessarily true! Suggesting to a friend that you don't find her acceptable as she is may be a good way to lose that friend.

Making people feel bad about themselves is not "motivating." If you are concerned about a person's health or **well-being**, the last thing you should do is shame them. Instead, you should aim to be a supportive friend. For example, if you notice that you have a friend who spends a lot of time on **social media** and this leads her to feel depressed, you may want to suggest that she take a social media break. If a friend is trying to pick up a new activity, such as volleyball, you may want to offer to practice with her.

- **My story:** In the process of writing this book, I've relied on scientific research that takes into account hundreds and thousands of girls' experiences. But I've also interviewed individual girls between the ages of 14 and 22 to hear about their specific experiences in detail. In this chapter, I feature Sage and Graciela. Each chapter will feature other real girls' experiences in their own voices. **The more that we all talk about body image and learn from each other, the easier it will be to feel supported and to develop a positive body image.**

- **Inspiration:** When it comes to feeling good about our bodies, all girls and women can use some inspiration. Each chapter will contain quotes, illustrations, and bits of information to help you think about your body in a positive way – and maybe even laugh about some of these issues.

- **Expert advice:** I've had the opportunity to connect with many different types of experts, from scientists to journalists to Olympic athletes, who have helped me think more deeply about the issues discussed in this book and have offered words of wisdom to help you think more about these issues too.

- **Surveys and activities:** There are many body image scientists who have developed ways to measure and improve body image. Some of these surveys and activities will be included throughout the book to provide you with some hands-on ways of working to understand and improve your body image.

EXPERT ADVICE

Jason Wood, *speaker and author, Director of Community Engagement at ANAD (The National Association for Anorexia Nervosa and Associated Disorders)*

"Who doesn't want to wake up and be proud of what they see in the mirror? Sadly, we live in a society that often values physical appearance above all else. This, combined with unrealistic and unhealthy stereotypes and expectations around body image, can have a devastating impact on our mental health. We need to remember that our bodies are our one true home. Rather than punish them, we should love, or at the very least accept them, as they are."

BODY IMAGE GOALS

Take some time to think about these questions and write out your answers.

How would you describe your current body image?

What thoughts and beliefs about my body image do I want to change? (Note: this is not what you want to change about your body, but what *thoughts and beliefs* you want to work on.)

What are three goals that you have for yourself as you work toward a positive body image?

Note: This activity was adapted from an exercise developed by Nichole Wood-Barcalow, Tracy Tylka, and Casey Judge in their *Positive Body Image Workbook*.

- **Find out more: The information in this book is evidence-based and scientific in nature.** In other words, it's not just my opinion but is based on thousands of scientists' research and understanding of body image and the other topics discussed. If you want to read more about a topic, these references at the end of each chapter will be a good place to look.

I want you to grow up to be strong, independent, and powerful. **Once you know the facts about the smartest way to nurture your positive body image, nothing will be able to hold you back!**

Graciela Marie, 18 years old, she/her, USA

I'm fairly certain that my cultural background has influenced my body image. A lot of formative body image experiences took place while I was growing up in Cuba; I didn't move to the USA until I was 9. In Hispanic families, family are involved in everything, especially the women, and they talk about your body openly. There are contradictions in the feedback you get because food is an important part of the culture, and you're encouraged to eat. But then, if you gain weight – even as a child! – family will comment on that. It's just normalized for people to comment on others' bodies.

After I moved to the USA, I started to take ballet lessons. Everyone in my classes was smaller than I was (and younger and hadn't gone through puberty yet). I became somewhat self-conscious of my body and tried to eat less. I ended up losing just a little bit of weight, but it attracted a lot of attention. I can remember my step-dad's brother saying, "You look so good. Whatever you are doing, it is working!" Even back then, I understood that this meant that I didn't look good before, but now I did.

A lot of my family members have gotten plastic surgery. Growing up in the Miami area, the focus on appearance and specific beauty ideals is inescapable. It can feel necessary to have a curvy (but skinny!) body as a woman, a body that is unobtainable without cosmetic surgery. My godmother (my mom's best friend) has had a lot of plastic surgery.

I appreciate that my mom has always seemed confident about herself and has not obtained surgery. When my godmother would go on a diet, my mom would say that she felt sorry for her; a diet can take so much joy out of life. My mom didn't move to the U.S. until she was in her late 30s, so I don't think she feels the same way about the beauty culture in Miami as a lot of other people. I know she just appreciates being able to go to a supermarket and get whatever she needs. It wasn't like that back in Cuba. She also loves cooking, and we never got take-out growing up. During COVID, I started to cook with my mom, and we'd make a new meal each day. This helped me learn to love cooking and really enjoy and appreciate food in a way I hadn't before.

If I could offer younger girls advice, I'd tell them that their bodies are going to go through so many changes as they grow up. Try not to be upset about these changes because your body is what is keeping you alive and allowing you to enjoy your days. It is cruel to starve your body of what it needs or even to talk down to your body. Your body is not just something to be looked at; it is so much more than that.

SUMMING UP #BodyImageBasics 

- Body image is sometimes defined as how you think and feel about your body.
- Your body image may affect your physical health, your mental and emotional well-being, and your health behaviors.
- Understanding your body image and knowing how to develop a positive body image will benefit you throughout your entire life.

FIND OUT MORE:

- *Fat Chance, Charlie Vega* is a book by Crystal Maldonado (2022, published by Holiday House) about a girl who struggles with her body image growing up. Her story is fun and inspiring to read.
- *The Skin I'm In* by Sharon Flake (1998, published by Little, Brown and Company) is another story of a young girl growing up and struggling to feel comfortable with herself. She learns a lot that you'll enjoy reading about.
- *Every Body: Celebrate, Respect, and Accept ALL Bodies – Especially Your Own* by Molly Forbes (2024, published by Puffin Books) is a book very much like *The Body Image Book for Girls*. If you want more information similar to what you see in this book, check out *Every Body*!
- References that support this chapter's content and additional resources can be found at the book's companion website: www.TheBodyImageBook.com.

CHAPTER 2

BODIES CHANGE

#GrowingUp

"Change is the law of life.
And those who look only to the past
or present are certain to miss
the future."

John F. Kennedy, 35th President of
the United States

Sabrina Ruth, 16 years old, she/her, USA

I feel pretty comfortable in my body these days, although I experience bursts of insecurity. I feel like I understand my body and what I need to do to feel pretty good psychologically and physically.

The pandemic and puberty collided for me when I was about 12. I noticed that my body was changing, and I found myself comparing my body to other people's. It's like I was trying to figure out what was going on for me. And then before you knew it, we were all in lockdown. Life moved online, and so did the people I compared myself to. I also had more time inside my own head, which I wouldn't say was ideal for my body image. The fact that TikTok really became popular around this time was also probably not ideal.

Social media definitely has contributed to my sense of what an ideal body looks like. Of course, there are celebrities on social media, but there are also girls my own age. Trying to be like the girls I see on social media who are my age feels like it should be possible, but I know it is unrealistic. Also, when you get to know someone in real life, you may pay attention to how they look, but the more you get to know them, the more their personality matters. On social media, you don't really get to know people, so it stays about appearances.

Recently, in art class, we were drawing each other's faces. It was interesting how my perception of someone's face rarely matched up exactly with the person whom I was drawing. People would tell me that they thought their face was wider or their eyes were smaller. It made me realize that, as an observer and artist, I create a holistic impression of another person. But as individuals, we tend to zoom in on our negative qualities and focus on pieces of ourselves and not our entire being. So much of how we view ourselves is subjective.

I think when we're growing up and our bodies are changing, it's hard to appreciate that it's normal to feel some insecurity — most people do! But then you start to feel more comfortable with yourself and realize that everybody is different. There are qualities you have that other people don't and some people probably envy you. People always want what they don't have.

What is puberty?

I'm sure you've heard the word **puberty**, but maybe you aren't sure exactly what it means. The word puberty comes from the Latin word *pubescere*, which means "to grow hairy." You probably already know (and maybe you've already experienced for yourself) that growing up does include getting hairier, but there's more to it than that.

IN THIS CHAPTER YOU'LL LEARN:

○ about the changes you will experience during puberty,

○ how puberty may affect your body image, and

○ how to cope with the physical changes you experience during puberty and keep a positive view of yourself.

What changes during puberty?

Skin

You've probably noticed that as kids become teenagers, they sometimes get pimples, or spots. This is related to changes in your skin that all teens experience. It's normal for your skin to get rougher and drier in some places, but also oilier in other places. This oiliness may lead you to break out and develop red bumps and patches on your skin. Pimples, or spots, can be a cause for concern or **self-consciousness** among teens, but in most cases they're treatable. Be sure to wash your face with a soap specifically intended for your face. These can be found in nearly any drugstore or grocery store. You may also want to treat pimples with a cream that contains **salicylic acid** or **benzoyl peroxide**. Both can cause your skin to get drier. If this doesn't help, you can ask your doctor (perhaps a **pediatrician** or a **dermatologist**, a doctor that specializes in skin care) for a more powerful skin treatment.

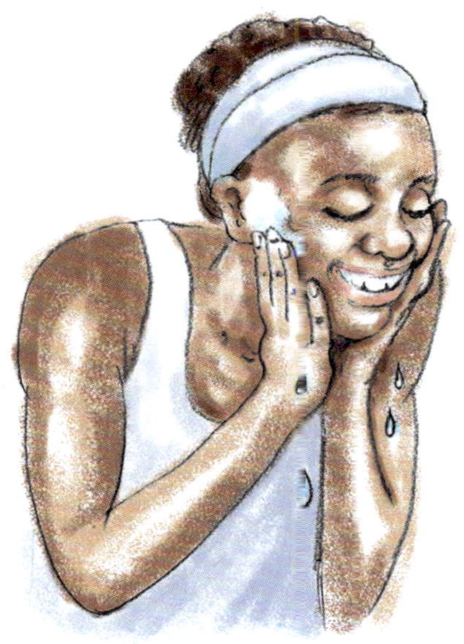

Changes in your skin also contribute to your likelihood of sweating more and having **body odor** (BO) more often. Most of the sweat occurs under

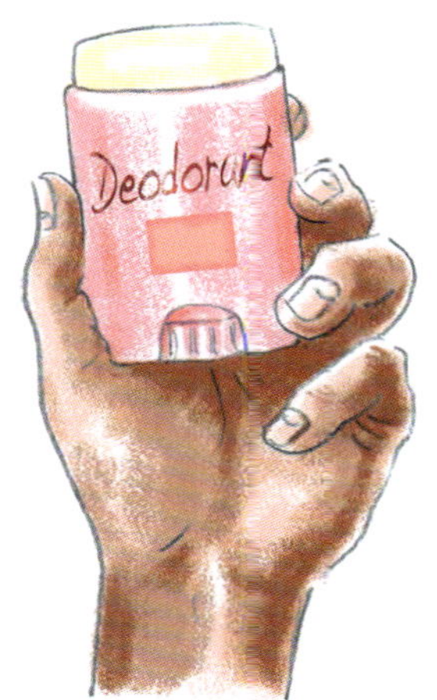

your arms, and deodorant can greatly help reduce the likelihood of smelling bad. If you don't like the smell of one particular deodorant, or it doesn't seem to work for you, then try another kind. There are tons of options to consider.

Eating chocolate can cause you to break out.

It seems pretty unfair that something as delicious as chocolate could make you break out in spots or pimples. Fortunately, this is mostly a myth. I say "mostly" because scientists have found that what you eat can affect your skin. Eating **nutritious** foods, including plenty of fruits and vegetables, can help your skin look healthier and may prevent breakouts. Some scientific research suggests that when people eat a lot of sugar and simple carbohydrates ("carbs," found in white bread and other **processed foods** like chips, or crisps), they may have an increased risk of getting **acne**. However, acne is caused by the many changes occurring in the body during **adolescence**, so a healthy diet may not prevent acne. In general, you probably shouldn't think about what you eat as a factor in how your skin looks.

Bones, heart, and lungs

Even body parts that don't seem related to puberty are affected by it. For example, your bones grow in length (how do you think you get taller?) and they become thicker. Your skeleton will be about twice the weight at the end of puberty as it was at the start, as you grow taller and your bones become stronger.

Your heart also nearly doubles in size over the course of puberty. This allows your heart to beat more slowly while still pumping blood as well as it did when you were younger. Your lungs also get much larger, which allows oxygen to move through your body more effectively. Overall, these physical changes can make you taller, bigger, and stronger. They can even make you more capable of doing well at a variety of sports.

Hair

Hair creeps up in all sorts of places when you go through puberty. This may be one of the first things you notice when you begin puberty. It may begin with a few hairs under your arms, or **pubic hair**, or hair on your legs, and maybe even on your face. Your hair also gets thicker and darker. Some of this new hair may be the same color as the hair on your head, but some may be a different color.

Often, girls and women will remove some of this newly appearing hair, but you absolutely do not have to do this. There are no health reasons for doing so, and body hair is completely natural and normal. Ask an adult you trust about this, whether it be your mom or dad, an older sister, an aunt, or a grandma. (Of course, you can talk to your friends about puberty, but friends may not always be as reliable and useful a resource as an adult.)

If you decide to remove body hair, there are lots of ways to go about it; two of the most common are shaving and **waxing**. Each has its pros and cons. Shaving can remove unwanted body hair quickly, but it's easy to accidentally cut yourself with a razor, so be careful. Before shaving body hair, be sure to consult with someone or look for a helpful YouTube video. Hot wax is also used for body hair removal. Usually, a professional will apply wax to unwanted hair, and when the wax is removed, the hair is also.

Keep in mind that a desire to get rid of hair probably comes from what you've learned from the people and **media** around you. In some cultures, hair removal isn't part of growing up. It's primarily in Western cultures that hair removal is common.

Breasts

A normal part of puberty for girls is breast growth. As you've probably noticed, some women have smaller breasts and some have larger breasts. You can't know how you're going to turn out until you've finished puberty, but your breasts will change at least a little bit. On average, breast development isn't finished for most girls until they're 16 or 17 years old. Scientists and doctors tend to describe breast growth in five stages. Basically, the process of going from a child's to a woman's breasts involves changes in both the **nipple** (which gets bigger) and the tissue surrounding and underneath the nipple (which also gets bigger). One of the first changes some girls notice to their breasts is often called **breast budding**, which is when a sensitive mound of tissue develops under the nipple when girls are around 8 or 9 years of age. These changes may occur at the same time for both breasts, or they may not. In fact, many women's breasts are not exactly the same size, and they may change slightly in size during the menstrual cycle (explained below).

Not every girl has the same experiences in terms of changes to their breasts. Changes may occur so slowly that you don't even realize they're happening, or they may occur so quickly that you grow out of shirts after a couple of months. As your breasts grow, you will probably notice them more. Running, for example, can cause breasts to move up and down in a way that's new to you. Many girls and women use special underwear to support their breasts. This may be a fitted tank top, a "**cami**," or a bra. There are a lot of options, and you should find what's comfortable for you. Even if you don't feel like you need the support, you may feel more comfortable with an extra layer between your breasts and your shirts.

A lot of the breasts you see on television, in movies, or even clothed in social media images may not look like your breasts and may not look very realistic. Those breasts may not be real! They may be **photoshopped**, edited, or enhanced through **cosmetic surgery**. Most women's breasts are not perfectly symmetrical (the exact same size and shape as each other) and they may seem floppy, flabby, smaller, or bigger than what you see in the media. Don't worry – you are perfectly fine just as you are!

There are five stages of breast development, as shown on this page, which are often called "Tanner stages" after the doctor (James Tanner) who first identified them. These stages are used by doctors and researchers to identify breast development. (There are also five stages of development for girls' and boys' genital areas.)

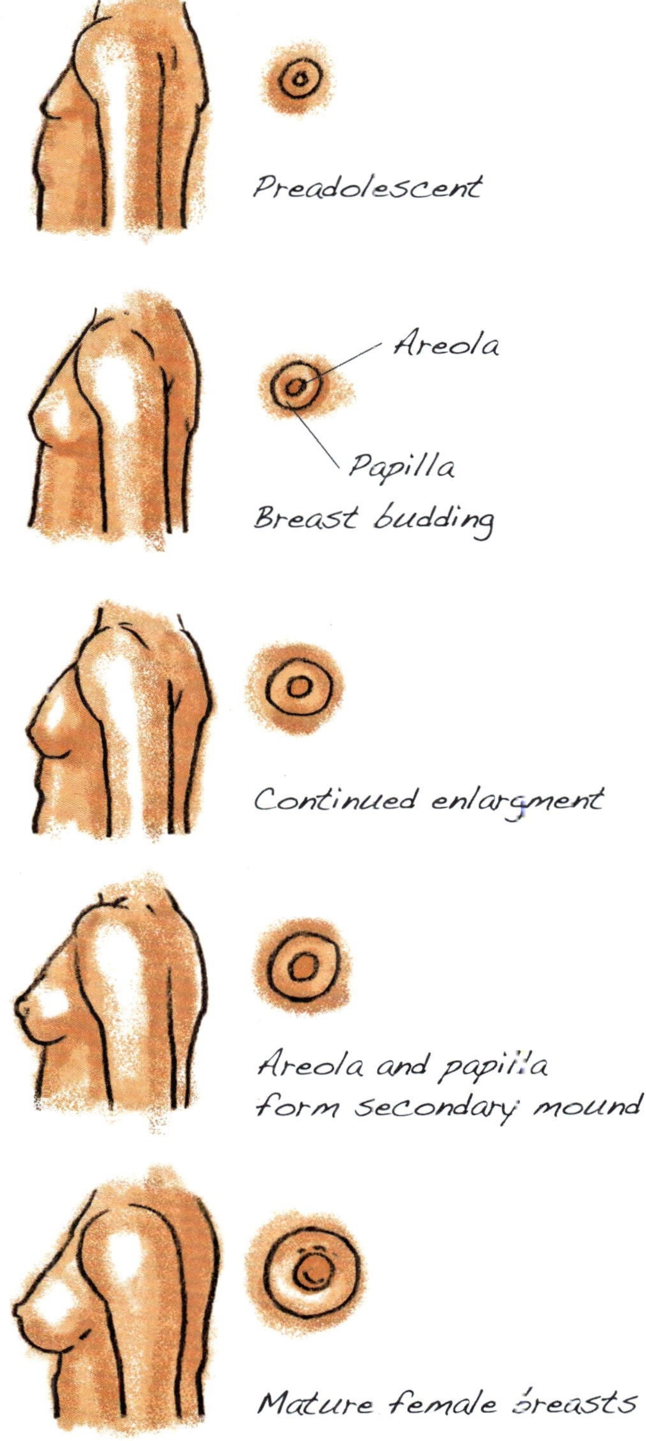

Genitals

Your **genitals** will also change during puberty. Unless you spend a lot of time looking at them with a mirror, you may not notice a lot of the changes that take place in your **vaginal** area. Some of the changes are hidden by the growth of pubic hair that will cover some of this area. (By the way, it's totally normal to be curious and get a mirror out to look.)

The primary changes include growth of the **labia majora** and **labia minora**. These external organs are together referred to as the **vulva**. These parts help to cover up and protect the urethra (where urine comes out) and vaginal opening (where **menstrual blood** comes out; more on this below). The **clitoris** also grows during puberty; the clitoris is the primary source of female sexual pleasure. The color of the vulva also deepens so that what was once similar in color to the rest of your skin is now typically a darker color.

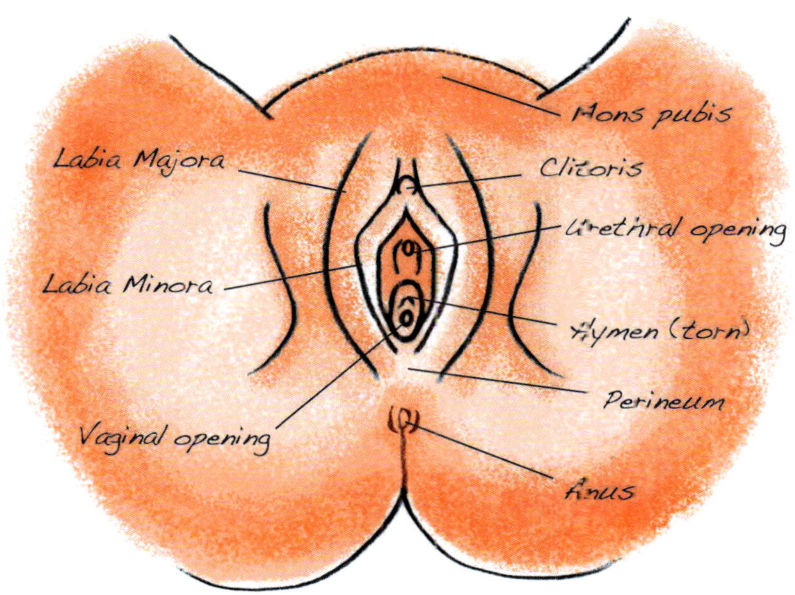

EXPERT ADVICE

Dr. Gemma Sharp, *Professor of Neuroscience, Monash University, Australia*

"Having a positive relationship with our bodies, including our genitalia, is really important for how we feel about ourselves overall and how we interact with other people. Unfortunately, young girls may not receive crucial information about the appearance, anatomy, and function of their own genitalia, which can leave them unnecessarily confused and worried about this crucial body part. I would like young girls to know that their genitals are just as important as any other body part. And, just like other body parts, they come in all shapes, sizes, and colors."

Hormones

Up until puberty, girls' and boys' **hormones** are very similar. This changes during puberty. At puberty, girls' levels of hormones, particularly female-specific hormones, increase dramatically.

Sometimes parents and other adults will say that the moodiness that develops during puberty is due to hormone changes. This may be partially true, but it's likely an overly simple explanation for a lot of the complicated changes that take place during puberty. For example, it's possible that you may feel hungry soon after eating, or tired despite sleeping a lot, due to changes in your hormones. In turn, hunger and fatigue may make you grouchy. Or maybe you feel **stressed** because you haven't been getting along with your friends at school and you don't have classes with the people you wish you did. Some of this may be related to your hormones, but a lot of it may not be. The **bottom line** is that you shouldn't feel like your life is out of control due to hormone changes that you can't help. **Your hormones play a really important role in your development, but they don't control everything.**

Your first period

Part of what is concerning about getting your period is not knowing what to expect and being worried that your experiences aren't "normal." Here are some things to be aware of when you get your period for the first time:

- It may not look like blood at all.
- It may be brown, thick, and goopy (when blood is exposed to oxygen, it oxidizes and changes color).
- You may see a brown stain on your underwear and not notice anything else.
- It may happen very irregularly and not occur again for a while, or it may occur again very soon.
- You may not realize it is happening.
- You may feel cramps or achy in your pelvic area, or even in your back.
- You may be 8 years old or 16 years old (but the average age is 12–12.5 years old).

Be sure you talk to someone – your mom, a doctor, an aunt, or even a teacher – if you have any questions or concerns. All women understand that this is a new experience and can be nerve-wracking and challenging to deal with.

Menstruation

Menstruation, or getting your menstrual period (aka your **period**), is a pretty big deal. Some girls worry because they don't know when it's going to happen for the first time. You may feel excited to get your period, or you may feel worried about this change. Either way, it's important to understand what your period is and what you can do to prepare for it.

At some point during puberty, your body will start to prepare for the day when you may want to have a baby. Don't worry! You probably don't want to consider having a baby until you're in your 20s, 30s, or 40s, but your body gets ready ahead of time (just 100 years ago it was common for girls to start having babies and families in their teens – that's less common now because girls often spend more years in school). In order for an egg to be fertilized by sperm and develop into a baby, eggs have to be released from your ovaries. This is called ovulation. You're born with all your eggs sitting there in your ovaries, where they remain until puberty. Then, once a month (about every 28 days) an egg is released. The egg travels down the **fallopian tube** and into your **uterus**, where it remains for a day or two. If it isn't fertilized by sperm, it flows out of your body through your vagina. These eggs are tiny, so you're unlikely to ever see one when this happens. What is all of the blood associated with getting your period? A blood-like substance lines your uterus in preparation for the possibility of a fertilized egg growing into a baby. If the egg is fertilized, this lining offers it protection and **nourishment**. However, if an egg is left unfertilized, this blood-like lining is not needed. Your uterus sheds this lining, and the lining plus your egg flow out through your vagina.

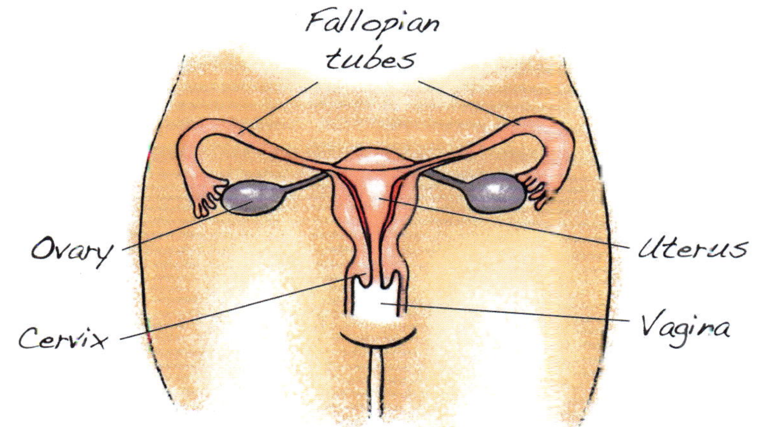

When you first get your period, you may notice that the blood is not quite red but more of a brownish color. You may see little spots of brown or red on your underwear (sometimes called spotting). During the first year or two of having your period, it's usually not quite "regular." You may experience a lot of blood flow on some days and not on others. You may get it every 25 days or every 60 days. This is all totally normal and nothing to be alarmed about. Girls usually settle into a regular pattern after the first year or two of having their period. If you don't, and the unpredictability of getting your period is stressful to you, this is a good thing to talk to your doctor about (either a pediatrician or a **gynecologist**, the type of doctor that takes care of girls' and women's **reproductive health**). Sometimes, medications can be used to help create regular menstrual cycles.

Girls can have very different experiences when it comes to getting their periods. Some may experience some cramps in their lower stomach. Some may experience lower back pain. Some may feel tired or cranky, and some may feel full of **energy**. Some will experience a lot of bleeding, and some will experience hardly any at all. Your body is different from everyone else's.

All girls can benefit by being prepared for their first period. You don't want blood to stain your underwear and clothes. There are a growing number of options for how to handle these practical issues that come with getting a period. It may be easiest when you first get your period to use a **pad** that you can stick to your underwear. The bottom side of these pads typically have a sticker-like surface that mostly keeps them from moving around. Once a pad gets moist with blood, you'll want to change it – usually a few times per day.

Another option is to use a **tampon**. Tampons are almost like a (small) stopper or plug you'd use to keep the water from going down the drain in a bathtub, but they're made of a substance that resembles the top of a Q-tip (aka cotton bud). A tampon is inserted into your vagina and will absorb the blood while keeping any from leaking out. Girls often find that tampons with plastic applicators are easier to use than tampons without applicators or with paper/cardboard applicators. (The front of any box of tampons will describe which type they are.) These also need to be changed a few times a day. Using a tampon for the first time can be a challenge,

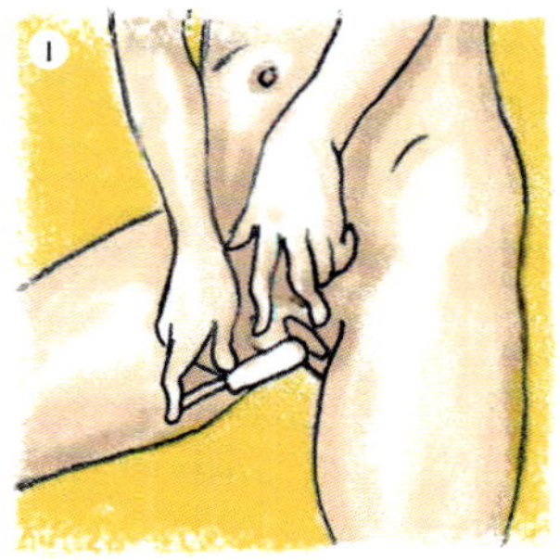
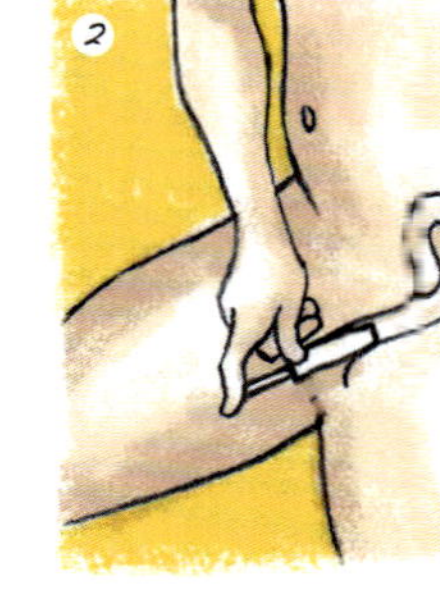
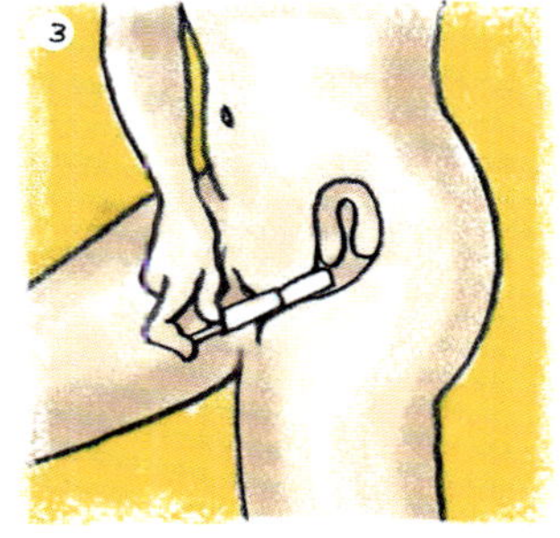
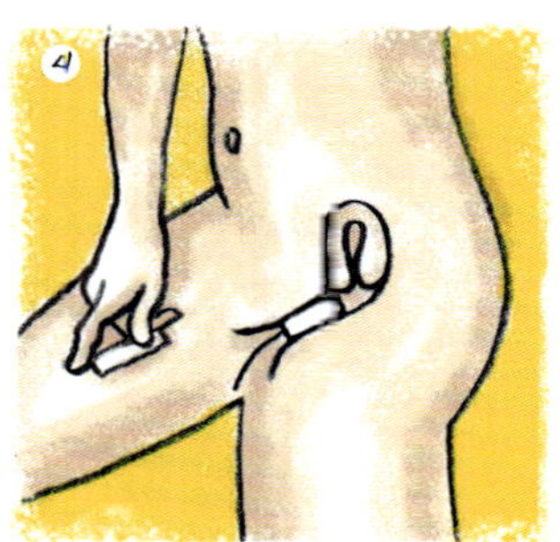

and you may want advice from someone who uses them. Tampons are generally very safe. This is why many women use them. However, it's important to change tampons regularly. There is a very small chance you could develop a bacterial infection (called toxic shock syndrome) if you don't change your tampon regularly.

Some girls and women use menstrual/period cups. These may be a bit trickier to use than a pad or a tampon because they need to be sort of folded up and then inserted into your vagina to catch the blood flow. They are removed and emptied a couple of times per day, or as needed. One of the benefits of using a cup is that it can be cleaned and reused day after day and month after month and so has less environmental impact.

Period cups

Disposable menstrual products like pads may seem cheaper and easier than reusable products, but they create a lot of waste. In the long run, they cost more than reusable products as well.

Another option is **period underwear**. These are underwear with built-in padding in the crotch. The advantage of period underwear is that the padding doesn't move around the way a removable pad can. The disadvantage is that, as you can imagine, this underwear needs to be cleaned really well between uses. Usually, this means rinsing them out in the sink and also washing them in a washing machine. They can also be fairly expensive (US$20 or more per pair).

Q&A

Q&A 

Every girl seems to worry about where they'll be when they first get their period. The problem, of course, is that there's no way to know. People around you understand this. If you're at school or camp, there is most likely a nurse who'd be more than happy to help you and will have pads and other supplies available. All female teachers and counselors have been through what you're going through at some point n their life, so they understand and are happy to help or to direct you to someone who can, like a nurse.

If your mom and dad live separately, and you're at your dad's house, you can always call your mom or another woman — a step-mom, aunt, grandma, or even a friend's mom — if you need help, or if you just want to talk to someone. You can also try to talk to your dad. He hasn't had the experience of getting a period, but he surely knows something about all of this and might be happy to talk to you. He is probably expecting this will be happening for you at some point soon, and he may just surprise you by being really helpful.

EXPERT ADVICE

Dena Moes, RN, CNM, author of *It's Your Body*

"It is important to develop healthy boundaries about your developing body. Spend time with people with whom you feel safe talking about your feelings, people who respect and consider you. Romantic partners may come and go, but your relationship with yourself is going to last a lifetime. Your number one love affair will be <u>you</u> with <u>you</u>."

Q&A

Some girls have told me that they're afraid to use tampons when they first get their period. It can be embarrassing to try to figure out something so personal, even if you have the advice and support of a good friend or another woman. Most boxes of tampons come with good instructions that include illustrations. The drawing in this book may also be helpful. Most tampons have an applicator to help you insert the tampon into your vagina. Once a tampon is in place, you won't feel it if it's securely in your vagina. This whole idea may seem strange at first and may require some practice to get right.

A lot of girls and women like tampons better than other options because they're hidden and allow participation in activities like swimming and gymnastics. Pads can feel bulky and would be seen in most bathing suits (and would absorb a lot of water, making them not really work in a pool), but tampons can allow you to sometimes forget you even have your period. However, it's important that you remember to change your tampons at least a few times per day, and more often (every couple of hours) if you have a heavy flow.

What's normal?

What sometimes gets missed in all the discussions of puberty and the physical changes is that every girl is unique. **No two girls' experiences are exactly the same and no two bodies are exactly the same.** If you get your period before you notice a growth spurt, that's OK. If you get pimples after you notice a growth spurt, that's OK, too. If you're 13, and you don't notice much about your body that has changed, there's nothing to stress about.

It's not uncommon for girls to notice some signs of puberty as early as 8 years of age, and it's also perfectly normal for girls to not have completed puberty until they're 16 years old. The majority of girls will start puberty before they turn 10, but that doesn't mean that these changes are necessarily visible (they may be just internal hormone changes). Most girls will begin to get their period around 12 years of age. There are many factors that influence when you will experience puberty, from your genes (aka biological factors) to your cultural environment. Your puberty experiences and the timing are out of your control. But it's important that you understand what to expect and are prepared for the changes that you'll experience.

The number on the scale

It's important for you to know that you will gain weight during puberty, and your body shape will change. This is totally normal. Everything about you is getting bigger, even your heart. Plus, you're probably going to be at least a few inches taller at the end of puberty. One estimate is that girls gain an average of 25 pounds (about 11 kg) during puberty.

Q&A

It's completely normal for your body to have wider hips; this is part of becoming a woman. Some girls like how their bodies change during puberty and some girls don't. Sometimes, it just takes getting used to your new body. If you feel upset about how your body has changed, it's a good idea to talk to someone about this, such as your friends, who will be having similar experiences. Talk to your mom or an aunt or another adult that you trust. If you feel like you want to talk to an expert, your doctor, school nurse, a counselor, or a therapist can be very helpful.

After high school

For most girls, puberty will be completed during your teen years, but this doesn't mean that your body stays the same for the rest of your life. There are a variety of things that can affect your hormones, and your body in general. Your weight will likely fluctuate from week to week and year to year. There are a lot of reasons for these fluctuations: changes in eating habits, **stress**, the amount you exercise, how much you sleep, changes in hormones, and even just your age (people tend to gain weight with age, even past puberty). Some day you may want to have a baby

EXPERT ADVICE

Dr. Zachary Souillard, *Assistant Professor of Psychology at Miami University and Director of the Body Image and Stigma among Queer Populations (BISQue) Lab*

"Body image diversity among young girls is the norm, not the exception. There's no one 'correct' way for girls to express their femininity or gender identity via their physical appearance. By embracing body image diversity from a young age, girls can challenge the rigid standards of beauty placed upon them and, instead, learn to celebrate the beauty in bodies of all different sizes and shapes."

and your body will change in dramatic ways again. Changes can sometimes make people anxious, but it's healthy to think of your body's ability to adjust and change in so many ways as pretty amazing.

How is this related to body image?

Research shows that most girls' understanding of themselves and their body image develops right around the same time that their bodies are changing due to puberty. These changes are likely to affect body image. Some scientists have suggested that because girls tend to gain weight and "fill out" during puberty (in other words, they're less likely to be lanky or skinny after puberty), they're also less likely to feel good about their bodies after puberty. It doesn't have to be this way. It's important to realize that changes to your body shape, growing taller, and gaining weight are all a normal part of growing up.

Self-acceptance

I discuss **self-acceptance** a lot more in the next chapter, but it's important to think about it in terms of puberty and the changes that will occur to your body as you age. To some, it feels completely natural to grow bigger and to mature, but to others, body changes feel strange and even embarrassing. **Remember that it's completely normal for your body to change as you age.** Even if you aren't sure you like all the changes that have occurred, there's nothing to be embarrassed about. There are great books written about puberty for girls that you can find in a library or online. (Be careful not to rely on the Internet too much; not all the information online is accurate.) Consult these books if you have further questions, and don't hesitate to talk to a trusted adult like a mother, father, sister, aunt, cousin, or even your doctor. Everyone goes through puberty eventually, and everyone has some questions about it, so no one will think any less of you for asking.

Twig Hill, 22 years old, she/her, USA

I am happier with my body image now than I probably ever have been. Being around more people who find all sorts of bodies beautiful has really helped me to internalize self-acceptance. Since I've been in college and found others that I relate to there and in online spaces, I feel much happier. I've also been on hormone therapy for almost a year now and that has changed a lot.

I had been wanting to start hormone therapy, but I had been really anxious about telling my parents about it. My parents are really accepting people, and they knew that I wasn't **cisgender**, but it was still hard to tell them for some reason. I finally built up the courage to tell them and they were really supportive of me! Fortunately, my university has a really streamlined process to make it possible to start HRT (**hormone replacement therapy**) faster than I expected.

It is strange to be in your 20s and going through a second puberty, but this time I'm much happier with what's happening to my body. I'm a little bit worried about breast cancer as I develop breasts, but I like putting on some weight and developing a bit of softness. I am glad to have a bit of a pudge in my tummy and weight in new places. My body feels more feminine to me. I hate how beauty ideals for women are so skinny when I really think that bodies with a good amount of fat look more real and more attractive.

Adolescence was rough for me because I was geeky and insecure, and, honestly, because other kids can suck and be mean. Growing up with lingering elements of **gender dysphoria** was hard because I didn't know that a lot of my experiences were atypical. It's like when I got new glasses and I realized the whole world was less blurry all of a sudden. Coming to terms with my **gender identity** was like that. Things made sense in a new way.

I never got the handbook on how to be a girl, but I'm learning. I'm working to change my name legally. Looking back, I wish I had known where I was heading, and that life would get so much better. I felt like a loser when I was an adolescent, but I think being yourself is more important than not being a loser. And you are not a loser to everyone, even if you aren't accepted by some people.

SUMMING UP #GrowingUp 

 Many aspects of your body will change during puberty. Some changes include getting taller, growing stronger bones and lungs, developing breasts, and getting your period.

Many aspects of your body will change during puberty. Some changes include getting taller, growing stronger bones and lungs, developing breasts, and getting your period.

It's completely normal to experience all the physical changes caused by puberty, but you may not necessarily experience them in the same ways that your friends do, or at the same time.

It's important to focus on accepting the physical changes that take place during puberty and maintain a positive body image. Reach out to trusted adults for guidance about any of the changes that you need help dealing with.

🔍 FIND OUT MORE:

- ✦ ***It's Your Body: The Young Woman's Guide to Empowered Sexual Health*** by Dena Moes (2024, published by Countrymen Press) contains so much easy-to-read information about your health that will empower you now and in the future.
- ✦ ***Celebrate Your Body (And Its Changes, Too!)*** by Sonya Renee Taylor (2018, published by Rockridge Press) will answer many of the questions you have about puberty.
- ✦ If you're looking for information about puberty and sexual health, check out: ***It's Perfectly Normal: Changing Bodies, Growing Up, Sex, Gender, and Sexual Health*** by Robie H. Harris and Michael Emberley (2021, published by Candlewick Press). I love the scientific detail and honesty in Robie Harris' books about growing up and you will, too.
- ✦ ***This is So Awkward: Modern Puberty Explained***, by Cara Natterson and Vanessa Kroll Bennett (2023, published by Rodale Books), is meant for adults but explains many aspects of pubertal development in an easy-to-follow manner. If you want more detail and scientific information about puberty, you may want to check out this book.
- ✦ Many books about puberty can be found in your local library, but don't be afraid to ask an adult to purchase these for you. For more scholarly articles and web pages with information about puberty, see the companion website for this book: www.TheBodyImageBook.com.

LOVE YOUR BODY

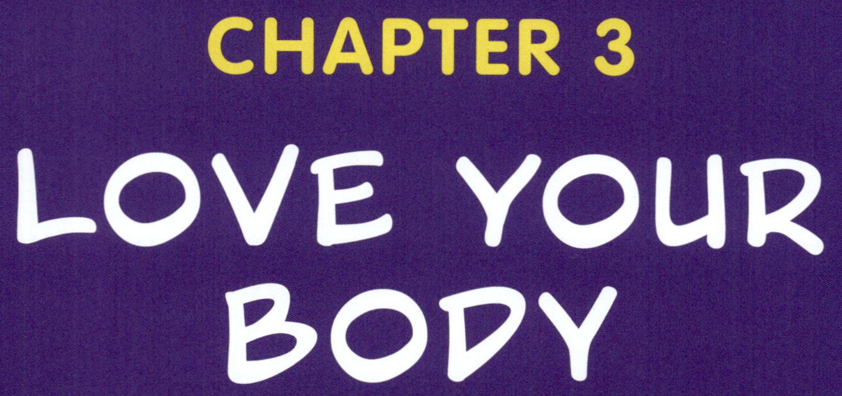

April Meyers, 14 years old, she/her, USA

I've been on the skinnier side my whole life, so in a way I guess I'm lucky. I've never felt "fat." However, I've always felt too skinny, and that my "stick arms and legs" were awkward and ugly. This makes me super self-conscious in bathing suits and tank tops. I've also always felt that my stomach "wasn't flat enough" and that I had too large of a stomach. I can find something wrong with every part of my body.

Over time I've realized that hating yourself shouldn't be the default. Although that's what's portrayed as normal in the media, it's not healthy. Everyone should love themselves no matter what. Even when I'm still uncomfortable with the way I look, I try to have this mindset, and then I feel better.

Something that has helped me understand I'm not as awkward and ugly as I feel is comparing myself to others. Not in a "Look at that girl, I'm prettier than her" way, because that's wrong and you should never, ever bring down other girls. But I find myself thinking, "Look, you think she's beautiful and she looks very similar to you, so why don't you think the same about yourself?" That has helped me realize that I'm just as beautiful as I think every other girl is.

I've thought a lot about how to talk with other girls about body issues: Don't comment on their body. Period. A good rule to live by is: If they can't change it within five minutes, don't mention it. That means that you can let your friend know they have something on their face or shirt but cannot tell them that "they are not too fat." Even if you think something is neutral or a compliment, still don't say it. You never know when you could hurt someone's feelings, and being a good friend is all about being supportive.

Sometimes I think your mind can be your worst enemy, and no one actually thinks about how you look except for yourself. Once you conquer the voices in your head, and convince them you're beautiful, no one can stop you.

Does anyone truly feel good about their body?

If you look on Instagram or TikTok, it seems like everyone is trying to change their bodies. Most people aren't all that satisfied with what they see when they look in the mirror, at least not after they hit adolescence.

Can you *learn* to feel good about your body? We don't think much about our bodies when we're young children, but as adolescence approaches, we begin to be critical. We wish our legs were longer or our bottoms bigger (or smaller). We wish for clearer skin and bigger (or smaller) breasts. But why? Long legs, or small bottoms, or clear skin don't make us smarter or nicer people. The desire for these physical features is learned. What has been learned can be *unlearned*.

IN THIS CHAPTER YOU'LL LEARN:

- some tips to help you stay positive about your body,
- the importance of protecting your body and keeping others from being negative influences on your body image, and
- the difference between **adaptive appearance investment** and caring too much about your appearance.

There is good scientific evidence that you can improve how you feel about your body. You can even LOVE your body. (At least a lot of the time!) It's not about changing your body so that you look more like Beyoncé or Taylor Swift. It's about changing how you think about your body. In an interview in *Seventeen* magazine, Emma Stone said, "My great hope for us as young women is to start being kinder to ourselves so that we can be kinder to each other. To stop **shaming** ourselves and other people for things we don't know the full story on – whether someone is too fat, too skinny, too short, too tall, too loud, too quiet, too anything. There's a sense that we're all 'too' something, and we're all not enough."

So how can you start feeling like enough? I have some ideas!

EXPERT ADVICE

Dr. Mary Himmelstein, *Associate Professor of Psychology, body image expert, Kent State University*

"When we love our body, we give permission for imperfection and learn to see beauty in all that we are."

Focus on functionality

What is **functionality**? Functionality refers to the ways in which your body moves, works, or functions. Our bodies perform all sorts of functions each and every day. We walk, run, jump, eat, sleep, breathe, dance, sing, swim, climb, and a million other things. Our bodies make all of these things possible.

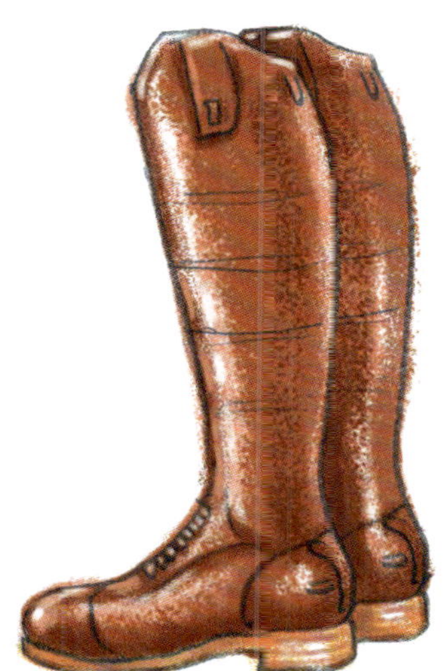

Scientists who study body image have found that thinking about our bodies' functionality is important. In fact, the more we think about functionality, the less we seem to get hung up on more **superficial** issues of appearance. If you're ever feeling discouraged about your body, it can be helpful to spend a bit of time thinking about the things your body does. Start with what you did when you woke up this morning and think about everything you did during your day. Maybe you woke up, showered, got dressed and ready for school, ate breakfast, rode your bike to school, read, wrote, completed a science experiment, talked to your friends, ate lunch, ran

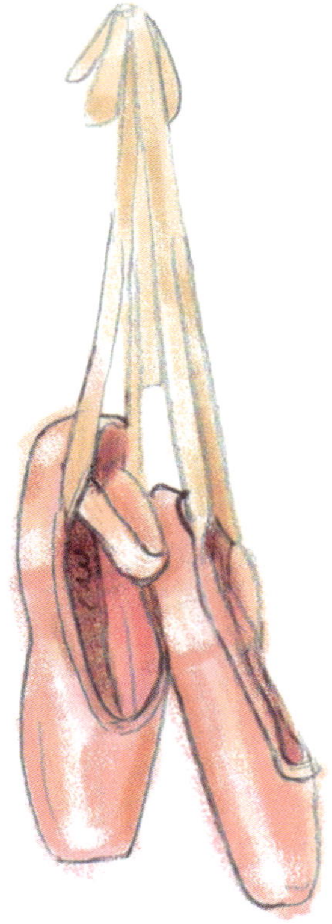

during gym class, played the piano, finished your homework, ate dinner, spent time with your family, watched television, and got ready for bed. Your body made all of that possible. That's a lot!

More specifically, your body digested your food and used that for energy to ride your bike and stay alert at school. Your brain allowed you to do your schoolwork and to have conversations with your friends and family. Coordination between your fingers and your brain allowed you to play the piano. **The human body is truly amazing!**

How do you help your body complete so many amazing tasks? You feed it, you keep it clean by bathing and following other good **hygiene** practices, and you sleep. When you think about it, you don't have to do all that much to end up with a body that can do so many incredible things.

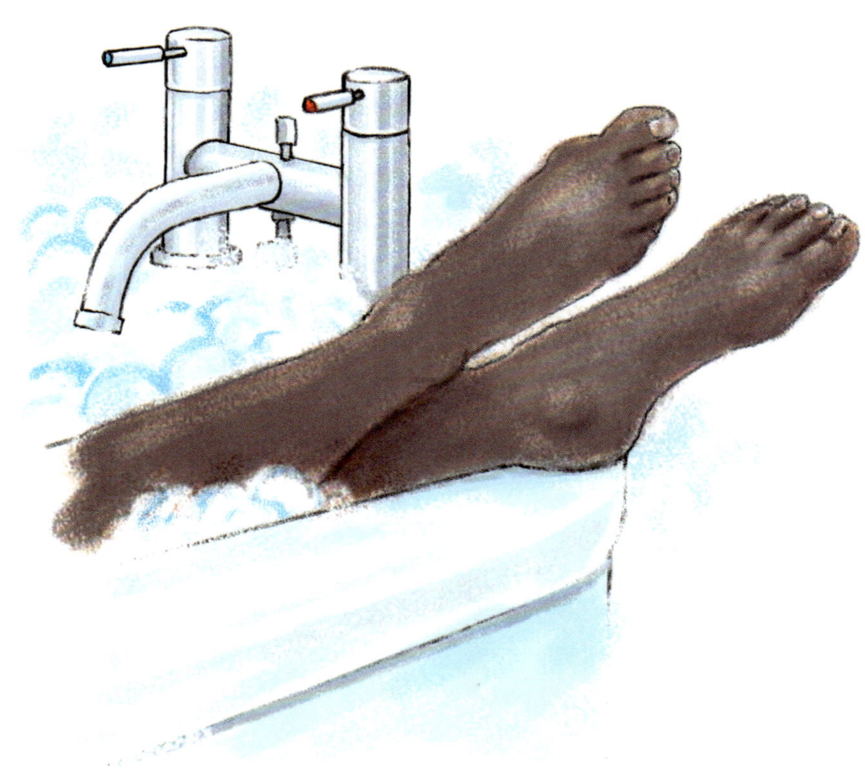

Appreciate your body

Even though your body is amazing, you may be able to come up with things you don't like about it. What things lead you to think negatively about your body? Can you avoid them? For example, if looking on Instagram leads you to feel bad about yourself, you might avoid Instagram, or at the very least, unfollow people who make you feel bad and replace them with body-positive accounts.

One activity that may help you feel better about your body is to make a list of the things that you **like** (or **love**) about your body and appearance. These can be anything: your eyes, lips, teeth, hair, fingernails, feet, stomach, calves, curves, muscles – anything at all. Add *why* you love these things to your list. Think about this for a few days and try to make the list as long as possible. You don't need to share this with anyone, so you can brag to yourself all you want. Keep your list someplace safe. When you feel down on yourself or upset about some aspect of your appearance, look at your list of the qualities you like about your body. Take a moment to feel grateful for them and try to push whatever negative thoughts you're having out of your mind.

Focusing on appreciating your body and being grateful for aspects of your appearance can improve how you feel about your body and appearance. In one of the studies I conducted with some other researchers, we asked people to list only three features they were grateful for about their appearance. Even just making this very short list had a positive impact on people's body image. It's a simple thing to do, but it just may work.

EXPERT ADVICE

Jaclyn Siegel, PhD, *body image scientist and social psychologist*

"When we think about our bodies, we often think about what they look like, rather than what they can do, feel, or experience. Because girls and women are held to impossible and ever-shifting beauty standards, there will always be something to dislike about our bodies when we're only focused on appearance. By shifting our focus to functionality — the hugs we get to feel, the hand games we get to play, the mountains we get to climb, or the pleasure we get to experience — we can begin to appreciate our bodies for what they really are: a way to experience the joys of being alive."

BODY APPRECIATION

Take some time to think about what you appreciate about your body. Don't just think about your physical appearance but all the things your body can do as well. Make a list of <u>at least three</u> things about your body that you appreciate.

1) ____

2) ____

3) ____

The Body Appreciation Scale is a survey used by body image scientists to determine the extent to which people feel good about their bodies. Specifically, do they *appreciate* their bodies? To complete the measure, circle your response to indicate whether the question is true about you never, seldom, sometimes, often, or always. The scoring information is below.

I respect my body.	Never 1	Seldom 2	Sometimes 3	Often 4	Always 5
I feel good about my body.	Never 1	Seldom 2	Sometimes 3	Often 4	Always 5
I feel that my body has at least some good qualities.	Never 1	Seldom 2	Sometimes 3	Often 4	Always 5
I take a positive attitude toward my body.	Never 1	Seldom 2	Sometimes 3	Often 4	Always 5
I am attentive to my body's needs.	Never 1	Seldom 2	Sometimes 3	Often 4	Always 5
I feel love for my body.	Never 1	Seldom 2	Sometimes 3	Often 4	Always 5
I appreciate the different and unique characteristics of my body.	Never 1	Seldom 2	Sometimes 3	Often 4	Always 5
My behavior reveals my positive attitudes toward my body; for example, I walk holding my head high and smiling.	Never 1	Seldom 2	Sometimes 3	Often 4	Always 5
I am comfortable in my body.	Never 1	Seldom 2	Sometimes 3	Often 4	Always 5
I feel like I am beautiful even if I am different from media images of attractive people (e.g. models, actresses/actors).	Never 1	Seldom 2	Sometimes 3	Often 4	Always 5

Note: This is actually a revised version of The Body Appreciation Scale (BAS-2), which was created by Tylka and Wood-Barcalow in 2015. To compute your score, sum up your responses and divide by 10. This gives you the average number for your response. In Tylka and Wood-Barcalow's original study examining this measure, the average person scored between 3 and 4 on this measure; in some research examining adolescent girls, the average score was closer to 4. Higher scores mean higher body appreciation. If your score is closer to 1, follow the tips in this chapter to work on appreciating your body more.

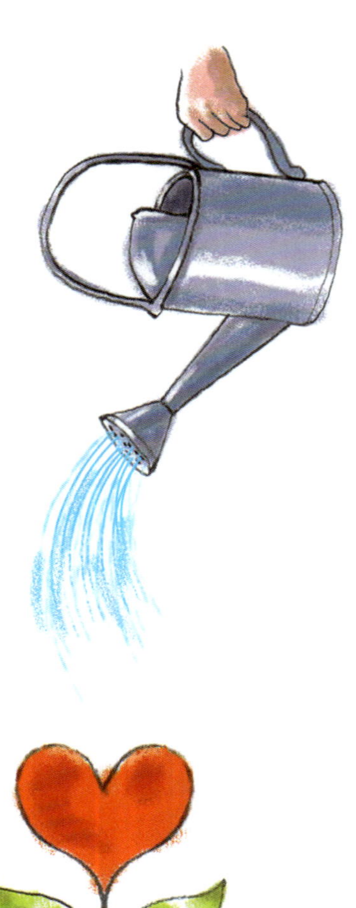

Self-compassion

Sometimes, many of us think about and treat ourselves worse than we would treat a friend. We may think that we're too short, too chubby, or not athletic enough. We wouldn't tell our friends that we think they're too short, too chubby, or not athletic enough. So, why do we "talk down" to ourselves like this?

There is evidence that people *think* they benefit from being hard on themselves. They think they'll improve themselves if they bully themselves. **However, people tend to benefit from self-compassion**. Self-compassion is basically being kind to yourself and treating yourself like you would treat a friend. Scientists have found that people who are self-compassionate tend to experience success because they don't waste energy getting upset with themselves; instead, they focus this energy toward **motivating** themselves to achieve self-acceptance and success.

Some new research suggests that people tend to feel bad about their bodies when they feel bad in general. In other words, negative emotions may be directed inwards toward the self. This research leads me to think that in addition to self-compassion, it may be helpful for some of us to work on having a positive mindset in general. What can we do to boost our mood and increase the number of positive experiences we have each day?

The next time you want to tell yourself that you're out of shape or unattractive, take a deep breath. Remember, this isn't a good use of your energy. Think of a close friend. You're as deserving as your friend, so don't say anything to yourself that you wouldn't say to a close friend. What can you do to improve your negative mindset?

If you're having a hard time feeling accepting of yourself, go back to the lists I suggested that you make earlier in this chapter and try to focus on your strengths.

Body respect

Your body is your home for the rest of your life. It's easy to get caught up in the present tense and not think long term, but you want your body to be a comfortable, **healthy** home for many years to come. To accomplish this, you need to treat yourself with respect and care.

Body respect is listening to your body's needs and honoring them. Body respect does not mean eating too little or avoiding entire food groups. Body respect is not pushing yourself too much when it comes to physical activity or leaving yourself tired out and unable to attend to other matters in your life. Body respect is not staying up all night or sleeping less than 7 or 8 hours per night; adequate rest and sleep are critical to showing yourself respect.

I know you know all of this; your mom, dad, teacher, and/or medical providers have been telling you all of this for as long as you can remember. However, sometimes, we hear this sort of advice so often that we don't frame it in terms of self-care. This can be surprisingly hard because we are often bombarded by cultural messages that suggest we should ignore our physical signals, such as signals of hunger or exhaustion. In order to take care of and respect our bodies, we can't ignore the messages they send us.

Keep a healthy mindset when it comes to food and physical activity

This book has entire chapters dedicated to your eating (Chapter 5) and exercise habits (Chapter 8), but it's important to mention both here as well. Your health habits can affect your body image, and so can how you think about these behaviors. For example, if you go for a run but you think of it as necessary, you're unlikely to enjoy that run. But if you think of running as something you do to help yourself feel good, improve your health, and take care of yourself, you might actually enjoy running more and find it easier to sustain this behavior. Furthermore, this mindset will likely support your positive body image instead of detracting from it.

The key is to reframe our behaviors in ways that make healthy, adaptive behaviors sustainable. Punishing or shaming ourselves for not doing all the "right" things is rarely an effective approach to health (mental or physical) and can reinforce negative body image. Furthermore, as I hope you learn in this book, there are no clear rules about what your body needs so that you feel your best; some of our bodies need more food than others, some need more sleep than others, and some will enjoy physical activity more than others.

People will think that you're bragging or full of yourself if you act happy about your body or appearance.

Have you ever heard someone say, "I feel soooo fat." Maybe you even responded by saying, "You are not! I am soooo fat!" When people talk like this, **psychologists** call this **fat talk**. Although extremely common, fat talk isn't good for our **mental health**. Talking negatively about our bodies with our family, friends, and even our acquaintances has been shown to make us feel bad about our bodies. The more we do it, the worse we feel.

What could we do instead?

It may be beneficial to be happy – confident, even – about our appearance. The next time someone you know says, "I feel sooo fat," you can respond by saying, "Let's focus on the positives. What are some things you like about your appearance? I like my…" The person you're talking with may be surprised but also relieved to have a different sort of conversation. They aren't likely to think that you're full of yourself, but instead, they're likely to think about their own appearance differently and more positively. In fact, a recent study showed that the best way to change this sort of fat talk is to confront it, not ignore it or join in with it. Changing the direction of your conversation could have real benefits for both you and your friend.

Feeling teased — or even harassed

It can be extremely hard to appreciate your body, practice self-compassion, and maintain a healthy mindset about your health behaviors when you sense a lack of support from the people surrounding you. In particular, if someone you care about teases you about your appearance, this may lead you to feel terrible. In one study, adult women were asked about being teased about their appearance in their childhood and adolescence. If they were teased, they remembered it! And they remembered who did the teasing (friends and brothers were the biggest **culprits**). The worst part is that these women were also less likely to feel good about themselves than women who weren't teased when they were younger.

You can't necessarily stop other people from teasing you, but you can change how you react to the teasing. It's a good idea to tell people if they're upsetting you. Your brother, your friend, or whoever is teasing you may not even mean anything by it; maybe they mean to be funny or affectionate. (People can have a strange way of showing that they care about you.) You can also choose not to internalize what they say. **Internalizing** means taking information that's outside of you and making it your own. If your brother tells you that your nose is too big, you can choose to ignore him or you can make his opinion your own opinion — meaning that you start to believe your nose is too big. But you don't have to share his (or anyone else's) opinion about yourself.

Sometimes, people can take teasing too far. Someone may even bully you about your appearance or some other quality. If someone says something mean, inappropriate, or sexual about you, it is **harassment**. Sometimes harassment is even **sexual harassment** if it includes things like commenting on your breasts, or it could include touching your body where you don't want to be touched (see the Q&A section below).

Unfortunately, sexual harassment is pretty common, especially among girls and women. According to RAINN.org, one in nine girls under the age of 18 will experience sexual abuse or assault. When a girl or woman experiences harassment, sometimes she is embarrassed to tell anyone what happened. Sometimes, she may not even be sure that what she experienced counts as harassment. She may feel angry and upset, but she doesn't always say something to an authority figure. It's important that you speak up if you ever feel harassed. Even if you aren't sure how to describe what happened to you, talk to an adult you trust as soon as possible. It may make sense to talk to the police or to a principal or other relevant authority figure. But you don't have to do this on your own. **Be sure to ask a parent or other trusted adult to help you figure out the best way to handle your experience.** And keep in mind that you're doing this for yourself – and to protect other girls and women out there from being mistreated. Better communication about harassment, and punishment of **offenders** can help to reduce the harm girls, women, and people of all gender and sexual identities experience.

Q&A ?!??

What should you do if your friends tease you about your looks?

Being teased about how you look can be incredibly painful – even if the people teasing you love you and are just joking around. A lot of people who develop low self-esteem and **eating disorders** report that they were once teased about their looks. It's important that you don't let some insulting and hurtful things that other people say rob you of your sense of self. No one looks perfect and we all have body parts that we don't like completely. (We also all have qualities that have nothing to do with our appearances that we don't like completely!) It's OK to tell your friends that you find their comments hurtful. If your friends don't listen to you, you may want to talk to an adult about this. It's also valuable to remind yourself that some of our "imperfections" make us unique. They make us who we are, and we shouldn't change these qualities.

Q&A

It's really important that you know that your body is your own. <u>You should never be touched in a way that makes you uncomfortable</u> (unless it's a medical exam at a doctor's office; sometimes those are not exactly fun). If a boyfriend or significant other touches you somewhere you don't want to be touched, or someplace where it doesn't feel good to you to be touched, it's important that you say something to that person. If a friend — or even a stranger — touches you someplace that makes you uncomfortable, it's very important that you say something to that person as well. But you should also talk to someone else about this. <u>So who can you talk to?</u> It's a good idea to talk to one of your parents or another trusted adult about what you've experienced. There is no reason to feel responsible or guilty about this. If you don't share what's happened to you, then the person who has mistreated you may go on to mistreat other people as well.

It's OK to care about how you look

Even though you shouldn't let others make you feel bad about your appearance — and you definitely shouldn't put up with any sort of harassment — this doesn't mean that you need to totally ignore how you look. It's completely normal to care about how you look. In 2022, US$496 billion were spent on beauty and personal care (for example, **cosmetics** and **toiletries**). Why do people spend so much money on these products? It seems that spending time and money to make ourselves look and smell nice is important to some of us because it reveals to the world that we care about ourselves. In fact, psychologists sometimes call this **self-care** (see Chapter 9 for a lot more about self-care). There is absolutely nothing wrong with taking good care of ourselves, whether that be taking some time to wash and style our hair, paint our nails, or select clothes that make us feel **fashionable**.

However, if you spend *a lot* of time looking in the mirror and worrying about your appearance, you may care a bit *too* much. What's "a lot" of time? It's hard to say in terms of an exact number of minutes or hours. It's probably safe to say that you don't need to spend more than about 30 minutes of mirror time to get ready in the morning and maybe a bit of time (minutes, not hours) later in the day if you need to change or get ready to go someplace different. Body image scientists refer to time spent looking in the mirror and **primping** as **body surveillance**. Body surveillance is associated with dissatisfaction with our bodies and disordered eating. Further, spending hours on your appearance

EXPERT ADVICE

Drs. Lindsay and Lexie Kite, body image advocates and authors of *More Than a Body*

"Positive body image is an inside job. When we keep attempting to fix an internal, psychological problem with outside, physical solutions, those quick fixes will never really solve our problem, nor will they prepare us to respond effectively to future body image concerns."

each day will cut into the time you can spend on homework, friendship, hobbies, and even sleep.

Of course, there's a reason we have mirrors in the first place. We want to see how we look – and that's not always a bad thing. For example, if you have braces, you may get food stuck in your braces. You may have to look in the mirror to get this food out. I suppose it would be distracting, and even **unhygienic**, if you don't pay attention to this issue with your teeth. And it would be embarrassing if people were always telling you (or afraid to tell you) about the food stuck in your braces.

Looking in the mirror doesn't need to be an opportunity for **self-criticism**. Girls on YouTube may indicate that they spend a lot of time selecting their outfits each day, checking how they look in a mirror, and changing their clothes more than once on some days. You can try to make an effort not to do any of this. Remind yourself that no one else probably notices or cares exactly how your jeans fit you or which top you wear on any given day. **You can choose to pay less attention to some details of your appearance and focus that time and energy on other aspects of your life.**

Q&A

I know I shouldn't care too much about how I look, and that there are more important things in life, but I do care about how I look. I think that if I were more attractive, I would worry less. What should I do?

It's hard to not care about how you look. Pretty much everyone does, to some extent. And you shouldn't be upset with yourself for caring. You receive all sorts of messages every day saying that it's appropriate — even important — to care about your appearance. Some scientists have even suggested that it's normal for girls and women to think about and talk about how they look — that it creates a sort of belonging or bonding among girls and women.

Of course, caring can go too far. There should be other things on your mind besides your appearance. I think the definition of **adaptive appearance investment** is useful for thinking about what is "good" and what is "too far" when it comes to caring about our appearance. Adaptive appearance investment is defined as "regularly engaging in appearance-related self-care, such as **grooming** behaviors that protect an individual's sense of style and **personality**; it's enhancing one's natural features via **benign** (not harmful) methods." According to this definition of what's good or healthy when it comes to caring about our appearance, it's fine to buy clothes that fit us well and are comfortable. It's reasonable to take time to style our hair or to use make-up. But it's probably unhealthy or risky to do things that pose some danger to you, like spending so much time exercising that you don't have time to do other important things (like get enough sleep) or putting your health at risk by following fad diets.

Even scientists who study body image issues admit that it can be hard to know what is "healthy" caring about your appearance and what is "unhealthy." If you feel that you're worried about how much you care about your appearance, try to spend some time on activities that are not appearance-focused. Hopefully, some of the ideas in this chapter will be useful. It may also be useful to talk to a counselor about your concerns. The **National Alliance for Eating Disorders** has a list of counselors on their web page (findedhelp.com) who are trained to help people deal with issues other than eating disorders, including concerns about appearance, weight, and body image. You may…

… want to check their web page or look at other resources mentioned at the end of each chapter of this book.

As you grow up, you'll need to figure out what makes sense for you and how much you want to **invest** in your appearance, both in terms of money and time. But never forget that the people who care about and love you will not think any differently of you if you wear make-up or not, or if you wear nice clothes or just comfy clothes.

Body neutrality

Some body image scholars and **activists** have suggested that when we think about our appearance and aim for a positive body image, we can be overly focused on our appearance. In other words, for some people, trying to feel good about how they look might involve too much thinking about how they look. If this sounds like you, then you might want to aim for **body neutrality**.

Whereas the goal of **body positivity** is to feel good about your body, the goal of body neutrality is to just not really think about your body. Both body neutrality and body positivity include a focus on body appreciation, gratitude, our body's functionality, self-care, and self-compassion. However, body positivity tends to involve more feelings of joy concerning our body and, for some, a greater sense of comfort in their own skin. For some people, body neutrality might be a stop on the way to a more positive body image. For others, body neutrality is a satisfactory endpoint.

Remember: this matters — a lot!

Focusing on the positive and working toward a positive (or at least neutral!) body image is very important. A big part of this is developing healthy

habits, such as good eating habits (see Chapter 5 for more about healthy eating). Loving your body isn't just a superficial concern. It isn't just about loving how you look. **Feeling good about your body and taking care of it is important to your long-term health, how you view yourself, and how you view the rest of the world.** It's worth investing some time in yourself and working on your body image. You only get one body to last you your entire lifetime. It's important that you're good to yourself!

Q&A

I look a lot like my older sister, but she seems to get a lot more attention from boys — they think she's prettier. I would like to have a boyfriend, too, and I feel bad being jealous of my sister. Help?

It can be very difficult to feel like you're in a sibling's shadow.

It's also normal to feel like you want to grow up and do the things that your older sister is doing.

Try to enjoy being the age that you are now. Boyfriends (or girlfriends) will come in time if you want them to.

Most importantly, try to use this situation as practice in <u>not</u> comparing yourself to others. Psychologists refer to our tendency to compare ourselves to others as social comparison and rarely does anything good come of it. In fact, research suggests that people tend to feel bad about themselves when they engage in social comparison.

It's easy to look at someone else's life and feel like it's better than your own, but that's usually because we make social comparisons on just one aspect of life. It may seem like someone else has a better life because she receives more attention from boys. However, maybe she doesn't do as well in school or isn't as good at sports as you are. Each of us has our own strengths, whether in terms of our ability to make friends, our fashion sense, or our sense of humor. Focus on your strengths and try to be happy for other people when they have success on the basketball court or with a new boyfriend.

Amelia Grace, 20 years old, she/her, USA

Right now, I'd say I have a pretty good relationship with my body. Of course, there have been some insecurities in the past, and my body is still changing, I know. I didn't realize that my body would continue to change into my twenties and, really, forever.

I've been a performer my whole life, pretty much, and I'm majoring in drama in college now. This has challenged my body image at times. I am not naturally extroverted, and people were surprised I wanted to act. But I've found my voice as an actor, and I think I am most confident when I'm sharing myself through my art. I love the collaborative nature of putting on a show, and I can usually leave my lingering insecurities off-stage.

I'm auditioning for some professional performances now, and I hope to work in theatre in the future. I know this means that my physical self will be critiqued from the moment I walk into an audition. I will be measured for costumes. I will be given certain roles because of how I look. But I know that I can't dwell on these negative thoughts because then I wouldn't be able to be an actor. I have performed Shakespeare and played the part of an older woman — even the part of a horse! My body allows me to do all of this.

Being a performer has helped me to live more boldly in other ways and to become more fearless. I have found myself to be more willing to meet new people, apply for a job, join a club, and even go to a college where I didn't know a single soul.

If I could offer my younger self some advice, I'd tell her to focus on what her body is capable of. You are strong <u>because of</u> your body; your body holds so much value. You are so much more than what you look like.

SUMMING UP #BeYoutiful

- Get into the habit of focusing on the parts of your body that you like and not the parts that you dislike.
- Think of the ways your body helps you – dancing, eating, sleeping, and laughing – and always be kind to yourself.
- Take good care of yourself and work toward maintaining healthy habits like exercising and eating healthfully.

FIND OUT MORE:

- The National Alliance for Eating Disorders (AllianceforEatingDisorders.com), F.E.A.S.T. (Feast-ED.org), and ANAD (Anad.org) are all organizations that have great resources on their web pages, including information about support groups and providers who help people work on their body images.

- RAINN.org or SafeHelpLine.org are web pages that contains a lot of valuable information in addition to hotline and chat features.

- ***Jemima Small Versus the Universe*** by Tamsin Winter (2019; Usborne Publishing Ltd.) is a great book that chronicles a young girl's development of body appreciation.

- For more scholarly articles and web pages with information about body image, see the companion website to this book: www.BodyImageBook.com.

CHAPTER 4

YOUR IMAGE

#BeYourOwnInfluencer

> "He that falls in love with himself will have no rivals."
>
> Benjamin Franklin

Tatum Hope, 14 years old, she/her, UK

Right now, I wouldn't say I'm especially confident about my body. I feel insecure about some things and some days are better than others, but I've come a long way.

When I was younger, I struggled a lot with my body image, and I was insecure about my weight. I was a bit of a chubby child, and family and friends didn't hesitate to comment on my body. I have an auntie who used to say things like, "You are looking really chubby this week!" These comments led me to research ways to lose weight as young as 8 years of age.

My body image insecurities led me to the Internet and social media. But then I ended up comparing my pre-adolescent body to that of 17-year-olds. It was really ridiculous and unrealistic and contributed to only making me feel worse about myself. Around this time, my mom bought me a positive mental health handbook that I read and learned a lot from. It helped me to put my insecurities into perspective and think about how to protect myself psychologically.

What I've come to realize in recent years is that people worry about their own body images much more than they worry about how other people look. And when people comment on others' bodies, it says much more about _them_ than the person they are talking about. I think settling into a close-knit, supportive friend group has helped me to think about these issues in a more mentally healthy manner. It's easier to feel good about yourself when you are surrounded by people who are so affirming.

These days, I also try to tune into social media content that is more body-positive. I like to see influencers normalizing different body types. I've also come to see that something you hate about yourself other people may like. Hardly anyone is fully happy with themselves!

If I could offer younger girls some advice, I'd tell them to try to worry less about their appearance. And remember that everyone else is so self-absorbed that they are probably not really looking at you or noticing the flaws you think you see in yourself!

I suspect that most of us have had some experiences similar to Tatum's. It's easy to feel **insecure** in this culture that is full of **unrealistic** beauty ideals. We look at Instagram or YouTube and see people who seem to look pretty, fit, and like they're living their best lives. They basically look perfect, but there's a good reason for that.

It's just not "real"

Have you ever played with a **filter** on your phone or computer to change how a picture looks? Tweaked a selfie so you look a little different? You've probably done this plenty of times. You've cropped a tree out of a picture or made a colored picture black and white. Now, imagine that you could hand your pictures over to a professional photographer. In fact, imagine that the professional photographer took the pictures in the first place and now she is going to edit them for you with all the latest **software**. Your hair will look smoother, your skin will look clearer, and your eyes will look brighter. Maybe your waist will look smaller, your legs longer, and your breasts bigger.

This is what happens to all the pictures that are posted by celebrities and **influencers** that you see on **social media**. I've talked with professional photographers in the process of doing my research over many years, and they all tell me the same thing: **everything** is edited. People who are good-looking to start with

IN THIS CHAPTER YOU'LL LEARN:

- how the media is incredibly deceptive in presenting images of ideal beauty that aren't real depictions of actual people,
- the role that social media may play in your body image and how to become **media literate**, and
- the importance of being thoughtful about self-acceptance when making appearance-related choices, from the clothes you select to the cosmetics you purchase.

end up looking stunningly beautiful as a result of computer editing. When you look at famous people online or in magazines or movies, you don't see what they really look like.

Why are all the pictures edited?

The answer is obvious: Who doesn't want a pimple **photoshopped** away or a stray hair removed? Unfortunately, the result of all this editing is that girls and women come to believe that there are a lot of real people who are physically perfect. This isn't true. Everyone – everyone! – has imperfections.

Movies and videos are edited and staged, as well. There's lighting, filters (yup, for video, too), and professional make-up artists. There are **stylists** and editors who can do all sorts of things to change the way a person looks. Off-screen, celebrities and influencers are able to change their appearance using other means such as cosmetic surgery (and other **enhancements** like **Botox**, veneers, permanent tattooing of eyebrows; more on all of that later in this chapter). The main point is this: **What you see is *not reality***. Because these images aren't accurate (and for a bunch of other reasons), you shouldn't compare yourself to them.

The images you see are **manipulated** for another reason, too. They're usually intended to sell you a product or a service. Sometimes you're being sold the idea that perfect beauty is possible. Celebrities and influencers appear on social media looking perfect to sell everything from make-up to clothes to household goods. That skin cream that you think you need now. Where did you first see it? Was it an ad on YouTube? An Instagram post by an influencer? It's all **advertising** and you probably don't *need* it.

But you're smart enough not to be fooled, right?

We like to think that we're unaffected by advertising. Because we know that people are trying to sell us products, we believe we can escape the influence. The problem, though, is that you see so many advertisements each day, in so many different forms of media, that it's virtually impossible to tune them all out. Furthermore, there is research that makes it clear that even if we are told that an image is edited, we are still likely to be negatively affected by it.

Researchers who study how the media contributes to body image have found, across many different studies, that the **media *does* affect body image**. The media presents an unrealistic ideal of beauty that affects us all. In particular, seeing "perfected" and photoshopped images of girls and women's bodies has a negative impact on girls' and women's feelings about their bodies, and their feelings in general. What this means is that looking at these sorts of images tends to make girls think, "I wish I looked like that" and "I don't like how I look because I'd rather look like that." Girls may also feel sad or anxious as a result of seeing these images and may attempt to change some of their habits when it comes to eating, exercise, or beauty routines.

A big part of the reason girls often feel bad when they view models on Instagram or movie stars in videos is due to **social comparison**, a concept first described in Chapter 3. Part of growing up is figuring out who you are and who you want to become. It's hard to sort these things out. You could ask your mom for help in figuring out who you are, but she may tell you that you're "nice" and "pretty." The problem is that you know she's probably biased because she's your mom. You could ask a friend how she views you, and she may tell you that you're "fun" and "talkative." She's probably biased, too. Most people who know you may offer only biased, positive

feedback about who you are. People who don't really know you can't help with this dilemma. You're likely to look around at other people when trying to figure out who you are and who you want to be. You may decide that you want to have a haircut like an influencer you follow and be bold and funny like an actress you admire. Maybe you want to buy clothes like a popular girl at school, and you want to be athletic like your older sister.

In the process of thinking about your own identity, you look around at others and compare yourself to them. This is what social comparison is, and it's a valuable way to acquire information about yourself. Obviously, it matters a lot whom you compare yourself with. If you want to do well as a student, it may be a good idea to compare your study habits with your successful classmates. Comparing your practice habits with those of the team captain may help you become better at field hockey. But you probably shouldn't compare yourself to celebrities and influencers. I already

noted that it's impossible to know what they really look like, because the images you see of them are edited. They are likely older than you and spend more time and money on their appearance. They have expensive hair stylists, photographers, photo editors, and even people who help manage their image using social media (in other words, the posts they put on Instagram and TikTok are often due to someone else posting for them). In addition to issues of **presentation**, famous people and influencers are unlikely to be like you in a whole bunch of other ways.

There's one other thing that you should keep in mind when it comes to comparing yourself to others or trying to achieve appearance ideals you see online or even in real life. These ideals are constantly changing. Even if you figured out how to curl your hair like your favorite influencer, she might start wearing her hair straight the next week. Once you order a pair of dark blue jeans that you love, light blue jeans will become more popular. Most of us want to keep up with some fashion trends, and there's nothing wrong with this. But it's important not to take any of it too seriously because the trends are a moving target.

Just be you

There's a good chance that if someone has become famous, they weren't all that average to start with. This may sound depressing – it's not meant to – but you're probably average because that's the definition of average! "Average" is the way we describe what *most people* are like. There is nothing wrong with being average. In fact, if you think about it, there's something freeing about accepting that you're a normal, average person. Sure, you're special in many ways that the people who care about you appreciate. But you don't have to be exceptional, especially unique, or strive for fame. You can just be you.

EXPERT ADVICE

Dr. Diane Rosenbaum, *Professor, body image researcher, clinical psychologist*

"We often compare our bodies to others that we see – on social media, in everyday situations, in movies, you name it! Focusing on what we believe we lack compared to other people can take a toll on our mental health. Research has shown that this type of thinking is associated with more negative emotions, less satisfaction with our bodies, and disordered eating. However, we have the power to make changes in how we think about our bodies. Loving our bodies, focusing on how much they do for us each day, and appreciating how they function is associated with positive mental health and well-being."

Instead of growing up comparing yourself to a model or superstar, maybe it makes sense to recognize that that's not who you are. It may even be valuable to appreciate what the average woman looks like when it comes to body size. The average woman in the USA is 5'4" (163 cm) tall and weighs about 170 pounds (77 kg). In the UK, the average woman is 5'4"(163 cm) tall and weighs about 159 pounds (72 kg). However, the average female model is 5'7" (170 cm) tall and weighs 114 pounds (52 kg). This means that the typical model you see online or in magazines is **underweight** (to a very unhealthy degree), according to the **Centers for Disease Control and Prevention**.

Where does that leave you? First of all, remember that the models you see may not only have make-up and filters making them look the way they do, but they also have body **proportions** that you're very unlikely to ever have. Female models are a small minority of all people who are likely to be naturally tall and relatively lean, and they may have relatively large breasts compared to the rest of their bodies. They're also probably not eating enough to properly nourish their bodies. It's important to appreciate that most women can never achieve the bodies that models have, and if they do, it is likely to be through drastic and really unhealthy strategies. Let that sink in.

"Liking," "friends," and "followers"

Even if you do your best to ignore celebrities in the media all together, you'll still be affected by other people around you. In fact, with social media a big part of many of our lives, we are connected to people we've never met from our schools and communities. We can be virtually connected with a large **social circle** of people we don't really "know."

A recent study of more than 1,300 girls (11–15 years) in the USA found that 86% use social media. Most teens report liking social media, which makes sense – otherwise you'd have to wonder why so many of them were using it! But girls also report that social media is not all positive; almost half said they felt "addicted" to TikTok and almost one-third of girls said that Snapchat made them feel like they had to be constantly available and responding to peers. Girls also reported that social media can be both helpful and harmful to their mental health. They feel they benefit from being able to connect with others who are similar to them, but sometimes engage with content that upsets them.

The issue of **self-presentation** on social media is also problematic. A lot of teens say that they only share information and pictures that make them appear better than they may actually be. Sometimes people refer to this use of social media as posting the **highlight reel** of their lives, similar to how a preview for a movie may show some of the highlights from the movie. However, when teens see only each other's best selves – a filtered, edited collection of the best things they do – it's easy to feel like they don't look as nice as others, and that their lives aren't as exciting as others' are. This has the potential to make teens feel bad about themselves. Here again, social comparison is mostly to blame.

In spite of this, teens tend to report that social media is an important part of their social lives, and it helps connect them to other people in ways that they like. However, a recent study of over 17,000 teenagers found that younger teens seemed to be more sensitive than older teens to the downsides of social media. Also, teens who seem to be more **vulnerable** because they don't have as many friends, or because they're anxious or depressed, don't always view social media as a positive part of their lives. For these teens, social media can be a painful reminder that they don't fit in in a variety of ways.

Become media literate

One way to counter the negative effects of social media on your own body image is to become media literate. "**Literate**" usually means that you can read. When someone has **media literacy**, it means that person can "read" what's going on in some form of media. In other words, they're critical of the media and try to decipher the intention of the media. This may be similar to what you're asked to do in school during reading comprehension exercises that involve reading a passage or story and deciphering what's going on in it.

Why would you need to analyze and **evaluate** what's going on in some form of media? As discussed in this chapter, the media isn't always honest in its **portrayal** of people and ideas. Social media may be the worst, as far as this is concerned. To be social media literate, you need to think about people's motivations for posting, the techniques they use to alter their pictures or posts, and how others may be presenting their best selves through their posts.

How do you become media literate?

First, every time you see an image in the media, remind yourself that the image *isn't* **realistic** and is probably edited and altered in a variety of ways. This is an important step in terms of maintaining a positive body image.

Second, think about *why* the image is presented the way it is and pay attention to how it makes you feel.

Third, stop comparing yourself to images you see and pay attention when images make you feel bad. Replace those bad feelings with positive feelings about yourself by focusing on some of your strengths and avoid the images that bring you down.

Fourth, remember that the media is used to sell products and promote the idea that people have perfect lives. No one has a perfect life, and no one needs most of the products advertised.

Fifth, remind yourself that you don't have to engage with any media. You don't have to be active on all types of social media; you can ease into it, out of it, or not use some apps. You can turn off the television, delete an app from your phone, or stop yourself from responding to others' comments on social media. **You have control.**

Research suggests that being media literate can help protect your body image. Girls who are more critical of the media and think about the issues discussed above tend to have more positive feelings about their bodies. It's important that when you engage with the media around you, you try to "read" it carefully.

FACE the media

To help you think about steps you can take to keep different forms of social media (or any media, for that matter) from affecting you, keep the acronym **FACE** (Filter, Avoid, Careful of comparisons, Evaluate) in mind.

FILTER

I'm not referring to filters in a photo editing tool or Snapchat. Body image researchers refer to something called **protective filtering**, which is essentially filtering out influences in your life that negatively affect your body image. Because most forms of social media select content based on your own interests and usage, you can shape your social media world to protect yourself. This might require unfollowing influencers, celebrities, and possibly even friends who have beliefs that do not help you to develop a positive body image. Instead of engaging with those on social media who focus on their own appearance – and cosmetics or clothing that they feel enhance it – you could engage with activists who promote a positive body image, mental health professionals, and others who offer tools and advice to aid you in your journey toward self-acceptance.

AVOID

We all need media breaks. Be sure to avoid your phone, tablet, computer, or other media device for some time every day. Eat dinner without texting your friends. Do homework or work for your job without videos playing in the background. Sleep without the distraction of alerts coming from your devices. Turn alerts off so that you aren't always being distracted by your phone beeping. Remove apps from your phone to keep you from spending too much time on them. One recent study confirms the importance of this time away from the media. In this study of adults in their late 20s (on average), participants first completed surveys measuring their mental health.

Then, half were asked to stop using social media for 1 week, while the other half continued to use social media as usual. At the end of the week, the group who had a social media break was less likely to be depressed and anxious and reported better overall well-being compared to their original survey scores. Although it can be difficult to disengage from social media, most people report it gets easier over time – and there are real benefits to spending less time with our screens.

CAREFUL OF COMPARISONS

As I've already mentioned in this chapter, one of the ways that the media can be most harmful is by prompting us to compare ourselves with celebrities and other unrealistic portrayals of attractive people. Remember that these are not appropriate people to compare yourself with! The images that prompt social comparisons are usually of adults who have teams of people – fitness trainers, chefs, make-up artists, and professional photographers – who help make them look good. Most of us do not have teams of people working on our image, nor is this necessary. It's also helpful to remember that it's essentially (most) celebrities' and influencers' job to look good. And they have a lot of help, so the people we see in the media rarely look like themselves in real life. And even if some of them do, it's worth recognizing that another's beauty doesn't detract from your own. Maybe it's even better to be in a position where our worth is not centered on our appearance, and we aren't going to lose our jobs for not looking a certain way or for just getting older.

EVALUATE

Not only do celebrities, athletes, and influencers have teams of people helping to make them look good, but photographers and publicists are also editing (and in some cases, distorting) their appearances to the point that these people don't even look like themselves. Why? In the places you see these people – Instagram, TikTok, or the Internet – they are very likely trying to sell you a product or promote themselves and their "brand." Be skeptical and evaluate what you see. Why does the person look the way they do? How realistic is the image? What values and lifestyles are being presented? Why was this message created? What is for sale?

It's important that we not only evaluate what we see in the media but also challenge it. In fact, one study suggests that challenging appearance ideals in the media (for example, "Does she look like that in real life?" and "He must have to spend a lot of time at the gym – and not with his friends and family – to look like that") helps people to disengage from appearance-centric media.

Q&A

Some of my friends have begun to post **revealing** pictures of themselves on Instagram and one has even sent a partially naked picture (**sext**) to her boyfriend. All of this makes me somewhat uncomfortable, but I'm not sure what (if anything) to say to them about this. It just seems like these may not be the best things to do.

Well, your **instincts** are probably correct that these aren't the safest things for girls to do. It's important to be proud of your body, but this doesn't necessarily mean that you should share it with the world (on social media) or even by sending photos to a boyfriend.

One of the greatest risks is that someone you don't want to see a picture of yourself only partially clothed will see it. Chances are you don't want the principal at your school, a future employer, or your parents to see you partially clothed (in other words, partially naked). Whenever you share a picture of yourself with anyone, you have to consider the possibility that he or she will share it with others or that it will end up archived online pretty much forever. You may adore your boyfriend, but your feelings (and his) could change. Plus, other people may have access to his phone or pictures. Think about your future!

In rare cases, teens have been charged with breaking child **pornography** laws when they've shared nude or sexually suggestive photos with others. This isn't what child pornography laws were designed for (they're meant to protect children and teens), but they were created before sexting existed. It's unlikely to happen, but because of these laws, it's possible that sexting by those under 18 years old can result in criminal charges.

If you ever feel pressured to send a friend, girlfriend, or boyfriend a picture — or even just a message — that you aren't comfortable sending, stand up for yourself and say no. <u>A person who cares about you will not bully you into doing something that's embarrassing or uncomfortable for you.</u>

If you ever receive a message that you didn't want to receive, like a picture of someone else partially naked, delete it immediately. You don't want to have "pornography" stored on your phone or computer, as this also could possibly result in criminal charges.

As far as what to say to your friends, if they aren't asking for your advice or aren't close friends, then you may want to keep your thoughts to yourself. But otherwise, perhaps you can share some of the above information, and this will encourage them to change their behaviors.

An X-rated media problem

Adult movies, X-rated movies, or **pornography** (i.e. **porn**) movies are all movies that contain explicit nudity and sexual interactions. In other words, the people are usually completely naked. How could that possibly pose any body image challenges?!

Porn is usually made by men for boys and men. In fact, in one recent study, the majority of men (over 90%) reported watching pornography in the last 6 months. However, some research indicates that over 70% of women have also viewed porn in the past 6 months. **Although pornography watching may be common, it has the potential to be very problematic.**

First, there's a fairly obvious body image connection between watching porn and body dissatisfaction. Most of the people featured in pornography do not look like the average person. In particular, their bodies are likely to be more slender, muscular, and hairless than the average person. Men who are porn stars are likely to have larger-than-average **pecs** and penises, while women who are porn stars are likely to have larger-than-average breasts. Many porn stars have had cosmetic surgery to look as they do. People you see in pornography are not your role models; trying to look like these people is likely to make you feel inferior and disappointed with your own appearance. Also, avoid holding other people (for example, your romantic partners) to the standards set by porn stars, or you are likely to find yourself disappointed.

Second, porn is not necessarily a good influence on the development of healthy physical **intimacy**. Pornography tends to feature sexual encounters in which women are portrayed in submissive roles (at least, this is generally true of pornography that features interactions between a man and woman). Women are often **objectified** or treated like objects, not like people with feelings. Men, more often than not, take control of the interaction, and women go along with the men's preferences. Frequently, pornography features interactions that are violent, not loving or gentle. This is not how most adults expect or hope their sexual encounters will be; people tend to want a loving, positive experience, and want their partner to have a positive experience. It is important for partners to communicate with each other about their preferences, likes, and dislikes if they are going to have a positive, intimate relationship.

Third, pornography usually features sexual encounters that are not a part of romantic or emotional relationships. Often, it is viewed as "manly" for men to have sex without becoming emotionally connected with the person they are physically involved with. Women sometimes view sex without commitment as an act of feminism or independence. However, there are risks that accompany sexual encounters – unintended pregnancy and **sexually transmitted infections** – that make it important not to treat sex casually. Make sure that your sexual partners are respectful of you emotionally and physically, and discuss what you expect from the relationship and what safety precautions you will use.

The Appearance-related Social Media Consciousness Scale

When researchers want to understand people's investment in **appearance culture** and how affected they seem to be by the media and other social messages, they sometimes use this questionnaire. You can complete the Sociocultural Attitudes Toward Appearance Questionnaire below and use the scoring information to gain a sense of how much you're under the influence of appearance culture.

This measure was created by researchers (S. Choukas-Bradley, J. Nesi, L. Widman, and B.M. Galla, 2020) trying to understand the extent to which teens and young adults are concerned about how they appear on social media. Test yourself!

	Never	Almost never	Rarely	Sometimes	Often	Almost always	Always
1. When people take pictures of me, I think about how I will look if the pictures are posted on social media.	1	2	3	4	5	6	7
2. I think about how specific parts of my body will look when people see my pictures on social media.	1	2	3	4	5	6	7
3. Even when I'm alone, I imagine how my body will look in a social media picture.	1	2	3	4	5	6	7
4. During the day, I spend time thinking about how attractive I might look when people see pictures of me on social media.	1	2	3	4	5	6	7
5. I try to guess how people on social media will react to my physical appearance in my pictures.	1	2	3	4	5	6	7
6. My attractiveness in pictures is more important than anything else I do on social media.	1	2	3	4	5	6	7

	Never	Almost never	Rarely	Sometimes	Often	Almost always	Always
7. When I go to social events, I care more about looking attractive in pictures people might post on social media than I care about having a fun time.	1	2	3	4	5	6	7
8. If an unattractive picture of me is posted on social media, I feel bad about myself.	1	2	3	4	5	6	7
9. I look at pictures of myself on social media again and again.	1	2	3	4	5	6	7
10. I zoom in to social media pictures to see what specific parts of my body look like.	1	2	3	4	5	6	7
11. If someone takes a picture of me that might be posted on social media, I ask to look at it first to make sure I look good.	1	2	3	4	5	6	7
12. Before I post pictures on social media, I crop them or apply filters to make myself look better.	1	2	3	4	5	6	7
13. If someone takes a picture of me that might be posted on social media, I pose in a particular way so that I'll look as attractive as possible.	1	2	3	4	5	6	7

Instructions for scoring: Sum all item answers and then divide by 13. In research using this measure among women, the average score was found to range from approximately 3.5 to 4.5. The average score was found to be closer to 3 among men.

What not to wear?

As you become a teenager, it's totally normal for you to become more concerned with your image and more interested in what you wear. After all, it's likely that, for most of your childhood, one of your parents bought your clothes and decided what you wore. It's time for you to take over those responsibilities. Your clothing choices may become an expression of your personality, identity, or preferences. For example, you may want to wear certain brands of clothing, or you may want to wear clothing items that say something on them – anything from your favorite sports team's logo to a favorite band's lyrics. You may enjoy shopping for clothes and selecting items to wear, or you may not. (Girls and women don't *all* enjoy these things, but it's OK if you do.)

You may also sometimes disagree with your parents about what you're allowed to wear. Maybe you want to wear a bikini, and your parents want you to wear a one-piece swimsuit. Maybe you want to wear a short skirt, and your parents want you to wear a longer skirt. Maybe you want to wear jeans with rips in them, and your parents want you to wear unripped jeans. When parents and their children disagree about clothing choices, it's rarely a disagreement only about clothing. Instead, children are pushing to make their own choices about something, and parents are pushing back, not quite ready for their children to have that independence.

Parents may want you to look your age and may feel anxious when you look more grown up than they're ready for. And people sometimes draw conclusions about others' personalities based on their clothes. Parents are likely to want you to wear clothes that are comfortable and functional. In other words, your parents probably want you to wear clothes that do the job that clothes are supposed to do: cover your body comfortably. You may be more interested in fashion and less interested in comfort. Sometimes, parents and their daughters also disagree about how much of their body needs to be covered up.

What's going on, and why does it matter how much of your body is covered?

Well, there are a few possibilities. You're probably going through puberty and your body is changing. Your parents may want to protect you from some of the attention that a changing body may attract. Wearing revealing clothes may result in you getting attention from friends or boys, but it may not be good attention. Your parents may not be comfortable with you revealing more of yourself than you used to, whether it's wearing a cropped top or short jean shorts. They also may not be as aware of what's fashionable as you are, and they may be paying more attention to what's practical.

Attention due to revealing clothes may lead others to conclude that you don't have respect for your body and don't expect others to have respect for your body either. When you're an adult, you can and will make choices about your clothing with less concern for what others think. However, when you're young and going through puberty, you may want to think about others' perceptions a little bit. You have a lot of your life ahead of you and many important decisions to make about your life. You don't want others to judge you based on what you're wearing and to limit your choices, whether it be to get work experience, an internship, or a position on your student council or student government association. Of course, the world *should not* work this way; *your clothing choices should not matter.*

Some body image researchers have found that girls' and women's interest in clothes and fashion isn't always about showing off their bodies but about hiding them. More specifically, hiding parts of their bodies that they're not comfortable with. There is nothing wrong with wanting to wear clothes that are comfortable and that you feel make you look your best.

Here's something interesting to think about, though, when it comes to clothing choices. A classic psychology study asked college-aged women to participate in an experiment that involved trying clothes on and then doing activities in those clothes. The researchers told study participants that it was a study about shopping and clothes, but it was really more of a study about body image. Some of the women in the study were asked to try on swimwear and some were asked to try on sweaters. There was no one else around them to see what they were doing in their "new clothes," and they were then asked to work on a math quiz while they tested the clothing's comfort (or lack of comfort). Guess what? The women wearing the swimwear did much worse on the quiz. In fact, they got nearly twice as many of the problems wrong as did the girls wearing bulky sweaters. How come? The researchers proposed that clothing that's revealing or less comfortable is also distracting. It's not that wearing swimwear decreases your IQ. Most people probably feel more insecure in swimwear than they do in loose, comfortable clothes. Wearing revealing clothing may make it more difficult for you to focus on other tasks.

If you feel uncomfortable with what you're wearing, not only may it be more difficult for you to do well on school tasks, but you may also spend time thinking about your appearance in a way that's distracting. Maybe you've found yourself in this situation before? Have you ever worn shoes that are cute but not very comfortable on an outing that requires a lot of walking? Instead of enjoying what you're doing (especially the walking), you may have found yourself thinking that you couldn't wait to go home. In other words, your cute shoes may ruin the outing for you.

What you wear matters for a variety of reasons, not just because of how fashionable others find you. Your clothes can signal to others that you respect and care about your body and that you think that being able to move comfortably is more important than just looking a certain way. There is nothing wrong with caring about your clothes and wanting to be fashionable, but you may want to consider what your clothes could say about you to other people. Make choices that make you feel good, not based on your favorite Instagram celebrity's clothing choices.

EXPERT ADVICE

Jo-Ann Finkelstein, PhD, clinical psychologist, author of *Sexism & Sensibility: Raising Empowered, Resilient Girls in the Modern World*

"Beauty culture makes us believe we have to look a certain way to be valued. Ads and influencers are always telling us what we can do and buy to be 'better.' Did you know that studies show the more we focus on our appearance, the more shame and anxiety we feel about our bodies? And not only that — worrying about our looks distracts us from reaching our goals and showing the world what we're capable of achieving, even if we don't think it does."

Q&A ?!?

If you want to wear make-up or use beauty products, you're not in the minority. One recent report indicated that 80% of girls between the ages of 9 and 11 use "beauty and personal care products." Ninety percent of girls between the ages of 9 and 17 use "beauty products." I would recommend talking with your parents about why you're interested in wearing make-up. Is it just because your friends are? It's likely that they're concerned with you appearing more grown up than you are, or maybe they even feel sad about you getting older. They may also feel that make-up is unnecessary, both because you're beautiful and don't need to "enhance" that beauty and because using make-up takes time and money that could be spent in other ways. You may be able to reach a compromise with your parents by suggesting that you purchase some tinted lip balm or some tinted moisturizer (a lightweight skin cosmetic that can also moisturize your skin). Maybe you need to ease your parents into the idea of make-up.

A lot of women use make-up, at least sometimes, but this doesn't mean that you should, and it definitely doesn't mean that you ever "need" to. Applying make-up can be fun and creative, but it shouldn't feel necessary. One report found that women spend about 55 minutes each day primping (doing their hair, make-up, and other parts of their beauty routines). That amounts to 14 full days of every year spent on primping. Other research suggests that girls spend double the time boys spend on their appearance; this frees boys up to study, play with friends, or learn new skills. And all these beauty products cost about US$15,000 across a woman's lifetime. That's a lot of money!

It may be worth thinking about other ways you could spend your time and money.

Accept it? or fix it?

Clothes are one way you may want to try to "fix yourself up." But there are other ways to change your appearance. For example, maybe you're interested in getting your hair cut a particular way or even changing the color of your hair. Maybe you want to wear make-up, or maybe you even want to permanently change some part of your appearance with surgery.

It's not uncommon for girls and women to think about permanently changing some part of their appearance – their nose, stomach, or breasts – with surgery. In fact, according to the most recent information available in 2023, almost 1.6 million surgical cosmetic procedures were performed in the USA. The **International Society for Aesthetic Plastic Surgery** estimates that about 15 million surgical procedures were performed worldwide in 2022. That amounts to a lot of nose jobs, **tummy tucks**, and breast implants.

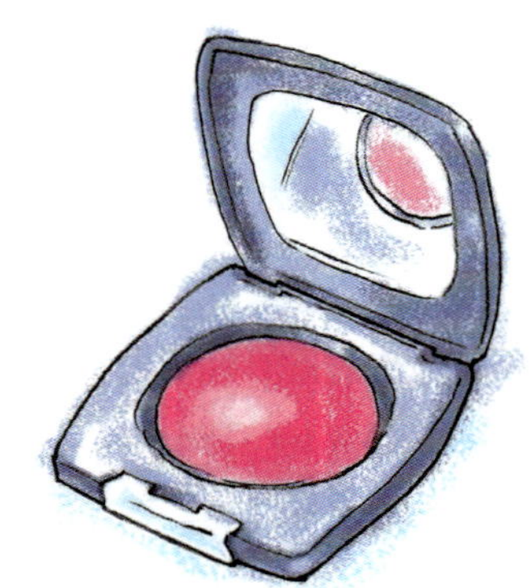

If you aren't happy with some aspect of your appearance, should you consider surgery? Well, there is a lot to say about **cosmetic surgery**.

First, cosmetic surgery can be very expensive. Some operations cost a few thousand dollars and most cost much more. According to the American Society of Plastic Surgeons, the average cost of a nose job (aka rhinoplasty) is more than US$7,000. Even though most surgeries are safe, there are always risks associated with pursuing surgery; these can range from not liking your new body part all the way to death. With surgery, there is always a slim chance that the medication used to put you to sleep during surgery (called anesthesia), or infections that are a result of surgery, could lead to serious and even deadly consequences.

EXPERT ADVICE

Dr. Aubrey Hoffer, *body image expert, Postdoctoral Fellow in the EAT Lab at the University of Louisville*

"You are almost certainly going to run into people in your life who will make you feel like you should change your body. They will make you feel like, by changing how you look — whether it's weight loss, a trendy hairstyle, or anything else — you will be more worthy of love and respect than if you didn't. Your worth as a person is not determined by what you look like. Genuinely, if people don't treat you well based on how you look, that's a "them" problem, not a "you" problem. You get to decide what you want to do with your body — whether that's decorating it with a bunch of piercings and tattoos or never doing anything at all! Don't let anyone take that from you."

Perhaps the most confusing issue when it comes to cosmetic surgery is whether or not it's psychologically beneficial. Some body image researchers believe that an important part of developing a positive body image is accepting yourself and avoiding extreme practices such as cosmetic surgery. Furthermore, research suggests that plastic surgery doesn't completely change how people feel about themselves. In other words, if you get a nose job, you're somewhat likely to like your new nose better than your old nose, but you aren't necessarily going to be happier overall. Your self-esteem is unlikely to be much higher. You may get used to your new nose and not feel like it has changed your life in any significant way once a few months (or years) have passed.

If you don't like one of your features, you should consider surgically changing it. Cosmetic surgery improves mental health.

Although there are a number of studies exploring the links between cosmetic surgery and mental health, the findings reveal inconsistent results. Some research suggests some improvements in satisfaction with the body or facial features that were changed with surgery. There are fewer studies to support the idea that cosmetic surgery improves mental health in general.

Some research has found that people may get depressed after surgery or experience some (mostly temporary) "post-surgery blues." This seems to be prompted by the pain following surgery, concerns about healing, and some reconsideration of pursuing surgery for cosmetic reasons. People who experience depression before undergoing cosmetic surgery do not necessarily experience improvement in their symptoms following surgery. Similarly, self-esteem does not necessarily show improvement following surgery.

Body dysmorphic disorder, which I discuss more in Chapter 7, is a body image disorder that may lead people to consider cosmetic surgery. Research does not suggest that surgery improves body image concerns among people with this disorder.

The bottom line is that cosmetic surgery may improve body image for some people but is less likely to benefit mental health in general.

The cosmetic surgery paradox

As cosmetic surgery has grown in popularity, most people tend to think of these procedures as safe and "effective." However, the safety of any procedure relies on the training and experience of the provider; not everyone who is willing to perform procedures is qualified to do so safely. As discussed above, the extent to which these procedures are "effective" at changing people's appearances in ways that satisfy them is also questionable.

Although beauty is desired by most of us, we tend to prefer natural beauty. In other words, we tend to think less favorably of beauty that is achieved through surgery or other "unnatural" procedures. Body image scientists have referred to this as the cosmetic surgery **paradox**: beauty is sometimes viewed as important enough to be pursued through surgical means, but artificial beauty is usually considered less acceptable. This is why people are often secretive about surgical procedures.

In spite of this paradox and people's secrecy, once people obtain cosmetic surgery, they are likely to pursue other procedures as well. Some research suggests that getting surgery actually leads people to be more focused on their appearance (not less focused or more content). Having one surgery often leads to having others. Multiple surgeries do not suggest that a person feels accepting or content with their appearance or body; it suggests that they view their body as a long-term project.

The advice that most body image researchers offer is to work toward **acceptance** of your "imperfections." It's good advice, to accept yourself as you are, but it can be very challenging. It is also important to keep in mind that you'll continue to change physically for most of your adolescence. Even after your adolescence, you'll keep changing physically in ways that you can't predict now.

You'll have to decide for yourself what sorts of changes to your appearance – if any – are right for you and at what point in your life. Someday, you may want to color your hair. Someday, you may want to change the shape of your nose. These are personal choices but make them for the right reason: because you want to do these things for yourself, not because anyone else wants you to. Always consider all the risks and consequences of these choices. **If you ever do decide to make a permanent change to your appearance, wait until after you've finished puberty, when you'll know yourself better and you're well on your way into adulthood.** Never forget that who you are and your body image aren't just a result of how you look. As Alice's story on the next page reminds us, **you're much more than your outward appearance**. You have many layers of thoughts, emotions, feelings, hopes, and dreams.

MY STORY

Alice Daphne, 22 years old, she/her, USA

My body image is better right now than it has been in the past. I feel pretty content these days and I don't worry much about my appearance. But starting in middle school and through most of college, I was pretty dissatisfied with my body and worried about my weight.

I started dieting in middle school. No one ever told me that I needed to lose weight; I wasn't bullied or teased. I became preoccupied with a beauty ideal that no one can achieve. I didn't appreciate that my body dissatisfaction was being driven by an impossible standard. I tried to be disciplined in my behaviors: drinking a certain amount of water each day, doing a set amount of exercise, keeping track of what I ate, going to bed at a certain time. I even remember learning about thermodynamics in school and trying to figure out how I could apply this to human metabolism so that I could burn more calories (turns out that it doesn't really work that way). At the time, I thought I was being healthy, but now I appreciate that my compulsions were disordered. I was aiming to be "perfect" and hadn't yet figured out that perfect doesn't exist in real life.

Social media used to add to my body dissatisfaction because I followed influencers who were really into fitness and nutrition. A few years ago, one of them switched her whole approach and began to focus on eating intuitively. Watching her transformation helped me to think about changing my life. I also started to take an antidepressant in college, and that helped me to have less anxiety in general and about my body in particular.

A few years ago, I watched my little sister, who's a serious dancer, start to lose weight. It was clear she wasn't eating enough, and she wasn't healthy. I was scared for her and realized I wanted to be a better role model for her. In some ways, I had been doing what she was, but I just had different "rules" I followed. Focusing on appreciating and loving myself more became important to me when I realized I wasn't just doing it for myself but for the example I could set for my sister and others.

Appearance goals can seem like obtainable goals, like there's an endpoint. But there's not. I've come to realize that I need to think of myself the way I think of others I care about. I want what is best for them and I don't want them to be constantly thinking about their appearance. I already think the people I love are beautiful — inside and out. They are amazing, and they don't need to change or fix themselves. I don't need to either.

SUMMING UP #BeYourOwnInfluencer

- Nearly all the pictures of girls and women in the media are edited, and celebrities have access to make-up artists and stylists. How you see them is not how they look "naturally."

- It's normal to compare yourself to others and to want to look like people you admire, but try your best to appreciate your own unique qualities and avoid feeling insecure if you don't look like someone else.

- It may be tempting to try to change your appearance, whether by wearing certain clothes or obtaining cosmetic surgery, but always keep in mind that how you look is only one part of who you are, and "perfection" is impossible.

🔍 FIND OUT MORE:

- There is a lot more about teens and social media in Common Sense Media's report *Teens and Mental Health: How Girls Really Feel About Social Media* (2023), available at: www.commonsensemedia.org/sites/default/files/research/report/how-girls-really-feel-about-social-media-researchreport_web_final_2.pdf

- *Growing Up in Public: Coming of Age in a Digital World* by Devorah Heitner (2023, published by Penguin Random House) is written mostly for parents but offers a lot of valuable insights about social media and how it affects all of our lives.

- The American Society of Plastic Surgeons posts yearly reports about the popularity of cosmetic surgery procedures, costs, and other interesting information: Plastic Surgery Statistics Report, available at: www.plasticsurgery.org/news/plastic-surgery-statistics

- Jo-Ann Finkelstein's book *Sexism & Sensibility: Raising Empowered, Resilient Girls in the Modern World* (2024, published by Harmony Books) contains thoughtful and useful information about many of the themes in this chapter: gender, body image, cosmetics, beautification, and a lot more.

- For more scholarly articles and web pages with information about body image, see the companion website for this book: www.TheBodyImageBook.com.

CHAPTER 5

NOURISH YOUR BODY

#Nutrition101

"Laughter is brightest where food is best"

Irish Proverb

Juliette Béatrice, 17 years old, she/her, Italy

Right now, I feel really good about my body image!

Growing up, I was a pretty skinny kid. In Italy, people often comment on my body. I think they mean to compliment me, but the comments often upset me. I've been told that I need to gain weight, but that was never possible for me, and it made me uncomfortable in my body to hear that.

And then I came to live in the US for a few months and I did gain weight — quickly. Food felt sort of magical at first; it was full of sugar and heavy and different from what I was used to. When I gained weight, I was overwhelmed by my changing body, and I tried to control what I was eating. Then, I realized that I actually liked my new body. And I liked eating all these different foods! I never liked hamburgers until I came to the US. And I had never tried Indian food, which is amazing!

In Italy, the food culture is so different. Family, school, and all sorts of activities revolve around food, and all of our meals are shared with friends or family. In the US, it doesn't always seem like meals are considered important, just something that has to be done. In Italy, every meal is important. But the food is fresher, lighter, and just different. It's so strange that food is taken so seriously in Italy but we actually may not eat as much of it as Americans do.

Social media is also different in Italy versus the US. In Italy, people only seem to post when we look super good — our absolute best. In the US., teenagers seem to post what they're doing and things that make them happy, like their pets and sports. Still, social media can feel toxic because we spend so much time on our phones. I can go from feeling like I'm the most beautiful person in the world to realizing that someone else is prettier than me. Of course, someone else is always prettier!

If I could offer my younger self some body image advice, I'd tell her that our bodies go through a lot of changes, and this is normal. You may not love your body right now, but it will change. Maybe it changes during puberty, when you move to a new place, or when you go to college. We don't have to try to have the same body all the time, but we should try to love ourselves no matter what.

What and how much you eat affect your body image and health in general. Girls and women often think about what they're eating and if they're making the "right" choices. But there are no simple right and wrong food choices. We need to nourish our bodies so that they can grow and thrive, but nutrition is a complex topic, and what works for one person may not work for another. And as Juliette's story reminds us, what works in one family or country may not work in another.

IN THIS CHAPTER YOU'LL LEARN:

- ○ why it's important to eat *intuitively* and to select **nutritious** foods to eat (at least some of the time),
- ○ basic nutritional information about different kinds of food: fat, carbs, sugar, salt, proteins, fiber, fruits, and vegetables, and
- ○ the information you need to think about food as nourishment for your body and mind and as contributing to a positive body image.

The "how much" of eating

Once you begin puberty, you may notice that on some days you feel really hungry, like a bottomless pit, and on other days you're hardly hungry at all. Believe it or not, this is totally normal. As you go through puberty, you'll grow a *lot* (see Chapter 2 for more information about puberty), and this growth is likely to make you hungry and lead you to eat. Unfortunately, although you'll need to eat more during puberty than you did before, there's no simple way to figure out how much to eat on any given day. One approach to figuring out how much to eat is to pay attention to the signals your body gives you. You can attend to cues like how full your stomach feels and how much hunger you experience. This is called **intuitive eating**.

We all learn food rules from our culture, like the rules to eat three meals a day, or not to eat before swimming or sleeping. If you're eating intuitively, you ignore most (if not all) of these rules. This doesn't necessarily mean that you just eat whatever you feel like whenever you feel like it. I'm sure you already know that doughnuts every day for breakfast, a burger and fries for every lunch, and spaghetti and meatballs for each dinner might leave you missing out on other foods that are good for your body – like vegetables. However, eating a fruit smoothie for breakfast, a kale salad for lunch, and grilled chicken for dinner may be nutritious but leave you both unsatisfied and hungry.

Intuitive eating is thoughtful eating. When you feel hungry, think "What would taste good right now?" and "What would feel good to my body right now?" Sometimes the answer may be ice cream, but it probably won't be ice cream all the time. Paying attention to your body and your habits is really important. **You want to feel nourished by food, to enjoy eating, and to create habits that are both psychologically and physically nourishing.**

EXPERT ADVICE

Yaffi Lvova, registered dietitian nutritionist, founder of *Baby Bloom Nutrition*

"People often want to know how much they need to eat, but it's impossible to accurately calculate the amount of energy any individual needs on a given day. Calorie expenditure — the amount your body burns — relies not only on physical movement but also on the things you might not consider: digestion, breathing, and even thinking. Even more than that, so many external factors account for the number of calories your body will burn in a day: sleep quality and quantity, emotional and intellectual stress, hormones, and even the weather affect the energy you need in a day. And that's not even a complete list. Your body is the only calculator fancy enough to take all of those data and communicate them. That communication is your appetite. By allowing your appetite to lead the way, being sure to eat when you're hungry, and eating until you're full and satisfied, you will give your body the amount of energy it needs."

Intuitive Eating Scale

The Intuitive Eating Scale (developed by T.L. Tylka in 2006) measures a person's likelihood of following their body's cues for physical hunger and determining when, what, and how much to eat. Before you read more about intuitive eating, you can test your own tendency to eat intuitively by answering these questions.

	Strongly Disagree	Disagree	Neutral	Agree	Strongly Agree
1. I try to avoid certain foods high in fat, carbohydrates, or calories.	5	4	3	2	1
2. I have forbidden foods that I don't allow myself to eat.	5	4	3	2	1
3. I get mad at myself for eating something unhealthy.	5	4	3	2	1

	Strongly Disagree	Disagree	Neutral	Agree	Strongly Agree
4. If I am craving a certain food, I allow myself to have it.	1	2	3	4	5
5. I allow myself to eat what food I desire at the moment.	1	2	3	4	5
6. I do NOT follow eating rules or dieting plans that dictate what, when, and/or how much to eat.	1	2	3	4	5
7. I find myself eating when I'm feeling emotional (e.g. anxious, depressed, sad), even when I'm not physically hungry.	5	4	3	2	1
8. I find myself eating when I am lonely, even when I'm not physically hungry.	5	4	3	2	1
9. I use food to help me soothe my negative emotions.	5	4	3	2	1
10. I find myself eating when I am stressed out, even when I'm not physically hungry.	5	4	3	2	1
11. I am able to cope with my negative emotions (e.g. anxiety, sadness) without turning to food for comfort.	1	2	3	4	5
12. When I am bored, I do NOT eat just for something to do.	1	2	3	4	5
13. When I am lonely, I do NOT turn to food for comfort.	1	2	3	4	5
14. I find other ways to cope with stress and anxiety than by eating.	1	2	3	4	5
15. I trust my body to tell me when to eat.	1	2	3	4	5
16. I trust my body to tell me what to eat.	1	2	3	4	5
17. I trust my body to tell me how much to eat.	1	2	3	4	5
18. I rely on my hunger signals to tell me when to eat.	1	2	3	4	5
19. I rely on my fullness (satiety) signals to tell me when to stop eating.	1	2	3	4	5

Table continues ...

20. I trust my body to tell me when to stop eating.	1	2	3	4	5
21. Most of the time, I desire to eat nutritious foods.	1	2	3	4	5
22. I mostly eat foods that make my body perform efficiently (well).	1	2	3	4	5
23. I mostly eat foods that give my body energy and stamina.	1	2	3	4	5

To find your total score, add together all the items and then divide by 23. Across several studies, the average score is typically around 3.4 for women and 3.7 for men. There is not a particular score that makes you an intuitive eater, but higher scores make you more likely to be an intuitive eater.

The Ten Principles of Intuitive Eating

Reject dieting Say no to dieting!	**Pay attention to your fullness** Listen to your body's signals of fullness.
Pay attention to your hunger Don't ignore hunger cues.	**Cope with your emotions** Food can be a source of comfort but there are other ways to cope also.
Make peace with food Give yourself permission to eat all foods.	**Respect your body** Your body size and appearance does not determine your worth.
All foods are good There are no "bad" foods.	**Exercise for the right reasons** Be active in ways you enjoy.
Feel satisfied Enjoy food!	**Gentle nutrition** Make food choices that are good for your body and mind.

Principles of intuitive eating

If you aren't supposed to follow "food rules," then how do you know when and how much to eat? I've already suggested that you pay attention to your sense of hunger and fullness, but there's more to intuitive eating than this. There are ten principles of intuitive eating that you may find helpful. These were first developed by registered d etitians Evelyn Tribole and Elyse Resch in 1995 in their book *Intuitive Eating*, which they have since revised (currently, *Intuitive Eating* is in its 4th edition). Some of these principles I discuss in entire chapters of their own; the problems with dieting (principle 1) and a positive way to view physical activity (principle 9) are discussed in Chapters 6 and 8 of this book, and the importance of body respect (principle 8) is discussed throughout this book.

Principles 2, 5, 6, and 7 have to do with attending to your body's cues and emotions. However, your body is not a perfectly consistent machine. All sorts of things affect your physical needs, from how much you sleep and exercise to how much you ate yesterday. This is totally normal. What is not normal is to expect your body to function well if you are hungry. One approach to figuring out how much to eat is to pay attention to the signals your body gives you. This is sometimes referred to as **interoceptive awareness**, which includes not just noticing internal physiological signals but also attending to these cues appropriately. You can make eating decisions by attending to cues like how full your stomach feels, whether or not your stomach is making noises (different noises may signal hunger, digestion, or upset), and your energy level.

Paying attention to your body may seem relatively simple, but our understanding of our own physical experiences is colored by our social and psychological experiences. Disordered eating, traumatic experiences, not having enough food to eat, **autism**, and **ADHD** may all be factors that make

it difficult to attend to your body's signals. Furthermore, if you haven't had much interoceptive awareness for a while, it may take some time – several months even – for you to develop this awareness. And it is possible to feel hungry but be upset or emotional and not want to eat. It's also possible to not feel hungry but want to eat something that you know will bring you joy. There's nothing wrong with your emotions influencing some of your eating patterns, but this can become problematic if eating (or skipping meals) serves as your go-to coping mechanism. I'll discuss maladaptive eating habits and eating disorders more in Chapter 7.

Principles 3 and 4 of intuitive eating are related: to make peace with food and refrain from thinking of food as "good" or "bad." These concepts may be difficult to adopt because it's likely you've grown up hearing that some foods should be avoided, and this may lead you to feel guilty if you eat these foods. Guilt rarely leads people to make healthy choices and can detract from your ability to enjoy a variety of foods. Scientific research suggests that it is typically better for both your psychological and physical health to allow yourself the freedom to eat all types of foods. This leads me to principle 10: gentle nutrition. What does this mean? It basically means that allowing yourself to eat all foods does not mean that you ignore the nutrition that these foods can offer your body. I talk about nutrition specifics for most of the rest of this chapter.

The "what" of eating

What should you eat? The simple answer to this question is: **Anything and nearly everything!** Some foods are better for your body than others, but this doesn't mean that you need to completely avoid any foods. As you've probably figured out by now, often the foods that may be less nutritious – sweets, cake, ice cream – taste good! The next chapter will discuss in more detail why it can actually be (psychologically) valuable to eat some of these foods even if they aren't the most nutritious options. The main point I want to make for now is that you don't need to give up any food that you enjoy (unless you are allergic to certain foods or have a religious reason to avoid them). Of course, you do want to be sure that you're eating enough foods that are nutritious so that you continue to grow and protect your health.

How exactly is the nutritional value of food measured? There are a variety of ways that foods can be categorized. What I mean by **nutritional value** is that foods provide various types of nutrition – through proteins, carbohydrates, fats, vitamins, and minerals – and these have an impact on our health. Below I describe these different types of nutrition so that you can be an educated eater, not because you should eliminate particular foods from your **diet** and not because you should feel guilty about what you eat.

Food's "energy value"

Food is often described by how many calories it contains. A **calorie** is a unit of measurement that indicates the energy potential of a substance. How much energy you need to get from your food depends on a lot of factors. Bigger people need more calories to keep their bodies running well. It's like when you heat a house: a bigger house will need more heat than a smaller house to keep it just as warm. If you're a very active person, you'll also need

more calories to keep your body working because you burn energy or calories when you exercise. Boys and men also tend to need more calories than girls and women. However, focusing on specific calorie information is usually not a great idea; listening to your body's signals of hunger and fullness can be useful in determining what your body needs.

Fat

Fat gets a lot of attention from nutrition experts, medical professionals, and even on social media. You've probably heard of fat as being mostly bad for you. Or maybe you've heard of **ketogenic diets**, which suggest it's healthiest to get most of your energy from fat. In other words, people who recommend ketogenic diets are saying that fat is good. If you're like most people, you may have no idea what to think about fat – how much of it to eat or how much of it to avoid.

This is what nutrition scientists currently know when it comes to fat: without any doubt, fat is more calorie-dense than other nutrients, such as protein. If you eat just a little bit of something high in fat, like a piece of cheese, it will likely be **dense** and provide you with a lot of energy. With that density comes a feeling of fullness, so if you eat something high in fat, you're likely to feel full faster and longer than if you eat something that's low in fat. This can be good, especially if you know that you won't be able to eat again for many hours.

But if you're going to eat every few hours or whenever you're hungry, do you need to consume fat? The answer is still "yes." Fat doesn't just make you feel full, it has benefits for brain health. There are actually different kinds of fat; for example, you may have heard that nuts contain unsaturated fat. Foods that contain **unsaturated fats**, such as avocados and sunflower seeds, don't have the same effect on your health as **saturated fats**. In contrast, saturated fats can raise your **blood cholesterol** over time; these are found in foods such as butter, cream, cheese, and most meat. Limiting your intake of foods high in saturated fats can lower your blood **cholesterol**, which may lower your risk of some health problems later in life, including **heart disease** and some **cancers**. Of course, we all eat some saturated fat, and there's nothing wrong with this!

The **bottom line** is that it's perfectly fine to consume foods containing fat. More "natural" foods (such as salmon, olives, and avocados) are likely to contain unsaturated fats, in contrast to processed foods (such as store-bought sweets or pizza), which are likely to contain saturated fats and may not be as good for your body.

EXPERT ADVICE

Jenna Werner, RD, owner of *Happy Strong Healthy* (www.happystronghealthyrd.com)

"One of the coolest things about nutrition is learning about what your body likes the most and knowing that this is different for everyone! Foods are not 'good' or 'bad,' but different meals and snacks and combinations all make each one of us feel different things. I like to tell my clients to picture themselves as explorers and consider every mealtime a mission. When it's over, check in with yourself to see how it went. How do you feel? Pleasant? Energized? Unpleasant? Uncomfortable? Happy? Hungry? Take note of those feelings, and for the less positive ones, ask yourself, 'What can I change next time?' Maybe it is the speed of consumption or the distractions around us; sometimes, something small can change the outcome of your next mission! Keep learning, keep listening, and remember food is meant to be enjoyed while it nourishes your amazing body."

Carbohydrates

Carbohydrates (aka "carbs") tend to get a bad rap. In fact, some diets (for example, the **Atkins** and **paleo diets**) focus on reducing carbs in order to lose weight. However, it's nearly impossible to completely eliminate carbs from your diet and you shouldn't try to.

Carbohydrates are an important part of your daily food intake for many reasons. Perhaps most importantly, carbs are an easy, fast source of energy for your body. This is partially why you may have heard of athletes "**carb loading**" or eating a lot of pasta before an athletic event. Having a lot of carbs in your system ready for use may improve athletic performance (although there are a lot of other things that affect athletic performance). Carbs are often tasty – think warm, fresh bread – and fill you up quickly.

Like fats, not all carbs are alike, and some are more nutritious than others. Plain white bread doesn't have as much nutritional value as wholegrain bread and may contain processed ingredients that aren't especially beneficial for your body. Doughnuts are delicious but are typically fried in oil, making them high in saturated (unhealthy) fat. So what carbs are best to eat?

Smart carbohydrate options include brown rice, oatmeal, and multigrain bread. Many fruits and vegetables (for example, apples and spinach) are also high in carbs and are a good source of other nutrients as well. These carbohydrates have been found to help promote heart health.

The **bottom line** is that carbohydrates are a great source of energy for our bodies. Carbs also help our bodies to create neurotransmitters (like serotonin) that affect mood and are our brain's preferred fuel. According to the **Mayo Clinic**, a respected medical institution in the USA, nearly half of your diet should be made up of carbs. It may be best for your body, however, to eat mostly whole grains and unprocessed types of carbs.

Salt

Salt may be one of the most misunderstood substances in our diet. Salt is made up of the chemical compounds sodium and chloride, which are both essential to human survival. And yet you've probably heard people around you mention their desire to reduce their salt intake.

Salt (aka sodium when it comes to food labels) helps to preserve (or keep from going bad) many foods we consume and makes most foods taste better, so it's everywhere. Even food that doesn't taste salty often has salt in it, including most bread, pizza, and sandwiches. If you look through the fridge and cabinets in your house and read some food labels, you may be surprised. You'll find some of what I did: one can of black beans = 120 mg of sodium, one piece of bread = 210 mg of sodium, one serving of mozzarella cheese = 170 mg of sodium, and one serving of chicken noodle soup = 700 mg of sodium.

Is there anything wrong with salt? Salt can contribute to **water retention** and **constipation**. More importantly, it has been associated with high blood pressure and heart disease. Because of this, the American Heart Association recommends that all of us keep our salt intake to around 1,500 milligrams a day. Most people consume 3,400 milligrams daily. One teaspoon of salt is approximately 2,300 milligrams of sodium.

Some doctors have recently suggested that the link between salt and heart health has been overstated and we shouldn't worry about eating salt. However, if you know that high blood pressure and heart problems run in your family, it makes sense to be cautious and not shake a lot of salt onto your food.

The **bottom line** is that salt makes food taste better and last longer, but it may be associated with high blood pressure and poor heart health when eaten in high amounts.

Sugar

Did you know that the average American eats 22 teaspoons of **sugar** per day? Like salt, sugar has a way of sneaking into foods you wouldn't expect. Bread, chicken nuggets, granola bars, and yogurt (and even ketchup) are all surprisingly high in sugar. You may not realize that sugar is in a lot of these products because sugar is often called other things: **high fructose corn syrup**, cane sugar, dextrose, fruit **juice concentrate**, or one of dozens of other names. Most of the sugar we consume doesn't come right out of a container of sugar but is found in processed foods. Soda, juice, and some breakfast cereals contain a lot of sugar. Sugar is in so many foods because it often makes them taste better. And as we all get used to eating packaged foods with a lot of sugar added, we seem to crave sugar more and more.

What's the problem with eating sugar? The biggest concern may be that eating processed, sugary foods is likely to take the place of healthier options. For example, a bowl of berries would be a nutritious and healthy dessert, but most of us would prefer to have those berries in a pie or on top of vanilla ice cream. The pie and ice cream would probably mean we'd eat fewer berries and more sugar.

The **bottom line** is that it would be difficult to avoid all sugar and it isn't necessary to do so. Natural sources of sugar like fruits and vegetables are often nutritious options, but this doesn't mean that you can't enjoy sugary foods that are less nutritious!

Fruits and vegetables

I'm sure you've heard that fruits and vegetables are good for you, but I bet you don't eat enough of them. Most people don't! In fact, it's nearly impossible to eat too many fruits and vegetables because they're such a good source of all kinds of nutrients.

The US Department of Agriculture recommends that about half of each meal and snacks be made up of fruits and/or vegetables. Half! This may not seem realistic – and other dietary recommendations suggest that carbohydrates make up half of our diet, which doesn't leave room for other important options (this stuff can get confusing!). Furthermore, a lot of us probably don't have time in the morning to eat a lot of fruit, and string beans probably don't seem appetizing at 7 am. Still, fruits and vegetables can be a nutritious and delicious part of our daily diet.

Why are fruits and vegetables important? They contain important nutrients, including folate, magnesium, **potassium**, fiber, vitamin A, vitamin C, and vitamin K. They also don't have a lot of the less desirable qualities, such as **preservatives**, additives, and salt and sugars that come with processed or packaged foods. It's also important to remember that fruits and vegetables can be delicious. You may want to explore new varieties and new ways of using them, such as dried, frozen, or canned (more on that below) and different ways of preparing them (roasting and stir frying, for example).

The **bottom line** is that fruits and vegetables are nutritious and delicious. Try to eat at least some sort of fruit and vegetable each day, and, ideally, at most meals.

Instead of eating fruit, it is just as healthy to drink fruit juice.

In recent years, **juicing** has become popular. This is just another way of saying "drinking juice" instead of eating solid foods. "Juicing" also refers to blending up fruits and vegetables in a blender and drinking them.

It's true that drinking nutrients can be faster and easier than eating them. If you're blending up fruits and vegetables at home, this may be a great way to drink nutrients. However, most store-bought juice isn't as nutritious as the fruit (or vegetables) it comes from. For one thing, most juice contains added sugars to make it taste sweeter. Although there is nothing wrong with consuming some sugar (see the section above about sugar), it's healthier to eat the whole fruit without the added sugar. Sometimes a lot of sugar is added to juice. In fact, some juices contain relatively little in the way of fruit or vegetables and as much sugar as a soda. In these cases, actual fruit and vegetables are definitely more nutritious than juice. Fruits and vegetables also typically contain some fiber, which is extracted (taken out) when juice is made. Fiber has health benefits that make solid fruits and vegetables a better choice than juice.

In sum, it's not true that drinking juice is typically as nutritious as eating fruits or vegetables. Juice can be delicious, but you may want to consider choosing juice that doesn't contain a lot of sugar or other additives and preservatives.

Protein

Protein is an important part of a balanced, healthy diet. Protein helps your bones, muscles, cartilage (soft, connective tissue found in the body), and skin to grow. It's also important for hormone functioning. Foods that are high in protein make you feel full more quickly than foods that are lower in protein.

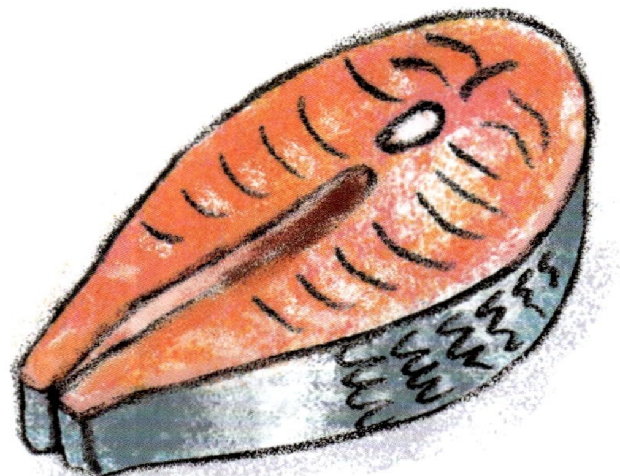

Eating protein is likely to keep you from feeling hungry. Unlike some of the other nutrients discussed in this chapter, it's usually pretty easy to get the daily recommended amount of protein. According to the US Department of Agriculture, most people eat enough protein without trying to.

Q&A ?!?

The short answers to these questions are "yes" and "no." Most nutritionists recommend that people drink water and milk because both are good for our bodies. Many other drinks tend to be high in sugar. Milk is a good source of protein and calcium, both of which are important to your body as you grow. Most milk is also high in potassium, vitamin A, and vitamin D. All of these nutrients can be hard to find in other foods, so it's wonderful if you can drink them in milk.

There are many different varieties of milk. They vary mostly on the percentage of fat included, from nonfat to full fat (3–4% fat) milk. The benefits of drinking milk outweigh any concerns about the fat content. Some people are lactose intolerant or may get an upset stomach when they drink milk. This condition is similar, although not exactly the same, as a food allergy. If you're one of these people, you may want to try lactose-free milk or other nondairy milk, like almond milk, soy milk, coconut milk, or oat milk. Most of these have nutritional benefits similar to regular milk. If you don't particularly like milk, you may like chocolate milk. There are other sorts of flavored milk, as well. Flavored milk, chocolate milk, and hot chocolate all contain a lot of nutrients, making them not just delicious but also nutritious.

Most of us are likely to get protein from meats like hamburgers and chicken, but there are many other kinds of protein as well. Beans, peas, soy products (for example, tofu), nuts, and seeds are all excellent sources of protein. Eating seafood such as salmon can also be a great way to increase the protein in your diet.

The **bottom line** is that protein is an important part of a healthy diet, but you're likely already eating plenty of protein. You may want to think about trying some new and different kinds of protein that come from vegetables and other plants to add variety to your diet.

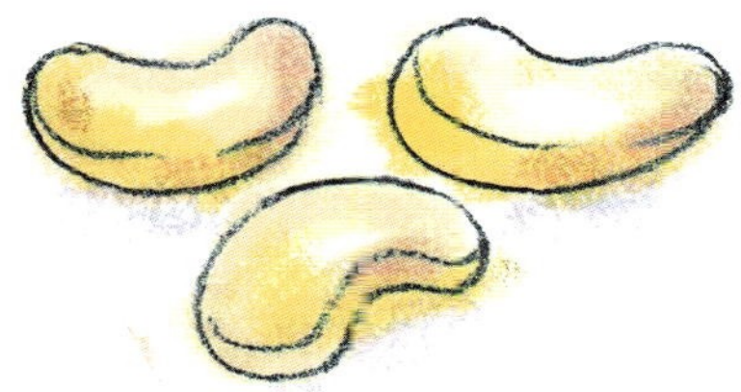

Fiber

Maybe you've heard the word **fiber** but don't know exactly what it is. Fiber is food that isn't digested or absorbed by the body. That probably sounds weird, but there are actually parts of foods that pass through your body without really changing much. These foods tend to be bulky, filling, and come from natural (not processed) sources. Foods that are high in fiber include apples, artichokes, barley, beans, Brussels sprouts, carrots, citrus fruits, nuts, oats, peas, prunes, raspberries, wheat bran, and whole-wheat flour.

There are many benefits to eating foods high in fiber, including healthy digestion, lowered risk of **diabetes**, heart health, lowered cholesterol, healthy blood sugar levels, and regular bowel movements (it's better than the alternative – constipation!).

The **bottom line** is that including foods high in fiber in your regular eating habits is good for your body. Foods that contain a lot of fiber, such as most fruits and vegetables, tend to contain many other nutrients as well.

Q&A ?!??

Vitamins and minerals

Vitamins and **minerals** – otherwise known as **micronutrients** – are dietary components that your body needs in order to grow, develop, and stay healthy. Some of the most important micronutrients are iron, vitamin A, iodine, and zinc. The catch? These aren't produced in the body but must be derived from food. Luckily, you don't need them in large quantities.

Most are easily available in foods and drinks you probably eat and drink regularly. For example, most salt has iodine added to it, so you're most likely getting more than enough iodine. Vitamin A is important for your eyesight and immune system, but you're likely getting enough vitamin A in the milk you drink. If you don't drink milk, try kale; it's also full of vitamin A. Iron is important to keep both your brain and your muscles functioning well and can be found in foods such as lentils (and other beans), spinach, quinoa, most meat, tofu, and even dark chocolate. Zinc is good for your immune system and nervous system and can be found in most meat and in vegetables such as spinach, broccoli, and kale, as well as in beans, lentils, nuts, and seeds.

There are many supplements available at grocery stores and at pharmacies that sell vitamins and minerals. However, most people do not need these and there is even some evidence to suggest that these supplements may cause more harm than good. In the USA (but not the UK), supplements are not regulated or checked by the **US Food and Drug Administration (FDA)**. This can lead to mislabeling of supplements, and sometimes these products are not safe, especially for growing bodies.

The **bottom line** is that if you live in the US or UK, the chances are you don't have to worry about your vitamin and mineral consumption. You're likely getting what you need through the foods you eat, and you don't need to take supplements to get these nutrients.

Vegetarianism and other similar diets

Maybe you've heard about celebrities such as Beyoncé choosing to eat vegan food. People often have very strong feelings about these issues. Most nutritionists would agree that there are pros and cons to avoiding meat and other animal products. I'll briefly describe them here, define some terms, and give you a sense of how they differ.

Vegetarians typically don't eat meat (for example, beef and pork), poultry (for example, chicken and turkey), or seafood (for example, salmon and shrimp). This may be a healthy – even moral – choice for many people, as eliminating meat, in particular, also eliminates a lot of saturated fat from most diets. There is evidence that the environmental toll of eating meat is much more significant than most people realize. Some people feel very strongly about not killing animals to provide a source of food for people. However, we also get a lot of nutrients from meat, seafood, and poultry; these foods can

Q&A

What are GMOs? Are they dangerous? Can they negatively affect my growth and development?

GMOs are genetically modified organisms. In other words, GMOs are living things that have had their genes altered in some way by humans. Usually, when people talk about GMOs, they're referring to plants that are modified as a part of food production, but other organisms are also modified to create medicines (such as insulin, which is used to treat diabetes).

People have been modifying the food supply in a variety of ways for hundreds (probably thousands) of years. Plants have been grown in certain soils, for example, and genes have been "chosen" through the process of breeding (having certain plants or animals fertilize others selected by scientists). It all seems a bit stranger when scientists modify genes in a laboratory, but it isn't all that different.

There is no scientific evidence that GMOs are dangerous, or even unhealthy. The American Medical Association, the National Academy of Sciences, the American Association for the Advancement of Science, and the World Health Organization (WHO) all agree that GMOs are safe. So what's the big deal about GMOs?

Some people worry that there could be risks associated with GMOs that just haven't been revealed yet. And people often fear what they don't totally understand. In fact, one recent scientific study showed that the people most opposed to GMOs were the people who understood them the least.

It's very unlikely that GMOs present any sort of risk or danger to your health, well-being, or development. In fact, by modifying fruits and vegetables, for example, in ways that make them easier to produce and get to us, GMOs may actually help to improve our health overall.

be very high in protein and iron (for example, in meat) and healthy fats (for example, in salmon). Human beings have been eating meat products since the beginning of recorded history, and there is likely a good reason for this. It's nutritious, filling, and can taste delicious.

Vegans are vegetarians who avoid all animal products. Not only do they not eat meat products, but they typically don't eat milk, cheese, eggs, and other dairy products. They also may avoid products that come from animals such as wool, silk, leather, and even honey. For some people, this may be a healthy way to eat, assuming they get plenty of nutrients from other foods such as nuts, beans, fruits, and vegetables. But it also may be impractical. Some of your favorite foods might be eliminated from your diet if you became vegan, including pizza, hamburgers, and fried chicken. Also, a lot of shoes are made of leather, so it may be impractical for you to totally avoid animal products.

Pescatarians are vegetarians who eat seafood. For these people, seafood may be a favored food, or they may believe that the health benefits of eating seafood and the lower environmental impact of producing seafood make it a morally acceptable source of food. **Macrobiotic** eaters are vegans who only eat **unprocessed foods** and sometimes fish; they also avoid sugar and refined oils. As with vegetarianism and veganism, these types of eaters tend to want to improve their health and avoid animal suffering and unnecessary environmental damage.

Keep in mind that most of these types of diets require extra work and planning to ensure that you get enough of the nutrients needed, such as protein and iron. Since most people do eat meat, it can be very inconvenient and impractical to give up the foods that most other people eat. If you're interested in trying a vegetarian or other similar diet, talk to the people you live with and see how they feel about this and what they're willing to do to support you. Unless you do your own grocery shopping, it may be difficult to make drastic changes to your diet without others' support.

"Superfoods"

Some foods are discussed in popular media as if they have superpowers. For example, kale, avocados, blueberries, salmon, açaí berries, Greek yogurt, and almonds are often described as "**superfoods**." It's not exactly an accident that these foods receive a lot of attention; they contain more vitamins and minerals than the average food. In other words, it's a good idea to eat these foods – at least sometimes.

However, as I already discussed in this chapter, it can be problematic to think about food as "good" or "bad" – or even "super." Putting foods into basic categories can leave you feeling like you must eat certain foods and avoid others. This is problematic because you should also enjoy the food you eat and adopt eating habits that nourish you both psychologically and physically. It's also not true that some foods are so amazing that eating them is all you need to do to protect your health. Health is most often achieved through the adoption of habits – behaviors you engage in most days – including your eating and activity habits. Our health is also affected by our circumstances, access to resources (açaí berries are not cheap!), and many other factors.

EXPERT ADVICE

Anna Lutz, MPH, RD, CEDS-S, founder of *Sunny Side Up Nutrition*

"It may seem confusing at times with all of the messages out there about 'healthy eating.' Although nutrition is important, eating well is not only about the nutrients that are on the table. Healthy eating involves feeling at ease around food and not stressing out about what you eat. Healthy eating includes making connections and memories with other people while eating special meals. Healthy eating is honoring what your body is telling you it needs and wants. Healthy eating is complex and multifaceted, just like you!"

Eating habits

Hopefully, after reading everything in this chapter, you will understand that you can eat anything you want to but that some foods have more (physical) health benefits than others. You also see that the way that different foods (for example, fats) are talked about by people and online isn't always accurate. **People can have very strong opinions about food, but this doesn't mean that these opinions are accurate.**

When I was growing up (probably around when your parents were also growing up), kids earned about basic nutrition in school using a "food pyramid." The foods on the bottom of the pyramid were the foods we were told to eat the most of, and the foods at the top we were told to eat the least of. As nutrition research has advanced, ideas about what we should aim to eat the most and the least has changed. It's important to remember that nutrition recommendations and guidelines are just advice about the sorts of eating habits that may be most beneficial to your physical health. For example, one current recommendation is to focus on eating as many fruits and vegetables as possible. Of course, this is only doable if you can afford to buy a lot of fruits and vegetables and you like to eat these foods. Another recommendation is to eat complex carbohydrates or grains (for example, whole-wheat bread). Sometimes you may just want French or sourdough bread, however.

Your body is unique and what works for you may not be what is recommended by some people. Furthermore, most people don't manage to put together each meal to include every nutritious food they enjoy eating. It's nice to have the goal of eating nutritious food, but it can be a complicated and difficult goal.

Caring for your body and respecting your body by nourishing it can be a part of developing a positive body image. As you'll learn in the other chapters of this book, there are many other factors that also contribute to the development of your body image.

Maira Kashvi, 22 years old, she/her, USA

These days, I try not to think about my body. I use the mirror to make sure that my clothes are on the right way and my hair isn't sticking up, but I try not to pay a lot of attention to my appearance.

A couple of years ago, after years of on-and-off disordered eating, I saw an amazing anti-diet dietitian. Her approach was all about separating who you are from what you look like. It was life-changing to have someone work intensely with me for a year and offer me a different way to think about my life.

When you have a maladaptive relationship with food, it takes over everything. I had started to feel like there was just no way out of it! My dietitian helped me to understand the science behind intuitive eating. She explained how humans have an innate ability to know when we are hungry and full. I had completely lost the ability to trust myself and my body. But, with time, I was able to regain that trust. I have a huge sweet tooth – especially for foods like chocolate cake, which made it hard not to worry about overindulging on sweets and skipping more nutritious foods. But it turns out that our bodies are really smart!

I now appreciate that my body will sort of tell me what it needs and wants. I think of my food cravings differently now. A craving used to be emotional, but now I don't really associate my feelings with food. I can want a salad because it would just taste good to me, not because of any other reason. I even crave spinach sometimes!

If I could offer advice to others, I'd say that being a good person is what matters most. You have to like yourself on the inside. My mom is Italian and my dad is Indian and people sometimes tell me that I'm "exotic" or even "beautiful." That's nice to hear, but it is not all that helpful to my mental health. I've had to put time and energy into taking care of myself and it's been really worth it.

SUMMING UP #Nutrition101

✓ It's important that you listen to your body and try to eat intuitively.

✓ You can eat all foods, but some foods, such as fruits and vegetables, may be more nourishing than others.

✓ Eating nutritious foods is one way you can care for your body, and treating yourself with care and respect can bring you closer to a positive body image.

🔍 FIND OUT MORE:

✦ To learn more about intuitive eating, especially the basic ten principles, you might be interested in exploring this page on the website *Intuitive Eating*: www.intuitiveeating.org/10-principles-of-intuitive-eating/

✦ The *Sunny Side Up Nutrition* web page has a lot of information about how to think about food that is nutritious and good for our bodies without stressing about food. They also share recipes: https://sunnysideupnutrition.com/

✦ The Mayo Clinic's web page has scientifically based information about nutrition, such as this page about carbohydrates: *How carbs fit into a healthy diet*: www.mayoclinic.org/healthy-lifestyle/nutrition-and-healthy-eating/in-depth/carbohydrates/art-20045705

✦ For more scholarly articles and web pages with information about healthy eating and nutrition, see the companion website for this book: www.TheBodyImageBook.com.

CHAPTER 6

DON'T DIET

"One cannot think well, love well, sleep well, if one has not dined well"

Virginia Woolf, English 20th-century writer

Hannah Elizabeth, 21 years old, she/her, USA

I've struggled with my body image pretty much my entire life. The struggle began in early childhood and coincided with my weight gain around then. My mom made it pretty clear that she hoped to save me from the concerns about her body and weight that consumed her (eventually leading to her own pursuit of weight-loss surgery). But her efforts seemed to have had the opposite of the desired effect.

By the time I was 7, my mom started to replace the "normal foods" in our house with "diet foods." There were Skinny Cow ice cream bars and 100-calorie snack packages. My older brother has always seemed to have a leaner body build and was allowed to have real food, but it has always been literally locked in the pantry away from me.

The day after 8th grade ended, I was sent to a 9-week weight-loss camp. On the car ride there, my mom offered me a "last meal" of all sorts of junk food. Once I got to "fat camp," I wasn't allowed to have much contact with the outside world. I could call my parents once a week for 15 minutes only. I think they were worried that we'd start to cry and our parents would come to get us. Two of the campers actually tried to escape the camp and ran away into the woods. I could hardly blame them; we were allowed to eat our three meals and two snacks each day, but there were some days that I didn't like any of the food and hardly ate at all. And we also exercised essentially all day long. I missed my friends and family so much! But I lost about one-quarter of my body weight that summer. I was thin for the first time in my life.

After my fat camp experience, I tried to stay in the routines I had learned, but I went back to a normal life of school, friends, and food my parents made. I tried to eat Lean Cuisine meals, but eventually, the weight came back on. This foreshadowed years of **yo-yo dieting** in high school.

I've tried low sugar, low cal, and keto. I've lost and gained weight and done it all again. But I've started to really work on developing a positive relationship with food. I now understand that what the adults in my life taught me as a child was wrong. I know my mom was doing her best to look out for me, and she worried because of our family history of heart disease. It has taken years of

My Story continues …

therapy to try to undo the guilt I still have about eating certain foods. I still live at home, and I am busy as a student who also works 15 hours per week, which makes it hard to find the time and energy to eat the way I'd like to.

If I could offer my younger self advice, I'd tell her that she's never going to obtain the perfect body, because it doesn't even exist! I'd beg her to avoid all of those fad diets. And I'd tell her to be really careful about the diet-related information she sees on social media. There are so few credible resources when it comes to how to eat, and the inaccurate advice can really mess with your head.

IN THIS CHAPTER YOU'LL LEARN:

- what diet culture is,
- why dieting is so harmful, and
- why you should resist dieting when you feel the urge to change your eating habits.

Like Hannah, most of us have grown up the victims of cultural messages indicating that it is important to control our appetites to look a certain way – to **diet**. We should monitor what we eat and how active we are. We should avoid certain foods altogether. We should "cleanse" our bodies of "bad" foods. All of these messages suggest that we can't trust ourselves. Our bodies will betray us! **These messages are incredibly misleading and harmful**.

Collectively, these **maladaptive** messages about food and our bodies are referred to as diet culture.

What exactly is "diet culture"?

Cultural messages tell us:
- we can control our bodies and our health,
- there is one right way to have a body, and
- we're obligated to fix our bodies when they don't fit cultural expectations.

All of these messages are pervasive and inaccurate. They suggest that we should just keep trying – doing the same thing over and over again with the hope of different results – to achieve the body we want. That body is slender in all the right places, muscular in all the right places, and voluptuous in all the right places. (The "right places" are different for individuals who identify as male versus female.)

Here's what psychological and medical research actually indicates:

1. We don't have total control over our health or the appearance of our bodies. With enough time, will, and money, you can exercise, alter your eating habits, get cosmetic surgery, consult with doctors and therapists, and alter your appearance and health. But the alterations may not be permanent and may require a great deal of effort. Other factors – from your **genes** to your access to resources – play a substantial role in your psychological health, as well as your physical health and physical appearance.

2. Every body is unique. You may have your dad's nose and your mom's vulnerability to experience an upset stomach when you're stressed, but you are your own unique person. You can try to look like a celebrity, influencer, or even a popular girl at school, but you won't ever be those people and you don't need to be. Even if you ate the exact same things as that girl and did the exact same physical activity program that she did, your body would look different!

3. "Fixing" or changing our health or appearance-related behaviors is not **obligatory**. We all tend to invest some time and energy into both how we look and how we feel (i.e. our health). However, diet culture suggests that we really should do a variety of things to "improve" ourselves. What if we are absolutely fine just the way we are? A lot of people make a lot of money by making us feel insecure and encouraging us to invest in these improvements, but no product, pill, or plan will produce happiness or perfection.

During the first year of the COVID-19 pandemic (2020), the weight-loss market in the USA declined, but this brief loss was restored in 2021 and the weight-loss market was estimated to be worth US$72.6 billion. The global weight-loss market was valued at US$192.7 billion in 2021, with projections indicating that this could grow to US$326 billion by 2028. In other words, dieting is big business; the "health" recommendations pertaining to our appearance, bodies, and weight are not typically offered by well-meaning health professionals seeking to help us feel good about ourselves and live long, healthy lives. They're offered by unregulated companies looking to make money; they contribute to the diet culture we live in.

Diet culture tells us we must control our bodies instead of caring for them. It leaves us feeling dissatisfied with who we are but offers a range of

Q&A

"solutions" for this dissatisfaction. Often these solutions are unhealthy and rarely are they based on scientific evidence. As you'll see in this chapter and later in this book (especially Chapter 7, which discusses eating disorders), many of the instructions for how we should behave that appear in diet culture messages are no different from the criteria that clinical psychologists use to diagnose eating disorders. What all diet culture messages tend to have in common is a focus on the importance of personal responsibility in how we look and feel. But the real problem is with the culture, not the individual! **Our bodies are not never-ending projects.**

The weight of the matter

It's important to remember that your weight is just a number. It doesn't determine your self-worth, and it is only *sometimes* associated with health. Also, there are a lot of things that contribute to your body size and shape, and some of them aren't within your control. Scientists estimate that 60–80% of your height is due to your genes. One large scientific study found that the majority of both your height and weight may be due to your genes (with the environment having more influence over your weight than your height). In other words, there's not much you can do to change your height, and there may not be a whole lot that can be done to modify your weight, either. You're however tall you are mostly due to how tall your parents are. Nutrition, medical care, and general health may affect your height a bit but not a whole lot.

Although weight is *somewhat* more easily changed than height, it's also very much influenced by our genes. Eating nutritious foods is important for your long-term health, but trying to change your body size or shape by changing what you eat can be very difficult and usually isn't a good idea. Recent research suggests that our body size has a lot to do with our appetites and that our appetites are also determined by **genetics**. Some people are more likely to feel hungry more often than others. Some people don't care as much about food because they don't feel hungry as often. Being hungry is a pretty miserable experience, and it's not a good idea to ignore hunger because you risk not only feeling very cranky but also not giving your body the nutrients it needs.

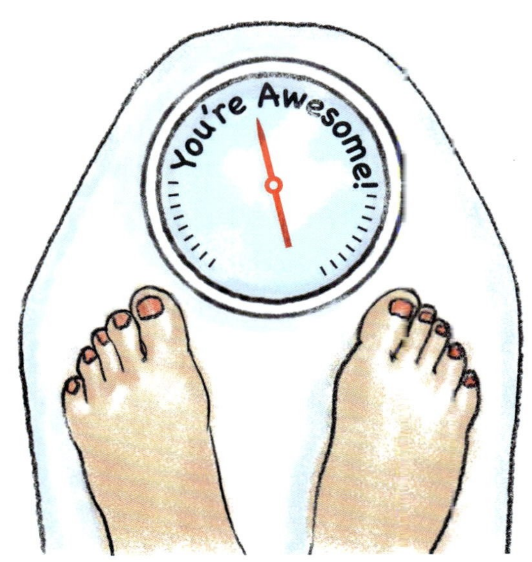

Q&A?!?

I know that **body mass index (BMI)** is used as a measure of whether or not a person is growing and weighs the "right" amount, but people just have different body types, right? Is there a "right" amount we should weigh?

You're absolutely right. BMI is often used as a measure of weight status — especially in medical settings — but it is just a very rough measure based on height and weight, and it can't account for people's different body builds. People obviously have very different body shapes. BMI was never intended to be a measure of health. Some scientists and doctors have argued that people who are classified as "overweight" according to their BMI are at risk for health problems associated with weight, such as type 2 diabetes, heart disease, and some forms of cancer. However, there are many things that contribute to our health! For example, if you exercise and are in good physical shape, you may improve your heart health, regardless of your body size.

There is not a "right" amount that any one person should weigh. Your weight should increase across your teen years because you are growing in so many ways during puberty. Your weight will also change across your life as your habits change, and you may experience pregnancy, illness, or aging. Your body will function best when you are eating (some) nutritious foods, being physically active (sometimes), coping with whatever stressors you experience, and getting plenty of sleep. Whatever you weigh when you are maintaining those habits is probably the right amount for you.

When your doctor tells you that you need to lose weight, you should go on a diet.

Most doctors become doctors because they want to help people achieve good health and recover from illness or injury. They make recommendations that they believe will be helpful. However, most doctors receive very little (if any) training about nutrition, diet, body image, and weight. They can document where you fall on a height–weight chart, but they may not know much about how to educate and support their patients concerning weight. In other words, although a doctor is a good person to turn to with questions about health and well-being, sometimes doctors offer bad advice when it comes to your weight.

If a doctor ever tells you that you need to lose weight, it's worth getting a second opinion from another medical professional. It may be most useful to talk to an expert who has been trained specifically to help people eat well and develop a healthy body image. A registered **dietician**, nutritionist, or even a psychologist with this specialty would be good options for people to consult. If you live near a university, check to see if they have a center or clinic that helps people with eating or body image concerns. Universities tend to be on top of the latest science and sometimes even offer free health services to people interested in trying out new medical **regimens**.

Most importantly, if you believe – because a doctor told you so, or your own research leads you to believe this – that you need to lose weight, **a diet is not the answer**. It may be a good idea to change your regular habits to be more physically active, for example, but only make changes that you plan to keep for the long term. As I'll explain more below, **if you go on a short-term diet of any kind, it's likely to lead to weight gain, not loss, over time**. It's also likely to be a miserable experience.

The problems with diets

They don't work – in fact, you'll probably gain weight

Let's say you decide to try a low-carb diet. You cut out most bread, pasta, and other grain-based foods from your diet. You'll miss those foods a lot! Assuming you replace those foods with healthy options like fruits and vegetables, you'll probably lose weight. For most people (and thousands of people have been studied), the weight-loss part of this experience lasts a few months, maybe 3 months if you're lucky. People will lose a couple of pounds a week for up to a few months and they'll think the diet is amazing. And then life gets in the way and it turns out that this diet is impossible to maintain. Maybe you'll be out to dinner with friends, and you won't be able to resist the rolls. Your dad will make your favorite pasta dinner, and you'll eat three servings. You'll have a bad day at school, and you'll eat a bagel for lunch. Gradually, the carbs will sneak back into your diet (as they should), and gradually, you'll gain whatever weight you lost. Typically, people gain even a bit more weight than they lost. **In studies that follow dieters across time, nearly all dieters gain back the weight they lost after 2 years, and most have gained back extra weight, too.**

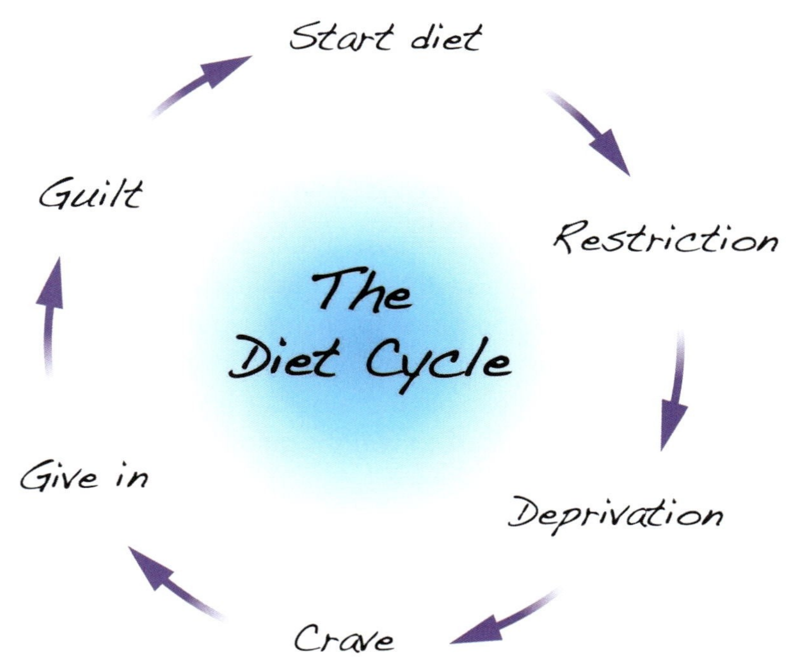

EXPERT ADVICE

Traci Mann, PhD, Professor of Psychology at the University of Minnesota and author of *Secrets from the Eating Lab*

"So many things I've heard about dieting my entire life are just plain wrong. I was told that losing weight was the hard part and keeping it off was the easy part, and that if you couldn't keep the weight off, it was because you were weak and had no willpower. In fact, losing weight is the easy part and keeping weight off is the hard part. Most people are unsuccessful at this in the long term, but it isn't because they are weak. It's because dieting — calorie deprivation — leads to all kinds of changes in your body and in your thinking that make it very difficult to keep dieting successfully. The problem isn't the dieter. The problem is diet<u>ing</u>."

They'll make you cranky

When people go on a diet, they often claim that they want to feel better. People usually expect to feel better both physically and psychologically. Research suggests that people feel good at the start of a diet. They tend to feel like they're committing to do something for themselves that's important.

The problem? These good feelings don't last very long at all, because none of us like to be deprived. In fact, feeling like we can't eat foods we want to eat is likely to lead to irritability. Although people often diet to feel better, within a few days they usually feel worse.

One of the first studies to examine how dieting makes people feel took place in the 1940s. The scientists conducting the study reduced the food that participants could eat, and people lost weight. That was expected. What wasn't expected was how

this experiment affected participants' mental health. They became obsessed with food and some even began to dream about food. They had a hard time focusing on regular activities and they became more socially withdrawn, depressed and very, very cranky. Recent studies confirm these early findings: **dieting isn't good for your mental health.**

They encourage body hate

The dieting industry attracts so many customers because it manages to convince us that there is something wrong with our bodies. The industry tells us there is something wrong with us – we're too heavy or we don't have the right shape – but they can help us fix it. Diets focus us on what we shouldn't do (and shouldn't eat) in order to be more attractive. This is an unhealthy way to think about ourselves.

A different way to think about our bodies is in a loving, caring way. We should think about the things we want to do to take care of ourselves, not the things (foods) we want to avoid. Psychologists have actually done research on goal setting and have found that goals such as this, focusing on what we do want to do, are usually easier to achieve than "avoidance goals" (as they're sometimes called). This is a much healthier way to think about our bodies. Avoiding food restriction and instead focusing on health make it more likely that we'll think of foods as nourishing our bodies and being a part of self-care. Plus, body hate is a waste of energy because it is generally unhelpful.

The physical consequences can be dangerous

If our bodies do not get the nutrients they need to sustain us, the physical consequences can be devastating and ultimately even deadly. As registered dieticians Evelyn Tribole and Elyse Resch have said, **"a dieting body is a starving body."**

When we do not eat enough, our bodies respond by putting our limited resources into the most essential functions of living, depriving other physical functions, and a variety of physical symptoms may follow. People who don't eat enough may be sensitive to cold, feel tired all the time, experience bone thinning and osteoporosis, and their reproductive health may suffer, resulting in menstrual period irregularities and infertility. Our bodies are also unable to protect us and heal when we are undernourished; wounds may heal slowly and we may be at heightened risk of contracting infections. Perhaps most serious can be the **cardiac** risks that may result, leading to dangerously low blood pressure and even arrhythmias (irregular heartbeat).

Some diets and food fads involve restricting certain types of foods, but not necessarily the amount of food. There is still danger in these approaches because our bodies need a variety of nutrients to function at their best. There are health risks associated with cutting out any category of food.

They use up valuable brain power

Although we all have the potential to keep learning throughout life and to continue to get smarter, our brains can only do so much at a time. Even if you're an excellent multi-tasker (which some research suggests is unlikely for all of us!), you probably can't cook a meal while reading a book while having a conversation with someone else. You can only think about and do a couple of things at a time. If you're focusing a lot on what you eat – eating being something you likely do throughout the day – this is going to distract from other things that you could (and possibly should) be doing. Sometimes scientists refer to this as "attentional focus" or "bandwidth." Your ability to focus your attention, or your bandwidth, is limited.

Research suggests that chronic dieters have a hard time completing some tasks as easily as people who aren't chronic dieters. In scientific studies, dieters have been found to be less able to exhibit self-control than nondieters, and even less able to speak in front of people than nondieters. As you grow up and you find yourself tempted by all sorts of diets, it's worth keeping in mind that **deciding to diet means deciding to not be able to do other things**, or not do other things as well as you could have. Is this a choice you want to make?

Ironic processing

Have you ever tried not to think about something and found that you couldn't get it out of your mind? Maybe you were irritated with a friend and you tried to clear your mind of this irritation to focus on a test at school, but your irritation kept creeping back into your mind. **Ironic processing** is the scientific term used for when you're trying to clear your mind of something, but it actually seems to have the opposite effect, and you often find yourself thinking about it more. (It's "ironic" because it's the opposite of what you'd expect, and the "processing" part refers to your thoughts or "cognitive processes.") How is this related to dieting? Well, dieting is all about trying not to think about foods that you like and probably want to eat. The more you try not to think about these foods, the more you may actually want them!

Don't believe me? You can try a little experiment on your own. Try not to think about anything to do with chocolate for the next 2 minutes. You can watch a clock to keep track of time and just sit still, relax, and try not to think about chocolate – cake, cookies, ice cream – put it all out of your mind. How did that turn out?

"What the hell!"

Nope. That's not a typo. Scientists who study dieting have discovered a **"What the hell" effect**. It goes something like this: you decide to go on a diet and limit your sugar intake. You start on Monday, the day that all diets seem to start (the beginning of the week is so hopeful). You're a perfect dieting angel on Monday and Tuesday. Then, on Wednesday, your friend at school upsets you by saying something mean about your shoes. You feel bad and weak-willed, so you get a cookie at lunch. Then you get home from school later that day and find some ice cream in the freezer. You haven't given up on your low-sugar diet, but you're craving sugar after not having any for 2 days. When Thursday rolls around, you have a big science test at school that you stayed up late studying for. You're tired and stressed and you go for a cookie at lunch again. At this point, you say to yourself, "What the hell!" and grab a soda too. Your short-lived attempt to limit how much sugar you eat is over.

See what happens in situations like this? By trying to eliminate something from your diet, you actually start to want to eat it more. You can successfully limit yourself for a short period of time, maybe 2 days or even 2 weeks, but usually you'll say "What the hell" at some point, and you'll end up eating more than if you had never tried to diet in the first place. This is one of the many ways that dieting can end up being totally counterproductive and unhealthy in the long run.

Diet or food fad? How to know when "health" advice is not actually healthy

If a celebrity, influencer, or even a doctor, describes an approach to body or weight transformation with any of the below wording, it's likely to be anything but evidence-based:

✘ **Results will be fast and easy to achieve!**

We all like the idea of feeling or looking better quickly, but changing our habits to feel or look different is only sometimes possible and usually takes months or even years.

✘ **It works for everyone!**

We are all unique, and a simple, one-size-fits-all approach to health is rarely possible. We all need different amounts of food and have different preferences in terms of what we eat and the physical activities we participate in. Any prescription that claims to meet everyone's needs can't possibly be accurate.

✘ **Just buy my...**

If a product is being sold, be suspicious. You don't need protein bars or juice blends to improve your health, lose weight, or gain muscle mass. It may seem cynical, but if something is being sold, the seller wants to make money and probably cares little about your health.

✘ **The product will "cleanse" or "detox" you.**

We have a natural system for detoxification; our kidneys remove waste products and excess fluid from the body. We do not need to use a product or follow a plan to cleanse or detox our bodies. We also do not need to eat "clean" food or "guilt-free" food. No food is "dirty" (unless it literally has dirt on it!), and no food should cause you to feel guilty.

✘ **It worked for me!**

As I've already mentioned, what works for one person is not necessarily what will work for another. This is part of what makes some social media posts so problematic. Just because your favorite influencer eats certain things does not mean that's what you should do!

✘ **The ingredients are "clinically proven" or "a proprietary blend."**

If a product doesn't offer information about how it is tested to ensure that it is safe and effective, or if it refers to its ingredients as secret or "proprietary" (which means that the recipe is owned by the creator and will not be shared), walk away.

Diets are part of a "for-profit" industry

Maybe you've heard of "nonprofit" organizations. A **nonprofit organization** is an organization of some sort that has a goal to help the world in some way, such as the Red Cross, which is dedicated to disaster relief. These organizations don't aim to make money, and any money they obtain through donations or fundraising is used to further the organization's goals.

The diet industry is not a nonprofit industry. Many diet plans are described as prescriptions for health, and opportunities to feel better. We tend to associate health organizations with nonprofit organizations and think of medical providers and medical plans as having the goal of helping us get healthier. But this isn't how diet plans work.

As I mentioned earlier in this chapter, the dieting industry is a multi-billion-dollar industry. People who come up with and sell diet plans don't necessarily care about your health, and they don't necessarily care if you lose weight. If you don't lose weight, you may need their "product" again that much sooner. I know this may sound a bit negative or cynical, but some have gone as far as to say that **the dieting industry is the only profitable industry in the world with a 98% failure rate**. Keep this in mind the next time you're tempted to diet: there are a lot of people who would be very happy to have you try their diet plans and pay for their book or other services. This doesn't mean they have your best interests in mind.

Q&A

What your metabolism has to do with it

Chances are you've heard people refer to their **metabolism** as "fast" or "slow." People seem to think that having a fast metabolism is a good thing, allowing them to eat more than those with a slow metabolism. There is no easy way, however, for most of us to know with any certainty about the complicated ways in which our bodies function. It turns out that our metabolism – essentially, the chemical processes that take place within our bodies that keep us living – doesn't stay the same all the time. The biology that we're born with affects our metabolism, but so do our behaviors. In general, when we eat less food, our metabolism slows down and processes that food more slowly. It's like our bodies want to make good use of the smaller amount of food we're offering them, and they use it more slowly. Scientists believe that our bodies work this way because in ancient times it was difficult for people to find enough food to eat. When there was less food around (i.e. plants to grow and animals to catch and kill), our metabolism protected us by needing less food.

This isn't to say that we must always eat a lot to keep our metabolism working at full speed – it's not that simple. But we should listen to our bodies and eat what we need to feel full and energetic. If we try to eat too little, our bodies go into a sort of "starvation mode," processing food slowly (and often making weight loss less likely). This is only one reason I say throughout this book that there is very good scientific evidence that dieting to lose weight isn't going to work; your metabolism works against weight loss. The best way to keep yourself and your metabolism happy is by nourishing yourself properly.

EXPERT ADVICE

Christy Harrison, MPH, RD, registered dietitian, journalist, and author of *Anti-Diet* and *The Wellness Trap*

"There may be a <u>correlation</u> between higher weight and certain health outcomes, such as developing cardiovascular disease and diabetes — but as the golden rule in statistics goes, correlation does not indicate causation. In fact, many chronic diseases blamed on weight could potentially be explained by other factors, such as the weight stigma and weight cycling that higher-weight people often experience — both of which are independent risk factors for heart disease, diabetes, mortality, some forms of cancer, and more. Also, people who increase their physical activity and fitness — without necessarily losing any weight — have been found to have a lower risk of death than those who intentionally lose weight. There's a lot more to health than the number on the scale and many ways to improve your well-being that have nothing to do with weight loss."

Q&A

My friend's mom is always on a diet. She constantly talks about the nutrients in different foods. Her mom says she's not on a diet but this is her **lifestyle**, and she's lost a lot of weight in the past few months. Doesn't that make it a diet? Is it healthy?

A lifestyle (change) can be defined as a set of habits you can adopt and maintain for the rest of your life. If the changes aren't the sort of things you can follow for the long term, they're only likely to lead to short-term changes in your life or health.

If your friend's mom loses weight, she is most likely dieting! Of course, it is possible for people to actually change their habits and stick with those changes. It just turns out that this is really rare and unlikely. Most changes in eating habits end up being only short-term, which, by definition, makes them a diet.

One final thought: you mentioned that your friend's mom is always talking about the nutrients in different foods. As I mention at different points in this book, when we spend time and energy thinking about our bodies and our weight, this is time and energy taken away from other things we could be doing, and we all have only a limited amount of time and energy in each day. It's important that we think about what's most important to us and how we want to spend our time and energy.

Just don't do it!

In spite of everything you've read in this chapter, I know that someday you'll see a **fad** diet and be tempted to try it. Unfortunately, the odds are against all of us avoiding diets because they're constantly marketed to us. There's always something new, some diet that promises to really "work" this time. It may seem easy, so you'll think, "What's the harm? Why not give it a try?"

It's possible that you'll be tricked into trying something because it sounds scientific. Or because no one calls it a "diet." It's a "juice cleanse," which is going to make you healthier. Maybe it's a "sugar fast," and you figure that you could cut back on how much sugar you eat. But all of these things are different kinds of diets. **The main reason they won't work is because they aren't sustainable.** You won't want to only drink juice forever, and you won't want to give up sugar forever, so eventually you'll gain back whatever weight you lost trying to "cleanse" or "**fast**."

Instead of falling for the latest fad, it's important to stay strong and take good care of your body.

EXPERT ADVICE

Amelia Sherry, MPH, RD, clinical nutritionist and author of *Diet-Proof Your Daughter*

"Whenever you have the urge to diet, ask yourself, 'What problem am I really trying to solve?' If you think losing weight will help you like your body more, boost your confidence, or help you make more friends, you'll be disappointed. Dieting doesn't give us those things over the long term. In fact, it often makes us feel worse. Dieting leaves us feeling hungry and deprived, causes brain fog and irritability, stresses relationships, and can weaken our bones, heart, muscles, and more. If you really want to feel good about yourself, dig deep to think about the things that make you feel proud or powerful and have zero to do with your weight or looks. Putting more energy and attention into that thing (or things) is the real secret to feeling confident. The best part? No mirror or scale in the world will ever be able to take that feeling away."

Is there anything you can do instead?

It is important to care about your health and to want to take care of your body. Sometimes, that may mean trying to change your habits. There is nothing wrong with aiming to improve your habits, but it is essential that you focus on habits that are sustainable and not short-term fads. It may make sense to consider some easy changes to your habits that would make you feel better. For example, if you never get any sort of physical activity, you may feel better if you try to walk your dog, take a dance class, or join a sports team of some sort. If you never eat fruits and vegetables, you may benefit – both in terms of how you feel and your physical health – by trying to get into the habit of eating fruits and vegetables. If you don't get at least 8 hours of sleep per night, you will feel better if you make it a habit to go to bed earlier.

Research suggests that if we want to change any of our habits, we are most likely to be successful if we just make small, gradual changes. The goal should be to feel better by adopting habits that we can maintain.

The bottom line

Diet culture suggests that drastic changes to your habits – removing an entire food group from what you eat, or keeping track of every morsel that passes your lips – come with rewards. Like many of us, Mare grew up feeling the intense pressure of diet culture and believing that the rewards associated with weight loss would be real and powerful. She also grew up to believe that having a body that falls outside of cultural ideals is undesirable. In some research, girls have indicated that they are more afraid of becoming fat than they are of cancer, nuclear war, or losing their parents. Think about that for a moment. Is the size or shape of your body really that important?

Mare Anna, 16 years old, she/her, USA

I think I have an average body shape, but when I look in the mirror, I see myself as 20 pounds heavier than I am. One of my earliest memories of this was when I was about 4 or 5, and I still had the baby fat that most of us eventually grow out of. I was standing in the bathroom after a bath, wearing a towel like a cape. I remember looking down at my belly and then looking up at my dad and asking, "Daddy, will I be fat forever?"

When I was 12 years old, just starting the process of puberty, my doctor told me I was fat and needed to start dieting. I had a relatively healthy diet at the time, and the only unhealthy thing I did was drink things other than water (occasionally). But I was a determined 12-year-old with a mission to be "beautiful." I made a complex diet plan with lists of things I should not eat. The only thing that this accomplished? It made me feel guilty and worthless.

Now, I currently eat with the mindset of being healthy, listening to my body, and eating things that make me feel energized and happy. I wouldn't say that my relationship with food is what I wish it was, though, and I blame that one doctor for a lot of my anxiety surrounding food.

It probably didn't help that growing up I took dance and gymnastics classes. I would compare myself to the other girls in class and feel awful because I didn't look like them. My younger sister has always been beautiful and skinny, and I always felt that I was compared to her when we were in public. My warped view of my body and constant comparison to others have been unhealthy, but I am trying to accept myself as being beautiful as I am.

So far, my junior year of high school is so much better. I feel like things have really started to change for me. I have a sense of identity, style, and I am beginning to accept myself. The biggest change that happened between this year and last year would have to be the people I hang out with. I now hang out with a group of people who are completely accepting and understanding. They accept me for me. I have never felt so close to other people before, and I am definitely happier.

Some lessons I'm learning that I wish I had learned earlier are:

- Strive to be the healthiest you, not the skinniest.
- The only person you should be comparing yourself to is you.
- Do everything possible to eliminate toxic people from your life.
- Your body is always changing, and how you see yourself will, too.

SUMMING UP #DitchDietCulture

- Diets typically don't work and are likely to lead to weight gain across time, not weight loss.
- Diets are likely to make you cranky and aren't good for your body image, mental well-being, or physical health.
- Focusing on your health and how you feel is much better for you than dieting.

FIND OUT MORE:

- The book *No Weigh! A Teen's Guide to Positive Body Image, Food, and Emotional Wisdom* by Signe Darpinian, Wendy Sterling, and Shelley Aggarwal (2018, published by Jessica Kingsley Publishers) covers some of the same information that I discuss in this chapter if you'd like to read more about these topics.

- Christy Harrison is a registered dietitian and journalist who has written a lot about food and dieting, including her book *Anti-Diet: Reclaim Your Time, Money, Well-Being, and Happiness Through Intuitive Eating* (2019, published by Yellow Kite). She also has two podcasts that are fun to listen to and really informative: *Food Psych* and *Rethinking Wellness*, which can be found wherever you listen to podcasts.

- There are more books for parents about helping young people avoid the dangers of dieting than there are books written for kids. But you may learn something from the books intended for parents. For example, *Raising Body Positive Teens* by Signe Darpinian, Wendy Sterling, and Shelley Aggarwal (2022, published by Jessica Kingsley Publishers) contains a ton of valuable information about how to avoid dieting. *Diet-Proof Your Daughter* by Amelia Sherry is another one of my favorites (2022, published by AS Nutrition Publishing) and picks up on the themes in this chapter – and many others across the chapters of this book.

- For more scholarly articles and web pages with information about healthy eating and the problems with dieting, see the companion website for this book: www.TheBodyImageBook.com.

CHAPTER 7
EATING DISORDERS

"Humor keeps us alive. Humor and food. Don't forget food. You can go a week without laughing."

Joss Whedon, US screenwriter, director and producer

Olivia Harper, 22 years old, she/her, USA

I've never been diagnosed with an eating disorder, but I have struggled with my eating and body image. For about 10 years, my weight has fluctuated up and down significantly. Not surprisingly, I get a lot of positive feedback when I lose weight.

I think I'm at a pretty healthy weight for me but I'm working to develop a healthy relationship with food and my body. I often end up busy throughout the day and don't eat much and then end up overeating at night. It can feel like a binge because I'm over-hungry and I just can't control how much I eat. I have thrown up from eating too much a few times, but I don't make myself sick on purpose. I hate throwing up.

I have looked into intuitive eating, but I don't really know if I could do it.

I have a hard time knowing when I'm hungry. I've ignored my body's needs for so long that I think I'd have to work to get in touch with my sense of hunger and fullness.

My disordered eating habits definitely started at home. I really loved food as a child, and I was always so excited about eating. I loved to try new foods. I became a chubby kid, and my mom, brother, and grandparents made fun of me. There was always a comment such as, "Are you going to eat all of that?" or "Do you need to eat all of that?" They even called me an "oinker," which was so hurtful.

When I began to do sports in high school and I grew taller, I became leaner. I got the most positive feedback about my body when I was exercising a lot and not eating enough. I know now that this is pretty messed up, but it was hard to see that back then. I don't play sports anymore and that has affected how I view my body. Fortunately, I have the most incredible friends now. I feel like we really look out for each other, and we make sure that we're taking care of ourselves.

If I had to offer my younger self advice, I'd tell her that people's comments about your body are meaningless. They don't understand if you are healthy and doing what is best for your body. Eating what you want to is OK. If you are hungry, you need to eat. I'd also tell her that our bodies change so much when you become a teenager; it's unrealistic to expect them to stay the same.

It would be easy to read Chapters 5 and 6 and start to think that eating can get pretty complicated. Maybe you already thought that. Eating may seem complicated because different people have different ideas about how to approach it. On top of that, our scientific understanding is always improving, and new research may lead to more information about food and eating. It's possible that trying to sort through all of the information available to you can make eating feel hard when it should usually be fun! As Olivia's story reminds us, sometimes it is easy to slip into **disordered eating** habits.

IN THIS CHAPTER YOU'LL LEARN:

- what defines disordered eating and eating disorders and how these problems can develop,
- treatment options for eating disorders, and
- how to improve your way of thinking about food and adopt habits to support a positive body image.

Eating should be fun

It's important to enjoy eating and it's equally important not to be too rigid about your food choices. As we discussed in Chapter 6, it can backfire if you spend too much energy trying to avoid foods you love.

There are a variety of potentially negative consequences of denying yourself foods that you enjoy. Aside from not being able to enjoy food, you may miss out on a lot, because food is often an important part of social and cultural experiences. A birthday cake or a wedding cake is considered an important part of a celebration. A big turkey or ham dinner is an important part of Thanksgiving or Christmas gatherings. Hotdogs, hamburgers, and pies can be favorite parts of a

backyard barbecue in the summer. These gatherings and celebrations are about the time spent with loved ones, the holidays, and the memories made. They are also, for many people, about the food. Of course, you can go to a barbecue and not eat a hamburger. However, if you spend the entire gathering avoiding hamburgers, feeling deprived, and wishing you could eat a hamburger, you aren't going to have a lot of fun. Furthermore, consistent **food restriction** is one type of disordered eating and can lead to the development of a life-threatening eating disorder.

Foods are not "good" and "bad"

Because we equate eating with guilt in many Western cultures (such as the USA and UK) and we spend a fair amount of energy concerned with how much and what we're eating, we miss out on a lot of the fun and enjoyment that food can bring us. Many of us have grown up thinking of some foods as "good" and some foods as "bad." I bet you could list five "good" and five "bad" foods without any trouble. Maybe you'd have milk, apples, broccoli, carrots, and Greek yogurt on your good list. Maybe you'd have French fries, pizza, ice cream, cake, and sweets on your bad list. But is food really this straightforward?

As I've discussed a bit in earlier chapters, there are a number of reasons why it's problematic to think of foods as "good" and "bad." First of all, most foods contain many different nutrients, so they're rarely entirely bad or entirely good. Second, when you feel like a food is bad and forbidden, it often makes you desire that food much more. (Remember the discussion of **ironic processing** from Chapter 6?) Imagine what would happen if your mom repeatedly told you that you must eat ice cream for dinner if you wanted broccoli for dessert. You'd probably start to think that broccoli must be pretty awesome if you had to earn it by eating ice cream, and ice cream must not be all that great. In other words, how we

think about and label food can change how much we want it. Also, when we label food as "bad," we're more likely to feel guilty for eating it. This label can change how much we enjoy food – in particular, the foods that are often meant to be special, or parts of celebrations. If your mom makes you a delicious chocolate cake for your birthday, enjoy it and relish this part of celebrating your special day. Don't feel guilty or think of your cake (or yourself!) as "bad."

Disordered eating and eating disorders

You've probably heard about eating disorders from the media or at some point in a health class at school, but you may not have known that there are several different kinds of eating disorders and that eating disorders can be *really* serious. In fact, they're the most deadly form of mental illness (aside from **opioid use disorder**). It's also likely that most of the information you're familiar with concerning eating disorders relates to girls and women. However, approximately 25–33% of all eating disorder patients are boys and men.

Disordered eating and eating disorders are not exactly the same. Most people probably engage in disordered eating at some time or another because most people fall prey to cultural messages suggesting they should skip meals or avoid certain food groups, or they feel guilty for eating certain foods. Other disordered eating behaviors may include using medications (or illegal drugs) to try to lose weight, chronic dieting, rigidity and strict routines surrounding food and exercise, and anxiety about eating or appearance. All of this may be described as problematic or disordered eating because it is psychologically stressful and often physically harmful. If these thoughts or behaviors become habits, they can lead to the development of an eating disorder.

There are significant consequences to engaging in disordered eating – even if you are never diagnosed with an eating disorder. If you skip breakfast occasionally because you're in a rush in the morning, that's unlikely to become a serious problem. But if you are constantly dieting or concerned about what you eat, your weight, or how much you exercise, your psychological health and quality of life are likely to suffer. You may also experience gastrointestinal problems, low heart rate and blood pressure, bone loss, and other physical health problems.

I'll review the most common eating disorders below. As you read, it is important to understand that the symptoms described can apply to boys, girls, men, women, nonbinary, and transgender people, and that anyone who experiences these symptoms should get professional help. It's also important to realize that the criteria for an eating disorder (versus disordered eating) are not always clear cut. The below categories of eating disorders are useful to clinicians and other medical professionals trying to treat patients, but in the real world, people rarely fit neatly into these categories. Some people have symptoms of various eating disorders at the same time. Even if you or someone you know doesn't fit perfectly into a specific eating disorder category, this doesn't mean that treatment wouldn't be beneficial. No one should feel that they need to wait until they are *really* suffering to get help!

Self-Assessment: Eating Attitudes Test

This questionnaire, the Eating Attitude Test-26 (EAT-26, created by Garner et al., 1982), is thought of as one of the best screening tools to assess "eating disorder risk."

Check a response for each of the following statements:	Always	Usually	Often	Sometimes	Rarely	Never
1. I am terrified about being overweight.	3	2	1	0	0	0
2. I avoid eating when I am hungry.	3	2	1	0	0	0
3. I find myself preoccupied with food.	3	2	1	0	0	0
4. I have gone on eating binges where I feel that I may not be able to stop.	3	2	1	0	0	0
5. I cut my food into small pieces.	3	2	1	0	0	0
6. I am aware of the calorie content of foods that I eat.	3	2	1	0	0	0

Check a response for each of the following statements:	Always	Usually	Often	Sometimes	Rarely	Never
7. I particularly avoid food with a high carbohydrate content (i.e. bread, rice, potatoes, etc.).	3	2	1	0	0	0
8. I feel that others would prefer if I ate more.	3	2	1	0	0	0
9. I vomit after I have eaten.	3	2	1	0	0	0
10. I feel extremely guilty after eating.	3	2	1	0	0	0
11. I am occupied with a desire to be thinner.	3	2	1	0	0	0
12. I think about burning up calories when I exercise.	3	2	1	0	0	0
13. Other people think that I am too thin.	3	2	1	0	0	0
14. I am preoccupied with the thought of having fat on my body.	3	2	1	0	0	0
15. I take longer than others to eat my meals.	3	2	1	0	0	0
16. I avoid foods with sugar in them.	3	2	1	0	0	0
17. I eat diet foods.	3	2	1	0	0	0
18. I feel that food controls my life.	3	2	1	0	0	0
19. I display self-control around food.	3	2	1	0	0	0
20. I feel that others pressure me to eat.	3	2	1	0	0	0
21. I give too much time and thought to food.	3	2	1	0	0	0
23. I engage in dieting behavior.	3	2	1	0	0	0
24. I like my stomach to be empty.	3	2	1	0	0	0
25. I have the impulse to vomit after meals.	3	2	1	0	0	0
26. I enjoy trying new rich foods.	0	0	0	1	2	3

Screening for eating disorders is important because, usually, early identification of disordered eating can lead to earlier treatment and a better chance of recovery. To determine your score, sum the values of all the items. Individuals who score 20 or more on the test should be interviewed by a qualified professional to determine if they meet the diagnostic criteria for an eating disorder. If you have a low score on the EAT-26 (below 20), you could still have a serious eating problem, so do not let the results deter you from seeking help.

Anorexia nervosa

Anorexia nervosa, usually referred to as anorexia, is an eating disorder that's relatively rare but extremely serious. Individuals who develop anorexia typically eat very little and often eat only certain types of foods. They may exercise excessively and tend to be obsessed with food, calories, and other qualities of foods, such as how much fat is in different types of foods. Patients with anorexia are usually concerned with trying to lose weight and tend to experience extreme body image concerns, although they very often are not overweight. Sometimes, people with anorexia will purge after they eat. **Purging** can take many forms, from overexercising (to "burn calories") to vomiting. Although individuals with anorexia are often seriously underweight, an individual can be overweight and have anorexia; you can't always determine who has an eating disorder by looking at a person.

The health consequences of anorexia can be very serious. When the body doesn't get enough of the nutrients it needs, a variety of problems may develop (in addition to what may be dramatic weight loss). Some of the many health concerns that can develop include stomach pain, weakness, lowered immune functioning (i.e. the body's ability to fight illness is reduced), slowed heart rate, overall feelings of coldness and difficulty with temperature regulation, difficulty sleeping, dizziness and fainting, difficulty concentrating, loss of menstrual periods, and even death. Some research indicates that 20% of people – one in five! – with anorexia will die due to complications of the disorder. Some of these deaths are due to **suicide**, and some are due to the body's undernourished state.

Q&A

I understand that people with anorexia often skip meals or eat very small meals, and that anorexia is a very dangerous disorder. But I've also read about people who use "intermittent fasting" for weight loss, which seems similar to skipping meals. What's the difference? And does intermittent fasting work?

Intermittent fasting has received a lot of attention in recent years as an approach to weight loss. It typically involves people eating as they regularly do for 5 days a week and then eating relatively little for a couple of days a week. Some people eat within a select window of time each day — for example, between 10 am and 5 pm. The general idea isn't to limit the food eaten overall but to reduce what is eaten to certain periods of time.

Research by nutritionists suggests that intermittent fasting can help people lose weight, but not any better than just changing the foods people eat (for example, eating more fruit and fewer sweets) or exercising more often. One of the biggest problems with intermittent fasting is that it leaves people hungry. It's a way of eating that requires people to ignore their bodies' cues when they are hungry. In other words, even if it helps people lose weight, they're likely to gain that weight back over time.

How is intermittent fasting different from an eating disorder? This is a good and complicated question. If someone is intermittent fasting because she is worried about her weight, avoids social situations so that it's easier to avoid food, feels concerned about her body size or shape, and has lost a lot of weight recently, then it's likely that this person has taken fasting way too far and has developed an eating disorder. If someone sometimes skips breakfast in the hope of losing weight, that's probably not indicative of an eating disorder but may still qualify as disordered eating.

Because intermittent fasting and eating disorders share some similar characteristics, I would never recommend that a child or an adolescent try this approach to weight loss. In fact, this could be an especially bad approach to weight loss for young people who are still growing and experiencing puberty because they consistently need a variety of nutrients to stay healthy. I'm not a fan of it as a way for adults to eat, either.

Bulimia nervosa

Bulimia nervosa, or "bulimia," typically involves **binging** and then purging food. When someone binges, they eat *much* more than is typical in one sitting. You may feel really full if you eat three or four pieces of pizza, but a binge would mean eating much more, in most cases. People with bulimia tend to feel a loss of control and an inability to stop eating when they binge. After a binge, a person with bulimia usually feels not just full but guilty, and then engages in some sort of purge. Purging can take different forms, including using medication that causes vomiting or diarrhea, or by exercising excessively.

The health consequences of bulimia are somewhat similar to the consequences of anorexia. In both disorders, individuals are unlikely to get the nutrients they need. Furthermore, for people with anorexia or bulimia, the time and energy focused on food and weight is a major distraction from the rest of their lives. However, unlike people with anorexia, people with bulimia often develop problems with their stomachs and digestive systems as a result of binging and purging. They may also have difficulty sleeping, difficulty concentrating, problems fighting infection, muscle weakness, and irregularities with their periods. Purging may result in other health concerns, including dental problems and very serious issues including chemical imbalances. These sorts of imbalances can lead to complications, including death, often without any warning.

Binge eating disorder

Binge eating disorder (BED) is the most common eating disorder. Individuals with BED tend to binge at least once a week without purging over a period of at least 3 months. These binges are described as excessive in terms of how much is eaten, and are experienced as uncontrollable. When people binge, they often describe the experience as if they're in a trance. They eat quickly and until they're uncomfortable, and then feel guilty and ashamed afterward.

People with BED often experience problems with their stomachs and digestive systems. They may get cramps, constipation, heartburn, or other symptoms as a result of their problematic eating habits. They often spend a lot of time and energy thinking about food and what they will eat. People with BED are at risk of weight gain due to their habits and may experience stigma and shame as a result of their body size.

Unspecified feeding or eating disorder

Sometimes people have unhealthy eating habits that are not exactly anorexia, bulimia, or binge-eating disorder, but their eating habits still disrupt their life. Their habits may lead to drastic weight gain or weight loss. Most importantly, these people are stressed out about their eating, body image, or weight (or all three). These individuals are often diagnosed as having an **unspecified feeding or eating disorder**.

To receive an official diagnosis of anorexia, for example, patients must have several specific symptoms. A patient may fall just short of the required number of symptoms, but she may clearly have serious concerns and unhealthy behaviors surrounding food, or a pattern of serious disordered eating. This patient would likely get diagnosed as having an unspecified feeding or eating disorder. This diagnosis helps different healthcare providers to realize the seriousness of the patient's symptoms and can help organize treatment for the patient.

Q&A ?!??

Food addiction isn't considered an eating disorder by psychologists. Addictions (often referred to as substance use disorder or other sorts of illnesses) can be extremely serious and even deadly. Usually, when psychologists discuss addiction, they mean addiction to chemicals or substances such as the nicotine found in cigarettes, or alcohol or other drugs. Regular overuse of these substances can affect nearly every part of the body and result in a **physical dependency** on them. In other words, once a person is used to regular drug use, for example, they'll experience **withdrawal** symptoms when the drug use stops. The person comes to need the drug, and without it they may experience symptoms ranging from flu-like symptoms and seizures to headaches and shaking. Although reducing consumption of a food you're used to eating regularly may result in cravings, it's unlikely to result in these sorts of serious physical withdrawal symptoms.

It's possible to be in the habit of eating a lot of sugar and to crave it. It's possible to like chocolate so much that you think of yourself as a **chocoholic**. Some research does suggest that similar areas of the brain are working when a person eats a food they crave and when a person uses a drug. But this doesn't mean that "addiction" to food is the same thing as addiction to a drug. Although habits can be persistent, it's typically easier to change an eating habit than it is to change a drug habit, for example. Food also has a nourishing and important role in sustaining our health. The same cannot be said of other truly addictive substances.

Body dysmorphic disorder

Body dysmorphic disorder (BDD) is not an eating disorder but often co-occurs with eating disorders. In other words, people who have eating disorders sometimes have BDD, but just having BDD is not an eating disorder.

BDD is actually a body image disorder. People with BDD are preoccupied with their body's defects and flaws. They are compulsive about tending to their appearance and may go to extremes to alter their appearance, such as obtaining extensive cosmetic surgery. At the heart of BDD is the inability for people to see themselves as others do and the tendency to be extremely critical of themselves. People with BDD may experience not only self-doubt but also anxiety and depression as a result of their preoccupation with their appearance.

There are subtypes of BDD that are characterized by different body image preoccupations. For example, the muscle dysmorphic subtype involves preoccupation with muscle size and shape. Another subtype includes delusional beliefs about appearance; people with this subtype are completely convinced that the way they experience their physical flaws is accurate.

As I discuss throughout this book, it is typical to have some concerns about your appearance and it is normal to attend to your appearance regularly – for example, bathing, grooming, and selecting clothes you like. However, BDD goes beyond all of this and, like most mental health problems, proves disruptive to an individual's life. It is one thing to be really focused on your hair or your clothes, but it is another not to want to leave the house ever unless those aspects of your appearance seem perfect to you.

You can never eat too healthily.

Eating nutritious foods is one good way to take care of your body. However, it is possible to eat too healthily. If you find yourself spending a lot of time thinking about what you are eating and feel guilty if you eat anything that is remotely unhealthy, you may have what is sometimes referred to as **orthorexia**. The American Psychological Association does not recognize orthorexia as a clinical disorder, but it is a term used to describe an overconcern with eating healthfully, avoidance of unhealthy foods, a rigidity about food choice, and often body image concerns. People with orthorexia often experience anxiety and obsessive–compulsive tendencies (aka OCD). Although you may benefit physically from a focus on foods that contain a lot of nutrients, taken to the extreme this can become problematic psychologically. Food should be enjoyed! Every meal does not need to include avocado, kale, and almonds.

EXPERT ADVICE

Oona Hanson, MA, MA, eating disorder educator and advocate

"There are a lot of myths and stereotypes out there about eating disorders. The most important thing to know is that recovery is possible. Getting the right support can make all the difference. And you might be surprised to learn that loving family members can often be a powerful part of that support system."

Organic foods are an important part of a healthy diet.

Sometimes, when people are aiming to eat "healthy foods," they become rigid – even disordered – in their food choices. This can evolve into a focus on eating organic or "**clean foods.**" Organic foods can be an important part of a healthy diet, but you don't need to eat only organic foods to have a healthy diet. Clean foods usually refer to unprocessed foods or organic foods.

What exactly are **organic foods**? Organic refers to a particular way in which foods such as fruits, vegetables, grains, dairy products, and meat are produced. In order to be considered organic, farmers are required to grow, handle, and process foods in ways that meet environmental and safety goals. For example, they must care for the soil so that they limit pollution and improve the quality of the soil. Farmers are also expected to allow natural livestock behavior (grazing and eating in a field, and not confining animals only to stalls).

What are the benefits of eating organic foods? They often taste better! Plus, they may be slightly more nutritious, although the science on this is fairly mixed right now. Organic foods are also less likely to be produced using **pesticides** or chemicals (for example, to keep insects from eating plants), so it's less likely that there are any chemicals on these foods. These practices are often environmentally friendly as well.

Perhaps the biggest downside to eating organic is that it can be expensive and challenging to find foods that have been produced organically.

Furthermore, most nonorganic fruits, vegetables, grains, dairy, and meat are equally nutritious. It's much better to eat nonorganic strawberries than no strawberries at all (assuming you like strawberries). Feel free to eat organic when you can, but you shouldn't feel that it's an important part of a healthy diet.

How does a person develop an eating disorder?

Like any mental health problem, no one wants to develop an eating disorder. It is possible that a person may have concerns about their body image or weight, but this doesn't mean they want to develop a serious disorder. It's important to keep this in mind if you encounter a friend or someone you know who has an eating disorder (see the Q&A, below).

There are many factors that can contribute to the development of an eating disorder. Usually, people who develop eating disorders are concerned about their weight and don't feel good about their bodies. Sometimes they're overweight, but more often they're not overweight but are still worried about what they eat and how they look. It turns out that usually a person's *actual* weight is much less relevant than a person's *feelings* about their weight in the development of eating disorders.

Many people who develop eating disorders live in families that talk a lot about food and dieting or in which others have eating disorder symptoms themselves. Sometimes, family members may tease and make a person feel bad about their food choices or weight. Sometimes parents really restrict their children's access to certain foods, whether it be fast food, dessert foods, or processed foods. This can have the opposite of the desired effect, making these foods more appealing and, in some cases, more binge-worthy. Eating disorders seem to run in families, but not only because of these experiences within families – there is also evidence of a genetic predisposition to eating disorders. The genes we inherit from family members may play a significant role in our vulnerability to eating disorders (and many other mental and physical health concerns).

Media influences are also relevant to individuals' development of eating disorders. As discussed in earlier chapters (see Chapter 4), girls and women see countless messages suggesting it is important that they be slender, with large breasts, and curvaceous hips and round bums. This combination of features very rarely occurs naturally among women (without surgical intervention). It's easy for people to believe that they'll be happiest if they look a certain way and feel willing to take drastic measures to achieve that look. The problem is that there are so many serious health problems associated with not taking good care of your body. Drastically altering your eating habits may result in weight loss or gain but can also contribute to an eating disorder that will cause many other problems.

Some research even suggests that people with certain personalities may be more vulnerable to developing eating disorders. People who are perfectionists or anxious are more likely to worry about things like fitting in with their peers and looking a certain way. This may lead them to be more at risk for an eating disorder. Some people with eating disorders also experience other mental health conditions, such as depression or **obsessive–compulsive disorder** (OCD). It's not always clear what comes first; an eating disorder may lead to depression (or another mental health condition), or depression may contribute to the development of an eating disorder.

Some people develop eating disorders and it is not clear what the causes were. It may be the combination of a number of minor experiences or one major life event. For some, it may be an illness, travel, or a break-up with a girlfriend or boyfriend that led them to change their habits and ultimately develop an eating disorder. Sometimes, people can't really articulate what happened or why before they ended up engaging in disordered eating or developed an eating disorder.

A lot of disordered eating is **normalized** in our culture. In other words, extreme diets and fads are viewed as normal and acceptable, so people may find no problems with trying them and may not realize that these place them at risk of developing an eating disorder.

Eating disorder treatment

Individuals suffering from an eating disorder usually require treatment by several healthcare professionals, including physicians, psychologists, and nutritionists. Early treatment is almost always more effective than waiting to see if a person grows out of an eating disorder. It's always safer to provide too much help and support to a person than not enough help and support. Unfortunately, not everyone gets the treatment they need. People who are heavier or who identify as male tend to be overlooked by medical professionals because it isn't expected that they will experience an eating disorder.

If you or someone you know needs body image or eating disorder treatment, you may need to talk to more than one doctor to get that help. The first part of eating disorder treatment will vary depending on the severity of the disorder. Often, when someone has been malnourished or is compulsively exercising, their pulse will be quite low. (The average resting heart rate of an 18-year-old girl is 72 beats per minute, and the average pulse of an 18-year-old boy is 79 beats per minute. Someone with an eating disorder may have a much lower resting heart rate.) Girls and women may stop getting their periods, and individuals who are weak from malnourishment may faint. When physical symptoms accompanying an eating disorder are concerning, an individual may be referred for inpatient treatment. In a hospital setting, the initial focus is often on nourishing patients so that they become physically stable. This can be uncomfortable to a person who is used to not eating a lot or exercising often; however, it is necessary.

After an individual is physically stable and the immediate risk of serious health issues such as a heart problem has been reduced, other aspects of treatment get more attention. Usually, this includes some form of psychotherapy, including one-on-one therapy and possibly family therapy or group therapy. Therapy can help patients address challenges they are having with recovery (for example, eating enough food to support their health) and factors that may have contributed to the rise of the eating disorder. It's not necessary for patients to understand exactly what led them to develop an eating disorder, but it can be helpful to consider whether there are factors that contributed that may make recovery difficult. For example, if a parent tends to be critical of their weight, learning how to handle this may be essential to recovery. Therapy can help with many other aspects of recovery by offering social support and strategies to help manage difficult times and relapses, and by helping to support mental health more generally.

A nutritionist or registered dietitian may be an important part of treatment for eating disorders. Many people who experience eating disorders lose touch with their body's nutritional needs. They've eaten (or not eaten) and ignored their body's signals of hunger and fullness, and those signals may no longer function especially well. Someone with training in nutrition science can help individuals with eating disorders learn what their body's nutritional needs are and help them adopt habits that are mentally and physically healthy. Many nutritionists and registered dietitians have training in intuitive eating and can help people eat more intuitively (see Chapter 5 for more information about intuitive eating). Many also have training in the Health at Every Size perspective and can help people appreciate that their body, weight, and eating concerns originate from a culture that offers many, many unhealthy and inaccurate messages about these issues (see Chapter 6 for more

information about the Health at Every Size movement). I highly recommend seeking out nutrition support from a specialist with training in intuitive eating and/or Health at Every Size.

Medication may also play a role in helping a person recover from an eating disorder. Often, eating disorders co-occur with anxiety, depression, or other mental health problems. Some of the medications, such as antidepressants, that are useful in treating one mental health condition can also help to alleviate eating disorders. They all affect the chemicals in our brain (aka neurotransmitters, including serotonin and dopamine) that influence our moods and emotions.

Our scientific understanding of the role of psychotropic medications, such as Prozac and Zoloft, continues to expand, as does their use for treating various illnesses. Some recent research suggests that a medication often used to treat attention-deficit/hyperactivity disorder (ADHD), lisdexamfetamine dimesylate (LDX), can be effective in treating binge eating disorder. However, there's a lot that is not completely understood about how these medications work or why certain medications work for some people and some conditions and not for others. Regardless, medication can be an important part of treatment for many people recovering from an eating disorder.

EXPERT ADVICE

Robyn Goldberg, RDN, CEDS-C, nutrition therapist and author of *The Eating Disorder Trap*

"If you have an eating disorder, a treatment team is necessary and important to support your journey toward recovery. It is important to make sure that you have a team that is trained in eating disorders. This team will include a doctor, mental healthcare provider, registered dietitian, and possibly a psychiatrist and a meal coach. Remember your family or chosen family is a part of your support team, too."

Q&A ? ? ?

I have a good friend who I think has an eating disorder. She's constantly talking about food and her weight, and she exercises for hours every day. I know that exercise can be good for you, but I think she's taking it too far. What should I do?

It's likely that at some point in your life, you'll know at least one person who has an eating disorder. It's important to think about how best to be helpful in these situations. First of all, you probably want to choose whether or not you want to talk to your friend directly or talk to an adult or professional who may be able to help. It may make sense to do both. If you aren't comfortable approaching your friend directly, you could talk to one of her parents, a psychologist, a counselor, or a teacher at your school. Sharing your concern with a caring adult can help ease your worry and allow someone else to step in and help.

If you're comfortable talking with your friend directly, be careful not to approach her by blaming her for her problem. No one wants to develop an eating disorder; she has an illness similar to other kinds of physical illnesses. It's often helpful to try to have a calm conversation that allows you to express your concern and worry about her. You may want to direct her to some helpful resources online, such as the **National Eating Disorders Association** eating disorders screening tool (www.nationaleatingdisorders.org/screening-tool). You may want to let her know that you're aware that eating disorders can be very serious — even deadly — and that you care about her getting better and enjoying food and a healthy future. Consider helping her to find a way to get professional help. It can be scary to ask for help, but it's probably a good idea for her to talk to her doctor and a psychologist. At the very least, she could call the **Anorexia Nervosa and Associated Disorders** (**ANAD**; https://ANAD.org) Helpline (USA: 1-888-375-7767) or the Beat Eating Disorders Helpline (UK: 0808 801 0677).

Sometimes people who need medical help aren't ready to get it. It's possible that you could talk to your friend, and she may not follow your advice at all. Try not to take this personally, but continue to express your concern to your friend. Most importantly, don't ever shame someone or make them feel bad for having a problem. This is unlikely to help and may only damage your relationship with the person.

EXPERT ADVICE

Cheri A. Levinson, PhD, Associate Professor, University of Louisville, founder and Clinical Director of the Louisville Center for Eating Disorders

"Often times, people with eating disorders have a hard time believing they are sick enough or that they really have an eating disorder. This is part of the illness. The eating disorder makes it hard to see that you are truly ill and deserving of help and support to get better."

How you eat is related to how you feel — mentally and physically

How you eat — even how you think about food — can significantly affect many areas of your life. The connection between how you eat and how you feel is physical; both your brain and your body react to what you eat (or don't eat). If you aren't eating enough and you're hungry, you're also more likely to be tired, unable to concentrate, and maybe even **hangry** (hungry + angry). If you're not eating nutritious foods, you may also find yourself feeling a lack of energy, be easily distracted, and find it difficult to learn. Poor nutrition is also associated with an inability to fight off illness and infection, which is part of why people who struggle with eating disorders may experience other physical illnesses and infections.

Your eating habits are also likely to affect how you feel about yourself and your psychological health, even if you never have anything resembling an eating disorder. For example, in one recent study researchers found that lower self-esteem seems to be associated with poorer eating habits. This may mean that people with low self-esteem don't eat as many nutritious foods, or it may mean that eating nutritious foods seems to have a positive impact on people's self-esteem. Most likely, both of these things are partly true.

In related research, an association has been found between self-compassion, eating behaviors, and body image. What is **self-compassion**? Well, if you're **compassionate**, you're concerned about others and you show them sympathy. Self-compassion is treating yourself with this same sort of concern and sympathy. People who think of themselves with kindness and caring are more likely to have more intuitive eating habits than people who think poorly of themselves. Self-compassion is also linked to a positive body image. This is just one more reason to treat yourself like you would a good friend (I discuss self-compassion more in Chapter 9).

As far as eating habits go, I think we're all works in progress. Most of us will have periods in our lives when we think we should change how we're eating, because we've been eating a lot of take-out food, we haven't been eating enough, or we've been eating a certain food more or less than we'd like to. Every now and then, I realize I am very busy and maybe I should get take-out food *more often* for a few weeks so that I can spend less time preparing food!

Many experts believe that although it's worthwhile to be thoughtful about our food choices, it's even more important *not to worry* about food and eating. Most – although not all – of us in the USA and Europe are lucky enough to have enough food to keep us alive, and this is what's most important. Food is the fuel that keeps our bodies working. It's good to give our body nutritious fuel, but it is as important to maintain a healthy relationship with food and enjoy eating without shame.

Maria Francesca, 19 years old, she/her, USA

Right now, I wouldn't say that I'm particularly happy with my body. I've had an eating disorder, and I'm still in the recovery process. I am working on building up my strength both by eating at least three meals a day and by lifting weights. I appreciate that I am feeling stronger, both physically and psychologically.

My eating disorder began when I was about 12 years old. I was part of a group of "friends" that were really mean, and I was fat-shamed by them. They made me believe that I needed to have abs or I was fat. But this may have just been the last straw because I grew up around a lot of talk about food. There were always comments about how much food was on my plate and what I was eating. I think this is partially because my mom has also always been on her own "weight loss journey." She's 60 years old (she was 40 when she had me) and still counting calories. I definitely learned to be insecure about my body by listening to my mom talk about her body. No matter how gorgeous or beautiful she tells me I am, I still feel concerned about my appearance because of how she talks about hers.

I don't think I've ever fitted neatly into any eating disorder diagnosis. I have had some qualities of anorexia and binge eating disorder across the years. Medical providers have never been that much help. One of my friends has had similar symptoms to me, and when she went to see a doctor, he told her she wasn't anorexic because her ribs weren't showing. Why wouldn't he have offered her help when she wanted it? Why does it seem like help only comes when people are really sick?

Part of my recovery has included avoiding most social media. Social media seems to be where beauty standards and self-consciousness emerge. A lot of what is shamed on social media is just normal body stuff. Everyone has stretch marks! Everyone has flabby parts! People don't need to follow diets to be healthy!

I know my body shape is not under my control. I want to just do what my body tells me to do. I want to eat when I'm hungry. And I want everyone to just look like themselves. We'd have more diversity and inclusivity if people weren't all trying to look like each other.

If I could offer younger girls advice, I'd tell them to work on being comfortable being themselves. People seem so committed to changing themselves instead of embracing who they are. And we all need friends who are uplifting and supportive. Find those people who won't judge or shame you but just understand you.

SUMMING UP #Livetoeat

✓ Eating should not be just about getting nutrients into your body but also about enjoying food and making it a fun part of your life.

✓ Always restricting yourself from foods you enjoy isn't healthy and may lead to disordered eating, or even a serious eating disorder. If you think that you or someone you know may have an eating disorder, talk to an adult and look for treatment right away.

✓ Eating disorders include anorexia nervosa, bulimia nervosa, and binge-eating disorder, but if you are spending a lot of time, energy, and brain power thinking about what you do or don't eat, you may have an eating disorder. It is best to get support if you have concerns about your eating habits so that you don't develop a serious, life-threatening problem.

🔍 FIND OUT MORE:

✦ If you have questions about eating disorders, you should spend some time on the Alliance for Eating Disorders or Beat Eating Disorders' webpages, available at: www.allianceforeatingdisorders.com and www.beateatingdisorders.org.uk. Both organizations have helplines and online resources, and offer virtual support groups.

✦ There are many free online sources of support on other web pages as well: https://anad.org, https://feast-ed.org, www.nationaleatingdisorders.org, and www.theprojectheal.org are webpages I would start with.

✦ There are great books written about eating disorder experiences and treatment. I love Jason Wood's **Starving for Survival** (2022, published by Orthorexia Bites), which focuses on his battle with orthorexia. **What's Eating Us: Women, Food, and the Epidemic of Body Anxiety** by Cole Kazdin (2023, published St Martin's Essentials) combines personal stories and investigative reporting to shed light on what it's like to recover from an eating disorder.

✦ For more scholarly articles and web pages with information about eating disorders, see the companion website for this book: www.TheBodyImageBook.com.

CHAPTER 8

BE ACTIVE

#MoveforFun

"The secret of getting ahead is getting started"

Mark Twain, American writer, humorist, essayist

Mila Ivy, 18 years old, she/her, USA

I feel pretty comfortable in my body these days, but I haven't always. Growing up, I studied ballet pretty seriously. I spent a lot of time looking in the mirror while wearing a leotard and tights — all while an instructor commented on what my body was doing. There was also plenty of discussion among dancers about restricting what they ate. I never restricted myself, but I wasn't immune to those conversations and the value placed on thinness. I just knew that I couldn't dance if I didn't have the energy that food provided. As I got older, I got more into jazz and contemporary dance and now I only dance hip hop for fun. One of the things I appreciate about hip hop is that there is so much more diversity amongst the dancers — in terms of both ethnicity and body size.

Growing up with Chinese parents, I was exposed to the idolization of the thin beauty ideal at home, too. I think my mom's eating habits and body image issues were an ever-present part of my childhood. My mom didn't really diet but was just very conscious of these issues. She'd make comments all the time about how much and what she was eating. She made it clear that it was important to keep her relatively petite body. I'm sure some of her beliefs were affected by her own childhood in China. When we go back to visit extended family in China, I'm struck by how open people are about making comments about others' bodies. People will just come out and say things like, "You're bigger than the last time I saw you." I'll be visiting family in China this summer for the first time since the pandemic and I'm already anticipating these somewhat different cultural norms surrounding body talk. As much as I will try not to let it affect me, I'm sure that I will spend some energy thinking about packing **flattering** clothes and worrying about what people will say.

Now that I go to college in Philadelphia, I'm surrounded by a lot more diversity. There's a level of comfort that comes from being surrounded by people who look like you. I've also noticed that I've found more influencers and creators online who are Asian and diverse in terms of body size. I was also introduced to weightlifting through social media and enjoy going to the gym to get strong. Lifting weights and seeing the weight go up over time makes me feel not just physically stronger but also psychologically stronger. I like feeling powerful.

If I could offer my younger self some advice, I'd let her know that she may feel self-conscious of her ethnic features now, but one day they'll be some of her favorite parts of herself. When you're young, you want to change yourself and you want to be like everyone else. Now I love that I'm ethnic and tall and strong and I'm not like everyone else. I feel like I stand out in a good way.

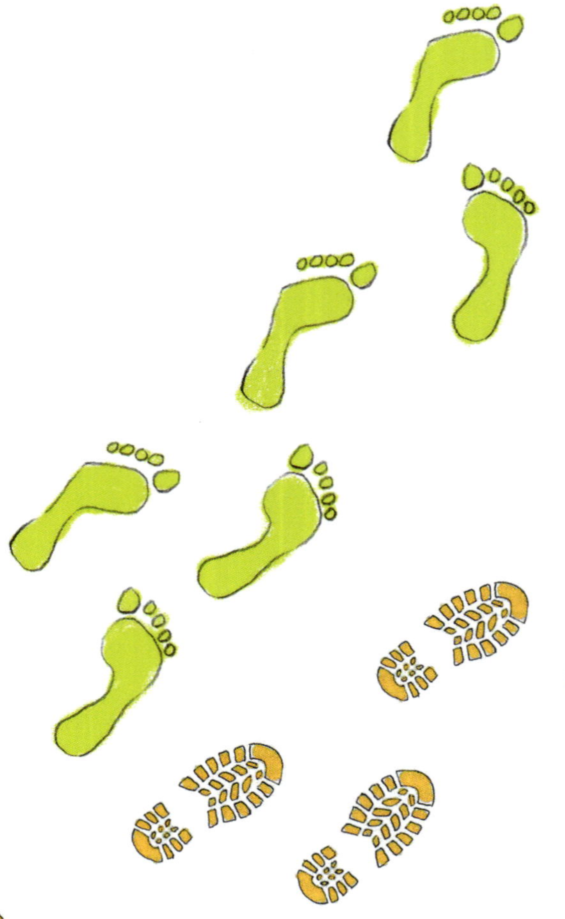

As you've probably noticed by now, a theme in this book is that it's important to take really good care of your body. One way to care for your body is to be physically active. As Mila's story suggests, physical activity may include dancing, weightlifting, and many other types of movement.

What is the difference between physical activity, exercise, and fitness?

Physical activity is pretty much any movement of your body. Nearly anything that requires energy is physical activity: walking, running, playing basketball, swimming, mowing the lawn, and even cleaning your bedroom. **Exercise** is a particular type of physical activity that's usually more planned and purposeful. In other words, playing on your school's volleyball team is exercise: you do it regularly, it's structured, and you intend to be doing it. On the other hand, you probably don't clean your room with the intention of "getting exercise."

Often people talk about engaging in physical activity or exercise with the goal of being fit. **Fitness** is a broad term with more than one definition. Often fitness refers to getting in shape. What counts as fitness for one person may look very different for another person. The word fitness has become popular in recent years, as has the word **fitspiration** (aka "fitspo"). Fitspiration refers to images, **memes**,

IN THIS CHAPTER YOU'LL LEARN:

- ○ about the benefits of physical activity for your body image and your health in general,
- ○ how much you should aim to be active, and the importance of balancing this with getting enough sleep and limiting other activities such as screen time, and
- ○ strategies for establishing good health habits for physical activity or anything else that could benefit your health.

or ideas, usually shared on social media, that are supposed to inspire fitness. Unfortunately, there is some research to suggest that fitspiration isn't actually always inspiring. In fact, sometimes seeing other fit (usually slender and toned) people just makes us feel bad about ourselves. Feeling bad about ourselves or feeling inferior to other people is rarely motivating.

Following fitness experts on Instagram will help motivate you to exercise regularly and get in shape.

Who doesn't like to feel inspired? Most people can use some inspiration (or fitspiration) to help them maintain good health habits, including regular physical activity. However, fitness experts on Instagram or other forms of social media may not be the best place to turn to for advice and inspiration. Many of these influencers do not have any actual expertise aside from their own experiences. Also, fitness "experts" are often incredibly toned and slim, and do little more than work on their fitness. That's their job! In contrast, you most likely go to school, study, hang out with your friends, and participate in other activities like your school's debate team, basketball team, or French club. You don't have time to exercise all day long and you have other important activities to prioritize. What this means is that fitness experts aren't usually a good source of comparison (or inspiration) because you're likely to feel like you don't measure up to these experts and that you never will.

When we compare ourselves to others and this results in us feeling worse about ourselves, this is one form of social comparison. Scientists refer to this particular kind of social comparison as **upward social comparison**. We're comparing ourselves to others who are "above" us or more accomplished than us in some way. The result is that we usually feel bad about ourselves. In fact, in one recent study examining women in their 20s, exposure to fitspiration images on social media was linked to higher rates of eating disorder symptoms. In other words, in this study, women not only felt bad about themselves after viewing what were intended to be inspirational images, but also may have been more likely to adopt unhealthy eating habits. Turns out, fitspiration is just not usually all that inspirational.

How much activity is ideal?

Any kind of movement is good for you and obsessing over how much you move is not, so it's best not to get hung up on numbers too much. However, the US Department of Health and Human Services recommends that kids aged 6–17 years engage in 1 hour of physical activity a day. That may sound like a lot, but remember that physical activity can include all sorts of things. If you walk to school, or even walk around while you're at school, you may easily find yourself active for 30 minutes most days.

Some of the activity you take part in is likely to be aerobic. If you're working up a sweat and breathing heavily, either because you ran up some stairs at school or because you've gone for a jog at home, then this is aerobic activity. Even a fast-paced walk is aerobic activity. But it's valuable to also take part in physical activity that's good for your muscles and bones. This can include stretching and working on flexibility or doing push-ups or sit-ups.

There are trends in fitness, from jazzercise (ask your mom or aunt if she ever went to a class) to aerobics classes to CrossFit. Sometimes these trends may seem enticing because they promise that you will get stronger and healthier in a short period of time (this is usually false advertising). Sometimes a "viral" challenge may prescribe two workouts per day or "streaks" of working out for a number of days in a row. Two workouts a day is more than you need to exercise for health benefits and may detract from other important things that you need to do in a day. Even though I will review some of the benefits of being active, it is important to remember that there are many other activities that you should spend your time on.

What are the benefits of physical activity?

There is a great deal of scientific research to suggest that regular physical activity is good for both your psychological and physical health. Physically active kids tend to have stronger bones and muscles. Being regularly physically active is also associated with better mental health – for example, lower rates of depression. Being physically active may even be good for your brain and your ability to learn.

Kids who are regularly active also tend to develop an appreciation for how good they feel when they move their bodies or participate in team sports. They may develop good activity habits that they stick with as they get older. If you develop a love for swimming when you're young, you're more likely to swim as a form of exercise when you're an adult. We all become more vulnerable to health problems as we get older, including heart disease, type 2 diabetes, and cancer. Being active can help prevent some of these health problems and may even help us live longer lives.

Finding what you love

I'm guessing that some of you reading this book will feel like you're not sure how to work physical activity into your life because you just don't like sports or don't feel like you're very good at any of them. I can relate to this. I was always chosen last for teams when I was a kid. I wasn't particularly athletic, and I always felt self-conscious when I tried to play sports. I wasn't against being physically active, but I felt stressed out by even the thought of playing sports.

Fortunately, being physically active doesn't have to mean that you play a sport. There are a lot of ways to get yourself moving. Here are some ideas, in ABC order: acrobatics, ballet, cycling, dance, exercise classes, fencing, gymnastics, horseback riding, ice skating, jumping rope, kickboxing, line dancing, martial arts, netball, Oztag (a type of rugby), Pilates, quoits, rock climbing, stretching, tai chi, ultimate frisbee, volleyball, walking, Xtreme paintball, yoga, and Zumba. Many people end up trying a lot of different activities out before they find something they love. At different stages in your life, you may try out different activities. Right now, being on your school's dance team or swim team may be a fun way to be active, but as you get older you may find yourself riding a bike to school or walking your dog to get exercise.

It's valuable to think outside the box when it comes to ways to move your body. Maybe you'll find that you love gardening or enjoy playing tennis with a friend. You don't have to be competitive (or even social) to be physically active, and there are countless options. Be creative in thinking about ways to keep your body moving and feeling good. And, of course, only be active in ways that are safe and healthy for your body as it changes, ages, and inevitably gets injured at times.

EXPERT ADVICE

Dr. Rachael Flatt, Olympic figure skater and clinical psychologist

"When we are physically active or playing a sport, it's so easy to get caught up in the idea that our bodies have to look a certain way. It doesn't help that what we see on social media — from revealing workout clothes to photoshopped and filtered workout images — is often unrealistic. In those moments, I find it helpful to think about all the incredible things my body can do for me, and I remember that being inclusive and celebrating all shapes, sizes, and abilities gives us all a chance to thrive and love what we do."

Why being active can make you feel good about your body

Although your social media feed may try to convince you that being athletic or fit looks a certain way, this is not true. People can be very physically capable without "looking the part." One fun example of this is a running group started by Martinus Evans called the Slow AF Run Club. (I'm sure you can figure out what AF stands for, but the link to his web page is at the end of this chapter.) This is an inclusive running community for people who don't necessarily look like runners. Their focus is on helping people to enjoy running – and focus on body functionality – without a focus on looking a certain way or weighing a certain amount. **This is body-positive exercise.**

You may recall the discussion of body **functionality** from Chapter 3. Basically, the idea is that girls tend to focus on how their bodies look far too often and instead should focus on how their bodies work or function because this can enable body positivity. You probably see so many advertisements for beauty products – make-up, hair and skin products, and perfume – that you hardly even think about them. However, all these products focus you on your appearance and how to change your appearance. This all comes at a cost, both the price of the products themselves, and the time and energy to use them. However, they may limit how you can move or function, whether because your shoes are uncomfortable or you don't want your hair to get messed up. The focus is all about how you look, whereas participation in sports and other physical activities leads to a focus on how you move. Exercising regularly so you can run or swim faster may take time, but it's also a good way to improve your health and fitness. And it's fun to see how much you can improve at an activity over time.

Scientific studies support the idea that focusing on functionality through participation in sports and other kinds of physical activities can be good for how girls think about their bodies. Girls who are athletes have been found to have higher self-esteem than girls who aren't athletes. Female university-age athletes have also been found to feel more appreciation of their bodies and to actually report valuing how their bodies function more than nonathletes. A large study also found that girls who are athletes have more overall positive body images than nonathletes. This doesn't mean that you need to be an athlete to reap the rewards of physical activity. Remember, any sort of movement counts as physical activity! One cool study called *This Girl Can* examined links between body image and viewing a video campaign of diverse women (in terms of size, shape, age, and ethnicity) exercising. When women in their 20s saw the video campaign of diverse – in other words, relatable! – women being active, they were more likely to appreciate their own bodies. This is important because when we feel appreciative of our bodies and not judgmental of ourselves, we're more likely to try new activities.

The **bottom line** is that any movement that you do regularly can help you think more about the many amazing things that your body can do, which is way more valuable than how your body looks.

Consider your reasons

Why are you physically active?

Check a box next to the reasons that you engage in physical activity:

- ☐ To reduce guilt
- ☐ To follow self-imposed rules
- ☐ To feel comfortable eating certain foods
- ☐ Because a friend/partner/coach says to
- ☐ So that you don't feel heavy

- ☐ Because it is fun
- ☐ For physical health improvement
- ☐ For stress-reduction
- ☐ To be with other people
- ☐ To feel good

There are many reasons why people choose to be active, and some reasons are healthier than others. Did you check more of the reasons in the left or the right column? Arguably, the reasons in the right column are indicative of a healthier mindset when it comes to physical activity. Notice, however, that reframing your reasons – focusing on feeling good as opposed to avoiding feeling bad – may make a meaningful difference. If you notice that you are participating in physical activity for the reasons in the left column, you may want to start to shift your approach to activity by choosing some activities that you enjoy more than what you are currently doing. More advice follows below for getting into activity habits that you both like and can sustain.

Establishing good habits

Maybe, as you read this chapter, the idea of being more physically active is growing on you. How do you get into the habit of being more active? It's typically difficult for people to change their habits, but there are some evidence-based practices that will help.

First of all, don't aim too high. That may sound sort of pessimistic, but it's too easy to set an unreasonable fitness goal and then find it impossible and give up all together. Set a small goal that you know that you can achieve. Maybe your goal is to walk your dog for 10 minutes each day, or to take a dance class with a friend each week. Do something that will be fairly easy. Once you do this new activity for a few weeks, consider adding another change. Maybe you walk your dog for 15 minutes per day or maybe you run with your dog instead of walking her. Maybe you add in a second dance class per week. When you set small, achievable goals and you're successful, that success will motivate you to do more. If it doesn't, then reconsider your goals. Maybe you don't really like dance. Maybe you'd rather go to a gym instead of walking your dog.

Another important thing to consider if you're trying to add physical activity to your regular routine is that this may mean you have to take something else out of your regular routine. As the saying goes, there are only so many hours in the day. If your schedule is already packed full, you may need to drop something to add in physical activity. Be sure you don't drop other valuable activities like spending enough time on your homework or getting enough sleep.

Telling people about your goals and asking for help in achieving them can also be helpful. Sometimes scientists call this a **commitment strategy**. We tend to be more likely to stick with a goal if other people know about it. We don't want to feel embarrassed if others realize we didn't stick with our goal. It can also be valuable to ask people for help in meeting our goals. Maybe you'd like a parent or a friend to remind you of your activity goals, or maybe you want a friend to exercise with you. Either way, it can be useful to have supportive people in your life helping you achieve any of the goals that you have.

Goals that are sustainable tend to be goals that make you feel good in the short term. Sometimes these are called **process goals**. Although long-term goals like your long-term health are important, these **performance goals** are rarely motivating in the present. Feeling tired but accomplished after a workout or noticing that you are stronger or more flexible after a couple of weeks at a new activity will help you to sustain that activity. Most fitness fads are flashy and dramatic; the goals are big and the timeline is short. This is rarely realistic, but *feeling good* after a hike outside with a friend is much more likely to help you want to go on another hike.

Be patient with yourself and don't give up. If you don't follow through with whatever activity goal you've set for yourself, this doesn't mean you throw in the towel forever. Maybe your life feels too busy right now, but once summer rolls around you'll have more time and you can work on setting new activity goals. Once you establish a habit for 2–3 months it tends to stick, but you have to keep at it before the sticking happens. People tend to be creatures of habit, and changing those habits isn't easy. Be patient with yourself if you don't meet your goals the first time you try. Most people have to try more than once to change any habit.

It's important for your health that you take 10,000 steps a day (and keep track of them)!

No one seems to know with absolute certainty where the idea that it is important to take 10,000 steps per day originated. Some have attributed it to a Japanese company that marketed a pedometer (an old-fashioned step counter) back in the 1960s as a device to measure 10,000 steps. Of course, today your phone or Fitbit may include 10,000 steps as your daily goal without you even suggesting this.

Recent research suggests that you probably don't need to take 10,000 steps per day to improve your health. In fact, pretty much any exercise may improve your health, and the benefits may level off at around 7,500 steps per day (at least, this seems to be the case in research examining women). Some studies indicate that about 5,000 steps is a good goal in terms of lowering mortality risk. This all depends on a variety of factors, of course. If you haven't been active in a while, going out and running 10,000 steps (4–5 miles) is probably not a great idea and could do more harm than good. However, walking half that distance may feel great.

The bottom line is that, although fitness goals may be motivating, it's important not to fixate on them. You want to enjoy being active and not spend mental energy obsessing about your exact number of steps per day.

Try taking it outside

One thing that may help you stick to a physical activity regimen is to try exercising outside. Several scientific studies have examined how people feel about exercise that's done outside versus inside. Usually, participants in this research are asked to do something like go for a walk outside or walk on a treadmill inside. Not only do people tend to say that they like walking outside more, but they also report feeling less tense and less depressed after a walk outside. The same doesn't seem to be true of walking on a treadmill. People seem to find outdoor physical activity easier, too. Walking on a treadmill is a good way to get some exercise, but if you don't enjoy it that much, it'll be hard to stick with it. One recent study found that natural environments may directly affect body image among kids, too. In this study, going for a walk in nature was more likely to improve body image than going for a walk inside. If being outside might make physical activity more pleasurable and improve body image, what else can you do outside? Walking, running, and hiking are all great outdoor activities. Nearly any sport can be played outside, too. Biking, football, and basketball are all possible outdoor activities. However, if the weather or other circumstances don't allow you to exercise outdoors, you should still try to find ways to move indoors. In research comparing people's moods after they sit around indoors versus exercise indoors, the folks who were active almost always seemed to be in a better mood and feel more relaxed than the people who were sitting around, even if they were allowed to play on a computer while they sat.

Can you exercise too much?

Watching professional athletes and people who enjoy being active can be so inspiring. It can make you want to devote more of your time and energy to achieving your own fitness potential. Physical activity is incredibly good for your body and your mind, but, as with anything, **there can be too much of a good thing.**

In terms of the physical benefits, some research suggests that participating in regular, vigorous exercise, like jogging, can add 5–6 years onto your lifespan. However, other research suggests that it may be better to be more moderate in your approach to exercise (for example, not exercising every day) to reap the most benefit in terms of how long you live. Even with some inconsistencies in the science, it's safe to conclude that exercise is nearly always good for you physically. However, it's important to listen to your body. If you're tired all the time, really hungry from exercising, or not enjoying exercising anymore, then you're probably overdoing it.

It also seems pretty clear that too much exercise can have a negative effect on your mental health. This is especially true if exercising feels like an obligation and is not something you enjoy. Psychologists sometimes refer to exercise that feels necessary, especially more than once per day, as **compulsive exercise**. If you feel like you're scheduling your day around exercise, worrying about how much you exercise, not eating unless you exercise a certain amount, or feeling guilty if you don't exercise, you may be a compulsive exerciser. Compulsive exercise can be dangerous for your mental health, and you should talk to someone – a parent, school counselor,

Q&A

Regular exercise can lead to your body looking different, and you certainly may acquire some muscle mass. In other words, where there was once fat, you may now see more muscles and definition. Most people like these changes in their body; they're proof of time spent exercising, and people may think that they look good. It's probably mostly a matter of opinion whether it's possible for girls and women to become too muscular. What is too muscular? Because of differences in girls' and boys' hormones following puberty (see Chapter 2), girls and women are less likely to develop the bulky muscles that boys and men may develop. Furthermore, in order to develop a lot of muscle mass, you would need to spend a fair amount of time lifting pretty heavy weights. Cardiovascular exercises like running or swimming are very unlikely to lead to the development of a lot of muscle mass.

So the short answer to this question is probably, no. It's also important to remember that muscles are about a lot more than how you look. They mean that you're strong, and strength means that can probably do a lot of useful things: carrying your own groceries or shopping bags at the mall, mowing the lawn, climbing up a flight of stairs without getting out of breath, and lifting heavy objects are just a few examples.

or therapist – if you think this describes you. **Being regularly physically active can be great, but if you end up pushing yourself all the time and not feeling like you're enjoying your activity, it's time to step back and rethink things**. Both your body and your mind need times of rest in order to reap the benefits of activity.

And make sure you rest, too

It's important to your health that you keep your body moving, but it's equally important that you make sure your body gets enough rest. Did you know that more than half of all middle schoolers and high schoolers in the USA don't get enough sleep? How much sleep do you get on most nights? Think about what time you usually get into bed, when you usually fall asleep, and when you usually wake up. Are you sleeping at least 8 or 9 hours each night?

The Centers for Disease Control and Prevention recommends that 6–12-year-olds need 9–12 hours of sleep each night, and 13–18-year-olds need 8–10 hours of sleep each night. Sleep is related to pretty much every aspect of your health and well-being. Although the relationship between sleep and different sorts of diseases is complicated, not getting enough sleep may place you at risk for type 2 diabetes, heart disease, weight gain, and even depression. At the very least, not sleeping enough is a way to feel miserable, tired, and cranky the next day. Making sure you get enough sleep is one thing you can do to take care of yourself and protect your mental and physical health.

If you aren't sure you're getting enough sleep, or you want to try to get more sleep (you can't sleep *too* much!), here are some things you might want to try to improve your **sleep hygiene**:

- Go to bed at the same time each night and wake up at the same time.
- Make sure your bed is comfortable to you.
- Make sure the room you sleep in is a comfortable temperature, not too hot or too cold.
- Don't eat a big meal too close to bedtime.
- Be careful not to drink anything with caffeine (such as soda or tea) in the afternoon or evening.
- Keep electronic devices out of your bedroom.
- Don't do other things in bed where you sleep – don't study, watch television, or eat on your bed.

EXPERT ADVICE

Lisa L. Lewis, MS, author of *The Sleep-Deprived Teen*

"It's so easy to get overscheduled, but make sure you leave enough time for sleep. Up until age 18, teens should be getting 8–10 hours. (And after that point, it's still 7–9 hours.) If you're regularly not getting enough sleep, everything becomes more difficult! You may have figured out how to manage, but you're not doing yourself any favors. If you're learning or studying for a test, you won't be as effective. And if you're working out or preparing for a big game, your coordination, accuracy, and even your recovery time will be impacted. There's also an important connection between sleep and mood, with sleep deprivation linked to depression, anxiety, and suicidality. Being well-rested boosts your emotional resiliency and your well-being, and makes it easier to deal with whatever stressors come your way."

Q&A

I know it's important to get enough sleep, but sometimes I just lie there at night thinking about everything that happened during the day. I worry about the next day. I start to worry about all sorts of things, and I can't sleep. What should I do?

It isn't uncommon for people to think about their days and even to worry a bit when they lie in bed at night. If you find yourself worrying a lot, then you may be experiencing anxiety that a professional can help you with. You may want to talk to a parent or other adult who you feel comfortable talking to, like an aunt or an older sibling. It also may be valuable to talk to a counselor at your school. Sometimes just talking about things that are on your mind can help a lot. Often, other people can help you understand that some of what you're worried about is unlikely to happen or unlikely to matter very much in the grand scheme of things. This isn't to say that your worries are anything to be embarrassed about, just that getting other people's perspectives can be valuable.

In terms of getting more sleep, consider the tips on page 174. You may want to try some relaxation exercises, or you could listen to relaxing music when you go to sleep. Sleeping well has a lot to do with forming good sleep habits and getting used to enjoying sleep, as opposed to feeling anxious in bed at night.

If talking with someone about your worries and adopting healthy sleep habits don't do the trick, then you may want to talk to a doctor. It's possible that you have a sleep disorder (although a true sleep disorder is fairly rare before adulthood, affecting just 4% of children, according to the Association of American Family Physicians), or that some medication may help you to cope with your anxiety (see also the discussion of anxiety in Chapter 9).

Don't sacrifice sleep for the screen

If you're like a lot of kids these days, you have parents who talk about **screen time** more that you would like them to. The American Academy of Pediatrics (AAP; the biggest organization of doctors that focus on kids' health in the USA) suggests that parents put limits on screen time and make sure their kids don't let screens interfere with sleep, physical activity, and health in general. They also suggest that parents make sure that kids experience media-free times with their families, such as dinner time. The AAP recommends that families sit down and talk about their media use and create a plan together.

Why am I talking about this in the chapter on physical activity? You've probably heard adults grumble that when they were kids they ran around outside and didn't spend all their time using a phone or a tablet. More screen time tends to mean less physical activity. Watching television or videos and playing video games can be entertaining, but **taking good care of your body means making it move most days**.

It's never too late

There's a chance that you're reading this and realizing that you aren't particularly interested in being more physically active than you already are, or that you just don't have the time, with school and other activities you're involved in. This is OK. Your goals and interests may change in the future, whether that means becoming more knowledgeable about a particular topic, more involved in a certain hobby, or more engaged in physical activity.

Being a kid means juggling school, relationships with family and friends, and other extracurricular activities. If you don't want to or just can't find the time to do *one more* activity or responsibility right now, this isn't a reason to feel guilty. As you get older, you're likely to find more occasions and opportunities to engage in physical activity of all types. I became a runner in my mid-30s after only a couple of years of running track as a kid. Running wasn't something I was that enthusiastic about or that committed to when I was younger. I can't even remember why I was on the track team for a few years – probably because I had some friends who did it, so I did, too. Now, running is an important part of my life and it's something I've done a lot more of than I ever expected I would when I was young. So even if you don't get into a particular form of exercise now, this doesn't mean that you won't when you're older. Most physical activity will benefit your mind and body, even if you don't make it a habit until you're an adult. I appreciate Kehinde's story (below) because she reminds us of the amazing things that our bodies can do and how wonderful it can feel to move our bodies.

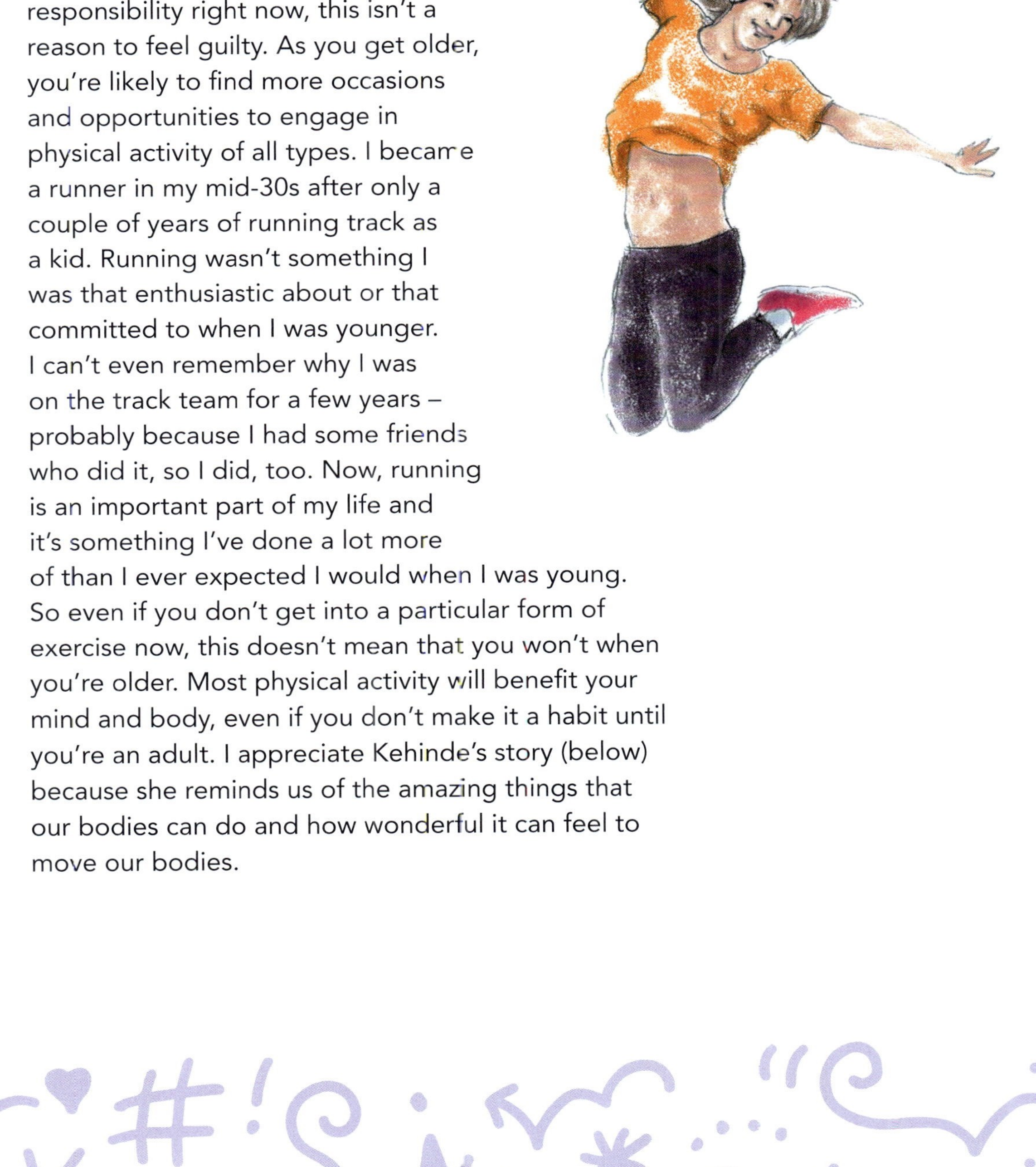

Kehinde Fatima, 18 years old, she/her, Nigeria

I'm really tall — over 6 feet — and thin. My body doesn't have a lot of shape and I've had a difficult time accepting it. My mom has helped me to feel better about how I look by comparing me to models, but sometimes people make fun of my height. I have started to try to get better about standing up for myself in these situations, even though I sometimes wish I had more weight in my hips and chest.

I'm currently attending the Nigeria College of Nursing. I don't know what sort of nurse I want to be yet, because my clinical training has just begun. It is somewhat scary to be responsible for helping people who are sick. Recently, I witnessed a woman giving birth; it wasn't what I expected. It was frightening to see the woman in pain as she tried to push out the baby. It was also amazing to understand that her body was able to do this — it accommodated growing a baby and delivering it. When she was done delivering the baby, her pain stopped, and her stomach deflated. The woman endured so much, and it all happened so fast. It was incredible.

I am busy as a student, but I try to take care of my body by exercising. I like to jog and feel the wind passing by my ear and my body move. I feel strong even though I am not fast. I also like to do yoga and try to do it a couple of times per week. I am somewhat flexible and good at yoga, and I find it relaxing.

My family has enough food to eat, but I sometimes feel too tired to eat. My advice for my younger self would be to learn to love food and to be sure to eat to take care of yourself. I also would tell her that if others say something negative about you, don't take it to heart.

This is not about you but a reflection of them.

SUMMING UP #MoveforFun

- ☑ Being regularly physically active is an important part of taking care of your body and nurturing a positive body image.
- ☑ Physical activity can improve not just how you feel about yourself but your mental and physical health as well.
- ☑ Don't sacrifice sleep to exercise and be careful not to let screen time take the place of sleep or physical activity. It's important to do things you enjoy (watching TV), things you have to do (homework), and things that are important for your health (physical activity and sleep). It can be difficult to achieve this balance, so be sure to ask friends or family for help establishing good habits.

FIND OUT MORE:

- ✦ The Centers for Disease Control and Prevention's website includes information about physical activity and sleep habits, such as www.cdc.gov/physicalactivity/index.html and www.cdc.gov/sleep/index.html.
- ✦ For more information about the Slow AF Run Club, check out their web page and Martinus Evans' book at: https://slowafrunclub.com/
- ✦ The American Academy of Pediatrics has an online worksheet that families can use to discuss the important issues around balancing media time: www.healthychildren.org/English/fmp/Pages/MediaPlan.aspx.
- ✦ Jaqueline Nesi is a psychologist who studies how technology affects kids. Her webpage contains some information that you may find interesting: www.techwithoutstress.com
- ✦ For more scholarly articles and web pages with information about physical activity, see the companion website for this book: www.TheBodyImageBook.com.

SELF-CARE

"There are only two ways to live your life. One is as though nothing is a miracle. The other is as though everything is a miracle."

Albert Einstein, German-born physicist

Emma Rene, 20 years old, she/her, USA

It has taken me a long time to accept my body for what it is. However, going to college has really helped change my level of confidence in myself. I started stepping outside of my comfort zone all around, including wearing clothes I would have never typically worn in high school. I remember the first time I wore a tube top to a party. I would have never worn a tube top in high school, especially not without a bra. For a girl who wears a 36D bra, sometimes you're told, "Oh you can't wear that, your boobs are too big." For me, my boobs were not the hardest part of wearing a tube top, it was my stomach. Ever in high-waisted jeans I was still concerned about how my stomach looked. It wasn't just about my stomach being fat, it was about the continuous glucose monitor I wear on my stomach for my diabetes that clearly sticks out like a sore thumb when I'm out. Sometimes I'll get lucky enough and I'll have placed it in a good enough spot that my jeans will come up high enough to cover it, but sometimes it still shows. It took me a while to be completely comfortable with wearing my glucose monitor on my stomach because I always worried about looking like a complete robot. I also wear an insulin pump on my arm that is completely noticeable 90% of the time, so I didn't want to have to wear anything else to make me stand out even more. But after a while of being on campus and seeing girls wear what they wanted to confidently, I decided to give it a try myself. One day, I went out and started buying different clothes that I would not have worn before. Now my closet is full of super-cute clothes that make me look and feel good.

My mom has always been my biggest supporter and very best friend. I think for her it all goes back to her own insecurities and making sure I never feel about myself the way she did about herself. Every day, my mom finds some way to remind me how beautiful I am, even if I look like I've just crawled out from under a rock. To take it a step further, when I'm feeling down on my body specifically, she tells me that my body is beautiful. She doesn't push me to do anything differently, she doesn't talk down to me or ever minimize how I'm feeling; she just supports me. Sometimes when I am wearing an outfit that looks really good on me, she'll ask me if people threw rose petals down on the ground for me when I walked in the room. I just laugh and tell her, "No." There are other times when she'll think an outfit looks really good on me and then

Story continues …

ask me if anyone else has told me how beautiful I was today. Again, I just laugh. It's so cute how she thinks everyone I will ever meet will think I am as beautiful as she thinks I am. But even if no one else besides her thinks that, that's all I need.

Being a girl is hard enough without having body image insecurities. I think it's really important to teach young girls to be nice to each other — and nice to themselves. It's our responsibility to be kind to one another. It doesn't need to be a competition with each other about who is more successful than the other. Instead, share your successes and accomplishments with other girls. Make your confidence your favorite accessory each day. Wear your beauty with pride and a big smile and hold your head up high. When I feel a little down on myself, I remember my favorite quote, "Confidence looks good on you girl!"

As Emma's story reminds us, nurturing a positive body image isn't only about feeling good about your appearance. It's about taking care of yourself — both your body and your mind. In this chapter, I discuss some strategies for self-care that you may want to adopt. I'll also review some things that may interfere with your ability to practice self-care so that you can combat them and be as healthy as possible for the rest of your life.

IN THIS CHAPTER YOU'LL LEARN:

- how to be mindful about your physical and mental needs and how to aim for positive embodiment,
- how to identify when you may need extra self-care, such as if you experience anxiety, depression, or a chronic health condition, and
- the importance of nurturing positive relationships with others who will support you on your journey to a positive body image.

What is mindfulness?

One way to care for yourself is to be mindful of your physical, psychological, social, and emotional needs. **Mindfulness** actually has two related definitions. To be mindful means to be aware. It's important to spend some time thinking about your needs; for example, you may find that you value some time alone each day. Or maybe you realize that you feel better when you get at least 8 hours of sleep each night.

Mindfulness also refers to being present in the moment, accepting your thoughts and feelings, and paying attention to yourself. There are different ways to try to achieve this sort of mindfulness, including yoga and meditation. A recent study provides some support for the usefulness of mindfulness for improving body image. In this study, young women were shown a series of brief videos about mindfulness, including videos about mindfulness in general, breathing exercises, and eating mindfully. At the end of the study, women's body image ratings showed some improvement, suggesting that learning about mindfulness was helpful.

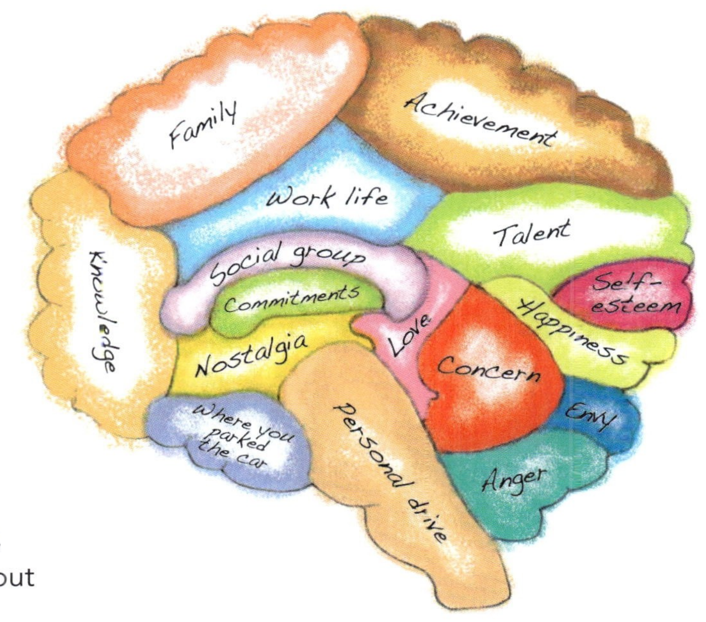

Yoga and meditation

Yoga has been popular with adults for a long time, and it's also becoming popular among children and teens. Yoga is a form of exercise, but it can also be a good way to increase mindfulness. Through stretches, poses, and breathing exercises, yoga

can help promote body awareness. Yoga can also encourage a focus on body functionality and acceptance. Because of all of this, researchers have begun to explore yoga as a way to improve body image.

Scientists have found that asking preteens to participate in a yoga program may increase their body appreciation. Among adults, practicing yoga has been shown to increase mindfulness and improve how people view themselves. Furthermore, practicing yoga may improve general body image. There is no guarantee that a weekly yoga class will dramatically alter how you feel about your body, but there is hardly any downside to trying yoga. You may improve your flexibility and strength, as well as your general well-being. Feeling better about your body could just be icing on the cake.

You've probably heard of **meditation** before, and you may have some basic idea of what it's all about. However, you may not realize that meditation is actually a broad term used to describe a variety of different techniques. All meditation techniques aim to train the mind, just as physical activity aims to train the body. Whereas physical activity is all about being active, meditation is about training the mind to be calm.

Meditation practices often involve breathing techniques to relax the body and calm the mind. Some forms of meditation involve stillness and focusing attention on a particular object while trying to clear thoughts from the mind. Meditation can also focus on acknowledging thoughts or concerns and working on accepting them or distancing yourself from them. Meditation includes listening to music that's enjoyable and soothing, and can even include reading, writing, or journaling. The goal of any sort of meditation is to feel calm, relaxed, and "**centered**."

What does this have to do with body image? For some people, meditation can help them feel not only calmer but also more in touch with their bodies. This sense of "being in touch with" or "happily living in" our bodies is sometimes referred to as **embodiment**. This may seem obvious, but we are our bodies. We cannot escape them. Feeling comfortable and accepting of our bodies is an important part of developing a positive body image.

Some people enjoy meditation but not everyone. You can get better at it with practice, but it also may not be for you. It typically involves stillness, reflection, and calmness. Some people don't like to be still, aren't particularly patient at reflecting on their experiences, and are naturally high energy. These people may grow to like meditation, but it also may not be a good fit for them. There are other ways to nurture yourself physically and emotionally, so don't worry if meditation doesn't seem to be for you.

Other ways to relax

Typical mindfulness techniques are not for everyone. There are many other ways to relax, feel in touch with yourself, and develop a positive body image. I already discussed exercise in detail in Chapter 8, but exercise can be a great way to relax for some people. Of course, you have to be doing some sort of exercise that you enjoy in order for it to relax you. Or, at the very least, the exercise needs to tire you out and force you to relax due to exhaustion. But even short walks, enjoying the scenery around you and taking a break from the rest of your day, can be a good way to de-stress.

Relaxation practices are often described as solitary activities that you must do alone. This is not necessarily true. If I meet a friend for lunch and we talk, catch up, and spend an hour or so just ignoring the stressors in our lives and enjoying each other's company, I feel relaxed afterward. I'm sure I'm not the only one who finds socializing to be a source of relaxation at times, and talking with others as a way to rethink things in your life that may be bothering you. Often, people we're close to can offer support and advice that makes us feel calmer and less frazzled by the demands of our lives.

For some people, grooming and hygiene practices can be a source of relaxation. A long, warm shower or a hot bath can feel soothing and relaxing. Filling a bathtub with bubbly water and listening to some music you enjoy can be a nice way to unwind. Spending time washing your hair or cleaning your face can even be a way to feel like you're caring for yourself. After all, that's what self-care is: nurturing yourself in ways that you enjoy and that make you feel good.

Self-compassion

Research has consistently established links between **self-compassion**, eating behaviors, and body image. If you're compassionate, you're concerned about others and show them sympathy. Self-compassion is treating yourself with this same sort of concern and sympathy. People who think of themselves with kindness and caring are more likely to have more intuitive and healthy eating habits than people who think poorly of themselves. Self-compassion is also linked to a positive body image.

If we're honest with ourselves, we know that we treat ourselves worse than we treat nearly anyone else. We may think critical thoughts ("You are the stupidest person in this room!") and try to motivate ourselves to maintain maladaptive behaviors ("You absolutely

Emotional self-care

Therapist Alli Spotts-De Lazzer helps people deal with body image and eating disorders all the time. Her work has taught her the importance of emotional self-care and she shares these tips:

To me, self-care is "what you do to care for and about yourself so that you can be your full self in the world." So, yes, that includes the usual stuff like sleeping and eating well enough to have steady moods, brain power, and energy. But what about emotional self-care?

Let's be real: feelings can be uncomfortable. We can have a bunch of feelings at the same moment, which can seem confusing (for example, you can't wait for something but are also scared about it). The complex world of emotions can beg for self-care. Here are three self-care strategies for your emotions that I call the three-D's (DISCOVER, DEAL, and DECODE):

1. As you age, do what you can to **DISCOVER** and learn about emotions in general. When they pop into your head or body, can you name what you are feeling? For example, "I feel sad, mad, glad, or rad!"

2. Then, if you have difficulty with feelings (most of us do at times), ask someone you trust for help to **DEAL** with them in healthy ways – especially the ones that feel big and icky. (When I feel bad, I like to dance. I might look silly if someone saw me, but it helps me settle inside a bit. Some people journal. You'll find your ways to deal with your feelings.)

3. Finally, it is really important to **DECODE** what your feelings are telling you. This takes practice and begs for your curiosity. Like if you get mad, glad, sad, or scared, those emotions are probably happening because something's going on that needs your attention.

Emotional self-care is an ongoing thing: I'm 50+ years old and still doing it. But here's the great news: I've learned that my feelings are my friend – even the ones that don't feel good in my body. Why? They tell me all sorts of important stuff. For example, they've helped me get great at knowing what matters to me, what I love to do, how to be safe in the world, and so much more. Emotional self-care is important even if society doesn't talk about it a lot!

have to walk 10,000 steps every day!"). Research examining self-compassion suggests that this self-criticism rarely accomplishes what we hope it will, and it is not motivating or good for our psychological health. What should we do instead?

One of the core tenets of self-compassion research is that we need to challenge our critical self-talk. Instead of being judgmental and harsh toward ourselves, we need to be more understanding. For example, if we usually like to exercise most days, but we choose not to exercise one day, instead of thinking of ourselves as "lazy," we should try to understand our behavior. We should appreciate that we were probably tired and needed a rest day. We don't need to feel guilty or condemn our behavior, we can accept it and work on viewing ourselves with kindness.

We all get messages that we shouldn't be kind to ourselves because being hard on ourselves is viewed as more effective. But the research suggests that this isn't true. Feeling down on ourselves or guilty is usually not motivating in the long run. These negative emotions may inspire some short-term behavior changes, like a long run after a rest day, but they don't usually inspire sustainable, healthy thoughts and behaviors. We need to think of ourselves with a gentler, more patient approach and greater acceptance of who we are.

Self-compassion scale (short form)

Are you wondering how self-compassionate you are?
Take this survey designed by psychologists to find out.

	Almost never	Seldom	Sometimes	Often	Almost always
1. When I fail at something important to me, I become consumed by feelings of inadequacy.	5	4	3	2	1
2. I try to be understanding and patient toward those aspects of my personality I don't like.	1	2	3	4	5
3. When something painful happens, I try to take a balanced view of the situation.	1	2	3	4	5
4. When I'm feeling down, I tend to feel like most other people are probably happier than I am.	5	4	3	2	1
5. I try to see my failings as part of the human condition.	1	2	3	4	5
6. When I'm going through a very hard time, I give myself the care and tenderness I need.	1	2	3	4	5
7. When something upsets me, I try to keep my emotions in balance.	1	2	3	4	5
8. When I fail at something that's important to me, I tend to feel alone in my failure.	5	4	3	2	1
9. When I'm feeling down, I tend to obsess and fixate on everything that's wrong.	5	4	3	2	1
10. When I feel inadequate in some way, I try to remind myself that feelings of inadequacy are shared by most people.	1	2	3	4	5
11. I'm disapproving and judgmental about my own flaws and inadequacies.	5	4	3	2	1
12. I'm intolerant and impatient toward those aspects of my personality I don't like.	5	4	3	2	1

Circle the answer to each item and sum up the numbers. Then divide by 12. If your total score is 4–5, you are high in self-compassion, 3–3.9 is indicative of moderate self-compassion, and a score below 3 suggests that you need to work on your self-compassion!

(This measure was originally published by Raes et al. in 2011.)

EXPERT ADVICE

Brian Pollack, CLSW, founder and director of Hilltop Behavioral Health in Summit, New Jersey

"Taking up space is not just about your body. Our views, values, words, reactions, and abilities are how we take up space and be present in our lives. Who we are goes beyond how we look. With practice, we become bigger in spirit and prouder of who we are. Our bodies allow all of this; they are vehicles that move us through our lives."

What if you feel like you need <u>extra</u> self-care?

There are a lot of great things about being a girl and a young woman, but there are also things that may feel challenging. The changes you experience physically as a result of puberty may feel strange and unsettling. Changes in your social world as you start a different school, participate in new activities, or make new friends can be exciting but also stressful. It's also during adolescence and early adulthood that some mental health disorders tend to emerge (in other words, people may have a biological tendency to experience these disorders that doesn't become obvious until adolescence or early adulthood). Three relatively common types of mental illness that you may experience are depression, anxiety, and substance use disorders. Fortunately, these disorders are treatable, and there is a lot you can do to feel better if you experience any of these.

Depression

Depression is the most common **psychological disorder**. We all feel sad sometimes, but depression is more than just sadness. Usually, when people experience depression, they experience physical, **cognitive**, and emotional symptoms. They may feel tired all the time or be unable to sleep. They may be hungry a lot or have no appetite at all, and may gain or lose weight. They may have a difficult time concentrating or completing tasks. They may also feel worthless and experience a sense of **despair**, as if life is not worth living.

Depression can be somewhat mild and last for a few months, or it may be severe and last for years. Sometimes, life experiences, such as the loss of a loved one, can lead to depression, but there is also believed to be a biological and genetic component to depression. Regardless of what leads someone to experience depression, it isn't their fault. No one wants to feel sad and hopeless, and anyone who does should consider seeking advice from a doctor or counselor – especially if the symptoms of depression last for more than a few weeks.

There are different treatments for depression, and often a combination of treatments works the best. Talking with a therapist can be an important part of treatment for depression (see Q&A below). **Antidepressant medication** can also be helpful. If you think you're depressed, be sure to talk to an adult that you trust about finding some treatment. There are some things you can do on your own – talk to friends, exercise, or participate in activities you enjoy – that may make you feel better, but don't try to tackle depression on your own.

> Vitamins and other natural supplements are the best and safest way to treat depression.

If you're concerned that you or someone you care about needs treatment for depression, the first step is probably for the depressed person to talk to a therapist. There are no downsides to talking to someone who can offer support, ways to rethink issues that may contribute to depression, and strategies for coping.

There are many types of therapists. Some may offer free services at your school or in a local clinic. Some may see patients in a private practice but typically charge by the hour. Some therapists are trained to help people cope specifically with depression (versus other mental health issues). Some are trained specifically to help children and adolescents. It can be important for patients to find someone to talk to who suits their needs in terms of where they provide treatment, what their fees may be, and their ability to help with depression in particular.

Some people who experience depression may benefit from antidepressant medications. The most well-known of these is probably Prozac, although there are many different kinds of antidepressants (most of which have been created more recently than Prozac). Antidepressant medication can be truly lifesaving for some people. However, these medications do sometimes come with undesirable side-effects, such as drowsiness, dry mouth, and even nausea.

Some people prefer not to take medications unless absolutely necessary. They may seek out a different sort of remedy, such as vitamins. Although there is not a lot of scientific evidence to suggest that vitamins will help someone cope with depression, according to the Mayo Clinic (a prestigious medical organization in the USA), vitamin B12 and other B vitamins may alter brain chemistry in such a way as to affect mood. Vitamin D has also received some attention as possibly being associated with mood.

However, here's something interesting that you probably didn't know: vitamins and **natural supplements** are mostly not regulated by the Food and Drug Administration in the USA (although they are in the UK and many other countries). What does that mean? It means that, unlike other medicine, there are no consistent quality checks on what contributes to the creation of vitamins and supplements in the USA. So, there may be risks associated with vitamins and supplements, as well. And in the case of vitamin D, most people get what they need just from sunlight.

Anxiety

Most likely, you have felt anxious at least once in your life. Maybe you've had to give a presentation at school and you felt yourself start to sweat a bit or felt your heart start to race. This is a normal emotional response to a stressful situation. However, if you feel anxious a lot of the time, then you may have an **anxiety disorder**. There are different types of anxiety disorders, but they all tend to affect people's ability to concentrate and focus, and often lead people to avoid certain situations. Anxiety can also affect sleep patterns (for example, making it difficult to sleep) and eating habits (leading people to eat more or less than they usually do). People who have anxiety disorders usually experience symptoms nearly every day for 6 months or more, and have a hard time keeping up with their daily routines at home, work, or school.

Anxiety can be very difficult to deal with, but it's treatable. Talking to a therapist can be a good first step toward coping with anxiety. A therapist can help you think through what's making you anxious and help you change habits and behaviors that may contribute to your anxiety. Therapists who specialize in treating anxiety can teach you strategies to help you cope with your symptoms. **Anti-anxiety medication** may also prove helpful. Similar to antidepressant medication, anti-anxiety medication alters the chemicals in a person's brain and can make a person feel calmer and happier. Stress management techniques, such as yoga and other approaches to mindfulness, can also help to reduce anxiety. But many people need more than mindfulness to cope with anxiety, and professionals can teach people strategies that can be really useful across different situations.

Substance use disorders

Addiction, or substance use disorders, occur when a person is unable to control their use of legal (for example, alcohol, or nicotine – the substance found

in cigarettes) or illegal (for example, cocaine) drugs or medication. These are complicated disorders that affect physical and mental health. Substance use disorders may occur for a variety of reasons. For example, a person may experiment with a substance and then become physically addicted to it. Or a person may use a drug to cope with stress, perhaps to help her feel relaxed or distracted, and then become addicted. It is also possible that a doctor may prescribe a medication, such as an opioid (pain killer) following surgery, and that leads to addiction. Scientists believe that there are biological and genetic factors that contribute to substance use disorders, with some people being more likely than others to develop substance use disorders. In other words, many environmental and personal influences may contribute to a substance use disorder.
If someone you know experiences a substance use disorder, it's not her fault; she was likely trying to cope as best she could and fell into addiction. No one wants to develop a life-threatening health problem. These problems are incredibly serious. They can lead people to make very poor life choices (for example, selling possessions so that they can afford drugs) and lose the ability to lead regular lives and maintain a job and family.

Treatment from trained medical professionals, therapists, and even treatment centers are often necessary for a person to recover from a substance use disorder. Some medications are also used to help treat substance use disorders. It is important that you seek help if you are concerned that you or someone you know has a substance use disorder because not only can the substance (such as alcohol or drugs) cause you direct harm and be fatal in some circumstances, but addictive substances also tend to damage different parts of the body (such as the liver and brain) with repeated use, and often that damage is not reversable.

Q&A

Other reasons for extra self-care

Some people need extra self-care, not because of their mental health but because of a physical health condition or disability. In fact, by adulthood, more than half of all people experience some type of chronic health condition. These conditions may be somewhat minor, such as seasonal allergies, or they may be more complicated and serious, such as diabetes or heart disease. Most of these conditions require some extra self-care for people to function well.

It can be very difficult to maintain the sort of health regimen that may be required if you have (or develop) a chronic condition or disability. Your doctor is likely to prescribe medicine that may be helpful. You may have more doctor appointments. You may need to make changes to your lifestyle, including changes to what you eat or what sort of exercise you do. It would also be normal to feel somewhat let down by your body, or to wish that you didn't have to deal with these things.

In recent research looking at body image among people who experience chronic pain, individuals who are more accepting of their pain tend to have more positive body images. It seems that health problems don't have to lead people to view their bodies negatively. It really matters how people think about their health. If they're accepting of their health problems – after all, most people will have some kind of health problem at some point – and understand that they need to cope with it, it's less disruptive to their feelings about their body overall. This isn't to say that you should feel glad about having to deal with a health problem. But if you do experience a health problem or disability, there are things you can do to help yourself cope. Never feel like you need to deal with this sort of thing alone. Support from caring others can be important if you find yourself in need of an extra dose of self-care.

Girl power

When I interviewed girls in the process of writing this book, one thing that came up over and over again was the importance of friends. Nearly everyone agreed that you don't need a dozen or two dozen friends or hundreds of followers on social media. One or two good friends goes a long way. **Girls can do anything! But they can't necessarily do it on their own. Everyone needs support, help, and love from others.**

Q&A

> I want to be accepting of myself, but I am relatively heavy and I feel like the rest of the world is not accepting of me. How do I work on self-compassion and acceptance in this hypercritical, appearance-driven world?

Of course, it is difficult to accept ourselves when the world doesn't seem to! This can be extremely difficult when it comes to body size, given that even most medical providers — the people we entrust with our physical and mental health — exhibit weight stigma (sometimes called anti-fat bias). Weight stigma is a term used to describe any bias against people because of their body size. We are all exposed to countless messages indicating that thinness is an important contributor to attractiveness, thus it is difficult for most of us to not have some weight stigma. Furthermore, there are misunderstandings held by many medical providers that include a focus on weight as a really important contributor to health. However, the latest research makes it clear that our weight is just one of many possible contributors to our health.

Given these popular beliefs, it makes sense that we would want to be thin! Why wouldn't we want to fit in, be liked, and be perceived as healthy and attractive?

Unfortunately, there are only a couple of options for managing this situation. You could try to change your body to be more acceptable to others, but this may only be possible by engaging in extreme physical activity or eating disordered behaviors. As I've stressed throughout this book, our body size is not totally under our control but is largely determined by our genes. Changing ourselves to please others may not be a good coping mechanism in general and is a strategy that is unlikely to succeed when it comes to our weight. Furthermore, it doesn't make much sense to go to unhealthy measures (such as skipping meals) to achieve health (or what some would perceive as healthy — a lower weight).

The only other option really is to accept ourselves while appreciating how difficult the world may make this for us. A supportive therapist may be helpful in the journey toward self-acceptance. And total self-acceptance isn't even necessarily the end goal. I'm not sure I know anyone who experiences complete self-acceptance, but a strong dose of self-compassion can get us closer to acceptance and farther from the desire to change ourselves to accommodate others.

Friends can be an important part of growing up and developing body positivity, for a variety of reasons. Feeling good about yourself – body and mind – can be easier when you feel like others feel good about you too. This isn't to say that you let other people determine your sense of yourself, just that we all find it helpful to feel supported by other people.
It's possible that you don't feel like you have a lot of close friends, and that's OK. It may be that you don't feel like you fit in well at your school, or that other kids don't share your interests. There are many successful adults who describe themselves as loners during their childhood. You may find enjoyment in developing a particular skill or hobby, and you may eventually meet more people who share your interests. Even if you don't feel like you have close friends now, this doesn't mean that you won't develop important friendships later, or that you shouldn't try to connect with people you enjoy spending time with.

Your family may be a valuable source of support, especially if you feel that your friendships are lacking in any way. However, it's totally normal for you to prefer the company of friends your own age to parents or other family members. It's also typical for teens to feel like their parents, in particular, don't understand what their life is like at school and with kids their age. To a certain extent, this is probably true. But in most cases, your family wants what is best for you, and they want you to grow up to be happy and healthy. Even if it doesn't feel like they "get you," they're usually happy to talk to you and offer whatever support they can. Sometimes, you just have to give them a chance.

Some people don't have close family relationships, and for a variety of reasons may not develop a lot of close friendships in their childhood and adolescence. However, there are a lot of other people who care about you and can be a friend to you. Maybe there is a teacher or a coach you admire and who seems invested in you. It's okay to turn to that person for advice. They probably chose that career because they enjoy hanging out with kids and want to be helpful to people just like you. There is good evidence that adult mentors (trusted adult advisors) can have very positive effects on young people's lives. I know that when my students ask me for advice, I always do my best to

be helpful, and I feel **flattered** that they want my advice. In other words, you're probably not going to burden a teacher, coach, or other adult in your life if you turn to them for advice or support. Remember, they were once kids too.

Q&A ?!?

Sharing the love

At some point during your teens, you're likely to want to form a romantic relationship with a boy or a girl. Maybe this relationship will turn serious, maybe it won't. Maybe there will be many of them while you're a teenager, maybe there won't be any until you're an adult. Why am I talking about this in a book about body image? Because all of our relationships impact us in different ways. Body image isn't just about how we look but how we feel about ourselves. Our relationships can play a role in all of this.

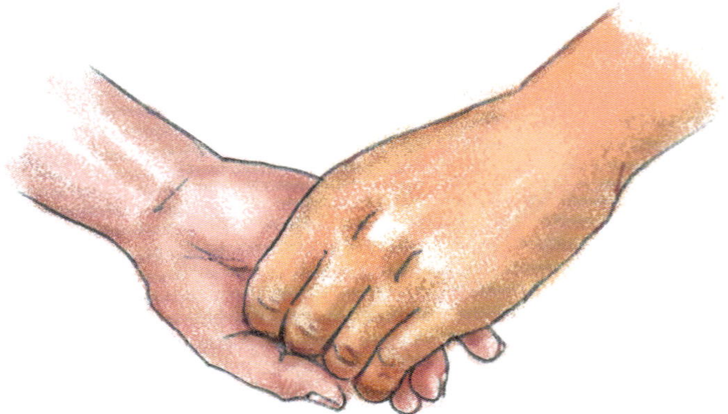

The start of a romantic relationship of any kind can affect how you think about yourself and may challenge who you are. You may feel like you should try to be someone different to be liked by someone you're interested in, or by your boyfriend/girlfriend. There is also scientific evidence to suggest that boys and men care more about how their girlfriends look than girls and women care about how their boyfriends look. If you feel like you're concerned about your appearance due to your interest in another person, this may be fairly normal. However – and this is important – you should never feel like you need to look or be someone different to attract someone else's interest. **A significant other *should* be a source of support and love and only add to your positive sense of yourself**. In fact, there is research to suggest that people who are in serious relationships typically feel better about their body image than people who are not.

Q&A

Intimacy and sex

Some relationships become physically **intimate**. Physical intimacy can take different forms and doesn't necessarily refer only to sexual intercourse or oral sex. Physical intimacy can open up a variety of body image questions and concerns. For example, some research suggests that feeling ashamed of one's body may make it hard to feel sexual excitement, and women who are dissatisfied with their bodies may have a more difficult time reaching **orgasm** or sexual excitement. This probably makes some sense – right? If you are distracted by worries about how you look and some (or all!) of your body is naked, it can be pretty hard to be "in the moment." It's not your fault if you feel uncomfortable with physical intimacy. There are many reasons why this may be. Nakedness can be awkward! Most real (nonphotoshopped) bodies have jiggly parts, **stretch marks**, bumps, and scars. These are not things to be embarrassed by, but the media messages we see lead many of us to believe that we should be embarrassed by any physical imperfections we have. Furthermore, if anyone has ever made you feel self-conscious about your body or weight, you may worry that a romantic partner doesn't find your body attractive, and this may be distracting. If you've spent a lot of time on social media, you may see a lot of images of beautiful, sexy people that lead you to question your own attractiveness. These are normal responses to social pressures to be and appear a certain way. It may help to keep in mind that your partner is also subjected to these social pressures and likely feels some self-consciousness as well.

Even though insecurity surrounding sexual intimacy is not your fault, it is something to remedy so that you can – should you choose to at some point – enjoy physical intimacy. A partner can make you feel safe and comfortable by taking the physical part of your relationship slowly. Communicating about your concerns is very important, as is communicating about safety and emotional issues relating to intimacy.

Respect and consent

Different families and religious and cultural groups have different understandings about when physical intimacy in relationships is appropriate. Because this is a health book, I will not address sex as a moral issue but as a physical and emotional health issue.

Sometimes partners do not communicate about where their physical relationship is heading, and one person ends up feeling (or being) hurt or taken advantage of.

When it comes to sexual encounters, it is incredibly important that you are sure that both you and

your partner want to have a sexual relationship.
I know that this may seem very basic, but **consent**
in sexual relationships is essential. When I say
"consent," I mean that you and your partner have
specifically talked about being sexually involved,
and you are sure that you are both comfortable with
this. **You have to have a discussion, and you and
your partner are allowed to change your minds.
Consensual physical encounters are the *minimum*
that you should expect from a partner.**

As you get older and your relationships change,
you have to determine what is comfortable and
important to you when it comes to physical intimacy.
You will likely need to talk to your partner about **safe
sex** and the protection you will use to avoid sexually
transmitted infections and un ntended pregnancies.
Do you want commitment from your partner? Is it
important to you to have sex only with partners that
you love?

As I discussed above, our relationships can influence
how we feel about ourselves. Having a romantic
partner may make you feel attractive, appreciated,
or even loved. But don't rely on others to feel those
things about yourself. And don't feel like you need
to engage in any type of sexual behavior to gain
anyone else's approval.

A final thought about self-care

Taking good care of yourself and nurturing your body
image will take some time and energy. It's OK to
think of this as a priority in your life; you shouldn't
feel guilty for spending this time on yourself. Girls
and women often find themselves in the position of
caring for others, including younger siblings, cousins,
and even their significant others. **In order to be
helpful to others, you need to take care of yourself
first. And you should expect that other people who
care about you will support your efforts at self-care
and the development of a positive body image.**

Sophie Jane, 17 years old, she/her, USA

It's a bit difficult for me to describe how I feel about my body because my feelings fluctuate. I think it's pretty common for girls my age, the ones I've talked to at least, to feel really self-conscious and to pick apart their appearance one day, and then to feel really amazing about themselves the next day. I think it's impossible to find a girl who feels great about her appearance 100% of the time. There are days where I look at myself in the mirror and only see the things that I don't like about my body. There used to be a lot more days where I felt like that, but I've reached a place emotionally where, even if I am having those intrusive negative thoughts about my body, I'm at least aware that those thoughts aren't accurate and I don't let them affect me as much.

One thing that's really affected my attitude toward my body is my interest in fashion. It's been both good and bad for me because, on the one hand, I do worry about how my body looks in the clothes that I'm wearing, but on the other hand, I now know how to dress in a way that makes me look good and feel confident. By developing a personal style that isn't based on what most girls (whose bodies typically look a lot different from mine) are wearing or what's trendy, I've learned to appreciate my body a lot more. There are certain things that I, a 5'9" girl, can pull off that shorter girls can't, and vice versa, and I've learned to accept that.

Going through puberty definitely impacted how I felt about my body. Puberty is an awkward time for everyone, including me. To sum up my puberty experience, I grew up before I grew out. So, when I turned 14, I was 5'9" and looked like an uncooked stick of linguini. I was thrilled when, about a year later, my hips got a bit wider, my legs looked more shapely, and my breasts were able to fill out my shirts.

My friends have influenced how I feel about my body significantly. I am really lucky to be friends with girls who don't judge or make fun of other girls' bodies. There were other groups of girls that I go to high school with who would feed each other's insecurities. If any of my friends express an insecurity about their body, the rest of us are quick to tell them that they're beautiful and that there is no reason for them to change a thing, whereas girls in other groups would encourage each other to try fad diets or to overexercise. I can't even imagine how messed up my perception of my body would be if I had friends like that.

My mom has also been influential when it comes to my body image. She doesn't make critical comments about my body, and she's tall too, so she understands the struggle of finding pants that are long enough. There are tons of people that I've never even met who influence me as well. Because of social media, I am exposed to pictures of girls with perfect hair, perfect make-up, and perfect bodies on a daily basis. It can be really hard not to compare yourself to them. I definitely do at times, and I know it's unhealthy.

If I were to give advice to other girls about body image it would be to talk about it with other girls as much as possible. By talking about it with girls that you love and trust, you can build an emotional support system and realize that you're not alone and that other girls feel the same way that you do about your body. It can be easy to assume that other girls who you think are prettier than you have no insecurities, but those same girls are probably looking at you and thinking the same thing.

I think that body image is a "grass is always greener" type of thing. For example, girls who are skinny are envious of curvier girls because they think curvier girls look sexier and look better in low-cut tops and tight skirts, but curvy girls are envious of skinnier girls because they think that skinnier girls look more like models and look better in short shorts and crop tops. Girls assume that if they had a "perfect" body, they would be happy all the time, and that's just not true. Though crash dieting and exercising way too much may seem like the best way to gain confidence, it definitely is not. Real confidence comes from a healthy body image, and that can be achieved no matter what you look like. It's not easy, but as long as you surround yourself with people who know that you're beautiful, you'll have a healthier body image.

SUMMING UP #BeMindful 

 Developing your positive body image means taking care of yourself – body and mind. Self-care can include everything from meditation to practicing self-compassion.

☑ If you feel that you need extra support as you try to care for yourself, be sure to talk to a counselor, therapist, doctor, or other adult who can offer that support or find helpful resources.

☑ Nurturing your relationships with other people is an important part of self-care. Your relationships should contribute to your positive body image and well-being.

🔍 FIND OUT MORE:

✦ For more information about therapists who can help people experiencing depression, anxiety, or a substance use disorder, look at the American Psychological Association's web page (https://locator.apa.org/) or the British Psychological Society's web page (www.bps.org.uk/find-psychologist).

✦ Dr. Kristin Neff is the originator of the concept of self-compassion and has written a number of books on the topic. I recommend starting with **Self-Compassion: The Proven Power of Being Kind to Yourself** (2015, published by William Morrow).

✦ **Anxiety Relief for Teens** by Regine Galanti (2020, published by Zeitgeist) offers a lot of information about coping skills that may be helpful even if you aren't super-anxious.

✦ For more scholarly articles and web pages with information about self-care, see the companion website for this book: www.TheBodyImageBook.com.

BE THE CHANGE

#ChangetheWorld

"Be the change
that you wish to see in
the world."

Mahatma Gandhi, Indian lawyer,
politician, social activist

Isabella Louise, 16 years old, she/her, UK

Right now, I feel really good about my body. I love it! I have had issues over the years but, mentally, I'm in a good place now.

I was very shy growing up, and I found it difficult to make friends. I was also taller than a lot of my peers, and this made me feel like I didn't fit in. I can still remember getting fitted for costumes for a dance performance, and another girl patted my stomach and said, "You won't fit into that."

This was a turning point for me and the beginning of many conversations about body image that I would have with my mom over the years. My mom was always willing to talk and support me. She let me know that she had also had body image concerns growing up and she wanted better for me.

I've always thought that my mom was the prettiest woman ever, and it was very strange to hear that she ever thought otherwise. Our conversations started to change how I viewed myself. One of the things she said to me is, "Different families are born with different bodies; some are born sparrows and some are eagles." My mom also told me that our ancestors gave us these bodies and we shouldn't be ashamed of them.

The summer before lockdown, when I was only 11, I had a really negative experience with a boy who was my friend and neighbor. He assaulted me and I felt like my body wasn't mine anymore. I couldn't look at myself without feeling sick. I hadn't even really come to appreciate that boys found me attractive or would want to touch me. As time has passed, I've mostly dealt with this experience. Talking with someone about it was the beginning of feeling better.

The lockdown during 2020 was hard on my mental health. I really shut myself away from everyone I knew and grew depressed. I think I needed to get out of the house and interact with people. I was so much inside my head when we were home that I started to think about harming myself and others. At some point, I became suicidal and finally told my mom. I ended up seeing a counselor and I was put on medication that I am still on. Things are so much better now.

There were a number of difficult things I dealt with before I was even a teenager. But fortunately, I've gotten help. I also think I got sick of hating myself. I just decided it was easier to love myself. When I get up in the morning, I make a conscious decision to choose to love myself.

If I could offer my younger self advice, I'd tell her that she is so beautiful. Even if she doesn't always feel beautiful and even if someone else makes her feel less than beautiful, she is — inside and out.

Loving yourself isn't easy, but it is really amazing when you do.

You and your body are inseparable; your body is the place where you "live." **Taking care of your body, accepting it, and protecting yourself are all important parts of developing a positive body image**. Our culture tends to emphasize the importance of women's appearances, making it easy for girls and women to doubt themselves and experience body dissatisfaction. Hopefully, after reading this far, you understand that you can work toward having a positive body image, even though it may not always feel easy.

Nurturing a positive body image is important because your body image affects many other aspects of your mental and physical health. It's also important because, by exhibiting a positive body image, you have the power to start to change how others think

about their bodies. If you think and talk differently about your body from how girls and women typically do (which, unfortunately, is usually quite negative), you can help promote positive change. Or, in the words of Gandhi, you can "be the change."

IN THIS CHAPTER YOU'LL LEARN:

- the importance of being kind and accepting of yourself and others, and not falling for other people's narrow ideas about what is beautiful or how you should look,
- how focusing on meaningful issues outside of yourself can contribute to your positive sense of yourself, and
- that you can play a part in helping others develop positive body images.

It's not always easy to do things differently from most other people. So, in this chapter, I want to leave you with some reminders of why this is so important, some potential obstacles on your personal journey, and some things to think about when you feel discouraged.

Remember: you are your own worst critic

We can be harder on ourselves than we ever are on anyone else. We feel bad about ourselves for not looking a certain way, and then we feel bad for caring that we don't look a certain way. Then we can feel even worse for spending time and energy on any of these worries.

If you feel like you're down on yourself, take a step back and try to quiet these negative thoughts. Remember the importance of **self-compassion** and **self-acceptance**. Both of these attitudes will do a lot more for you than self-hate ever will. No one is perfect by everyone's standards, so you can stop aiming for perfection. You can either be upset about this, or you can work toward treating yourself with kindness and acceptance.

Don't compare or despair

It's natural for us to compare ourselves to other people, but this tendency to compare ourselves to others, or **social comparison**, can be problematic. We're all unique in our own ways, and trying to be like someone else will rarely work. Changing our looks (or our personalities, for that matter) is harder than it appears. Most of our qualities have a strong biological component that makes them only partially changeable. We can get cosmetic surgery and change our nose, but it's nearly impossible to get longer legs, narrower hips, or a different sense of humor.

The science examining social comparison is pretty convincing, too. Most recently, researchers have examined how comparing ourselves to others on social media can be a negative experience but doesn't have to be. It turns out that not everyone who sees something positive on others' social media newsfeeds is then discouraged about their own lives. The key seems to be to focus on the emotional message in posts, not the content so much. People who see positive things ("Look at how happy she looks!") and think about the positive emotions shown ("It's great to see someone looking happy!") have a more positive experience using social media. They actual report an improvement in their own mood. The trick is to not take it that one step further and think, "She looks so happy, and I'm not that happy – what's wrong with me?" In other words, comparing is what leads to despairing, so don't go there.

EXPERT ADVICE

Jennifer B. Webb, PhD, Associate Professor and body image scientist, University of North Carolina at Charlotte

"Committing to actively choose freedom from the binds of diet culture is an ongoing daily practice. Doing so reveals the light inside you that can serve as a beacon of hope that encourages others to do the same. It is the realization that your freedom and their freedom depend upon one another. You're in this together."

Don't stigmatize

Another problem with our cultural focus on beauty is that it's usually all about one (or a few) particular look(s). It's rarely about diversity and inclusion — accepting everyone as they are. So few people can fit into the exact "looks" deemed beautiful by our culture because we all come in different shapes and sizes. Most of us aren't light-skinned, long-legged, and blond. We have different colored skin, hair, and eyes. We have different-sized noses, ears, and breasts. Defining beauty more broadly, including some of these variations, is an important way to appreciate one another and work toward accepting ourselves.

Unfortunately, there is often far more cultural focus on **stigmatizing** people who don't fit society's views of beauty than in accepting people who look different. Stigma is probably a word you've heard before, but maybe you aren't sure exactly what it means. People can be stigmatized or experience stigma for a variety of qualities they may possess: their race, gender, disability status, or weight are some of the most common qualities that may lead to stigma. If someone is stigmatized, they are mistreated due to these qualities and are often assumed to have negative characteristics associated with these qualities. **Weight stigma** (also referred to as **weight bias**, **weight-based discrimination**, and **anti-fat bias**) occurs when a person is mistreated because she is relatively heavy. (Although it's possible to experience stigma for being relatively slender, this is much less common). The person may be assumed to be lazy or addicted to junk food, for example, just because she has a larger body.

Weight stigma is incredibly problematic, not just because it's unfair to mistreat anyone based on how they look, but because it's associated with other problems. When a person experiences stigma, they often start to believe others' negative views of them. Experiencing weight stigma has also been associated with the development of body dissatisfaction, eating disorders, and depression. Unfortunately, the rates of weight stigma have risen dramatically in recent years. In fact, some scientists who study weight stigma describe it as the last acceptable form of discrimination. What they mean by this is that people often feel that it's acceptable to mistreat heavy people because it's their fault that they're heavy. Hopefully, after reading this book, you understand that weight is a much more complicated issue, and our size has a lot to do with our biology. **Furthermore, blaming or mistreating people for anything is rarely a helpful way to interact with them. Just as self-compassion is incredibly important, compassion for others is essential, too.**

Don't let body positivity become toxic

You may recall that I introduced the idea of body neutrality back in Chapter 3. Body neutrality, or focusing on self-acceptance and contentedness, may be a really valuable approach for many people, especially when body positivity just doesn't feel realistic (yet?!). Furthermore, although there is evidence that body-positive messages tend to have a positive impact on most of our feelings about our bodies, the positive body image movement has its critics.

One critique has to do with body positivity being interpreted to mean that you love how you look always. That isn't the broad definition I've offered in this book, but if you believe this then you may think you are supposed to love yourself all the time. This focus can actually lead to more body anxiety if you don't feel self-love, which is the opposite of what the body-positivity movement claims to want for people! The antidote to appearance concerns is not "fixing" your appearance but working on your mindset about these issues.

The focus of the original body-positive movement was on size diversity and gaining equal treatment and rights for people living in larger bodies. Some critics believe that the current body-positivity movement has moved too far away from these original goals and focuses too much on self-acceptance among relatively thin people. I believe that **body positivity is for everyone**. I think that *most* people struggle with body image concerns – and the research backs me up here – but I also think it is essential that we appreciate that some of us are more likely than others to experience anti-fat bias. We need to work toward equal treatment for all, while being mindful of those who need the most support.

We do not need to *always* feel good about *everything* about ourselves, nor do we need to put so much pressure on ourselves to be "positive" that we then feel guilty or ashamed when we can't stay positive. The last thing we want is for all of this positivity to feel toxic. Being comfortable in our skin and no longer feeling held back by body image concerns is where we ultimately want to end up.

Q&A

I don't want to care about material things like clothes and make-up, but I do. How do I change the way I think about these things?

It's important to realize that many — perhaps most — people care about material items. How we present ourselves to the world, with the clothes we wear and the other ways that we try to look nice, matters to most people. Don't feel bad for wanting to look nice or for caring about material things.

What's important to realize is that these material things are unlikely to bring you lasting happiness. A new pair of designer jeans may make you feel good for a few weeks or months, but they're unlikely to make you feel all that special years later. A stylish haircut may grant you some attention for days or weeks, but then you'll get used to it and your hair will grow out.

We're all bombarded with so many advertisements for material goods and beauty products that it's easy to feel like there is something wrong with us and we need to "fix" ourselves by dressing a certain way or using certain cosmetics. It can seem like success in life is all about having certain things. But all of these things change us only temporarily and in superficial ways. It's important, but sometimes very difficult, to keep this in perspective and realize that who we are — what makes us a caring person, a valued friend, and a decent human being — has very little to do with material things.

Don't add to the appearance conversation

When we keep our comments focused on our appearance, we leave out conversations about more important things in our lives. Challenge yourself to ask people about their hobbies, interests, and what they are doing, without focusing so much on how people are looking. This may feel strange at first because even a stranger is likely to respond positively when you tell her that you like her shirt. But you may be surprised at how positively strangers, friends, and acquaintances may respond to a conversation about the weather, a movie you've seen recently, or even a new recipe you tried the other night. This isn't to say that you can't ever comment on others' appearance, but instead you could try to shift the majority of your conversations to other topics.

Remember, be careful not to assume that weight loss is always good! Be very careful about commenting on changes in people's body size. Often, weight gain or loss is a sign of a health problem or a disordered relationship with food. Also, when we compliment weight loss, we reinforce the cultural value system that links weight, health, and attractiveness. We can push back against all the cultural messages surrounding diet products and plans by taking care not to celebrate our own or others' weight loss. After all, our body size is not the most important thing about us!

Try to think outside yourself

It may seem like your appearance is a "project" that requires a lot of time and energy. But it doesn't have to. What if you invested more of that energy into other hobbies, interests, and even volunteer work? In research that aims to understand why some people have more positive body images than others, scientists have found that focusing outside yourself

Q&A

Part of what leads girls to develop body image concerns is feeling that how they look is incredibly important. Our culture gives girls this idea through advertising, music, movies, and social media. What if we all tried to talk to other girls less about their appearance and focused more on other things?

It seems to come naturally to us to compliment our friends and other girls on their appearance, whether it's their hair, clothes, or make-up. In some ways, this is how girls and women connect with each other — and who doesn't like compliments? But we could all get a bit better about starting conversations about other topics. We could talk about books we're reading, things we've done recently, hobbies, and our goals and aspirations. If we value other girls for their brains over their bodies more often, their focus will be different as well.

can be good for how you feel about yourself. In this research, people who engaged with projects or causes that they thought were important, including focusing on schoolwork or volunteering at an animal shelter, spent less energy concerned about themselves. It seems that thinking about issues bigger than oneself may be important for keeping some perspective.

It makes sense, right? There are only so many hours in the day, and if you fill those hours with work or causes that are meaningful to you, there will be less time to worry about whether or not you're wearing the most stylish brand of jeans. And you may feel less inclined to care!

To improve your body image, you should change your body, even if this requires surgery or medication.

It is easy to think that changing yourself physically will change your body image; this is what endless advertisements, weight-loss campaigns, social media posts, and before-and-after images of celebrities seem to suggest. But believe it or not, there is not a lot of evidence to suggest that this is the way most people experience their bodies.

Changing your hair, or losing or gaining a few pounds may be a body image boost, but it's usually just temporary. We all tend to engage in some beautifying activities, whether it be how we dress or styling our hair a certain way. Reread the discussion of adaptive (and maladaptive) appearance investment in Chapter 3 when you feel uncertain about your motivation for and expectations surrounding trying to change your body.

As I've tried to explain throughout this book, body image is much more psychological – how you perceive yourself and how comfortable you are with yourself – than it is based on anything objective about your appearance. Diet culture and advertisements for weight loss drugs like **Wegovy** may try to convince you that all you need to do is change your body to be a happier person, but life is much more complicated than this! Beware of any "quick-fix" solutions you hear about, because when something seems too good to be true, it usually is!

Reasons for hope

Some days, it's hard not to feel like we live in a superficial world. The statistics about people who suffer from body dissatisfaction and disordered eating are discouraging. Many of the issues I discuss in this book are serious and worrisome, but I also deeply believe that there are reasons for hope.
I am incredibly grateful that my work has put me in touch with outstanding individuals and organizations

who are working to improve people's relationships with food and their bodies. I want to tell you about some of my favorite organizations here because you may find them inspiring and even want to get involved with some of their efforts.

Be Real (www.berealusa.org) is a nonprofit organization in the USA focused on body image improvement among adolescents. Founded by Denise Hamburger, Be Real partners with psychologists, educators, dietitians, and other community members to bring evidence-based education about body image issues to school settings. Be Real has created curriculum content for students and information on how to create body-confident environments for the adults in their lives. It also has a curriculum for kids about how to develop a healthy relationship with food. I love its interactive approach to helping kids reconsider what they see in the media and appreciate how amazing their bodies are.

F.E.A.S.T. (www.feast-ed.org) stands for Families Empowered and Supporting Treatment for Eating Disorders and is an organization dedicated to helping families and caregivers who have a loved one affected by an eating disorder. Its web page includes evidence-based guides, which offer information about diagnosis, nutrition, treatment choices, and many other topics. Videos, educational and support resources, and information about webinars are also included on its web page, which is a great place to spend time if you are interested in learning more about supporting someone with an eating disorder.

Project HEAL (www.theprojectheal.org) is an organization that helps people in the USA who are struggling with disordered eating. Because a minority of people with an eating disorder receive treatment, millions are left without the resources for recovery each year. Project HEAL is especially focused on helping those who tend to be systemically left out

of treatment due to age, race, gender identity, sexual identity, size, ability, or financial means to find support. Project HEAL offers clinical assessment, treatment placement, financial assistance, and community for those who are struggling. Its web page offers information, resources, and links to additional sources of support.

The Body Positive (https://thebodypositive.org) was created by Connie Sobczak and Elizabeth Scott, LCSW, CEDS-S, over 25 years ago to train educators, student leaders, and mental health providers to use their Be Body Positive curriculum in the USA and other countries worldwide. The Body Positive was ahead of its time in trying to spread these messages of hope and self-acceptance to people of all ages but especially kids and teens in school settings. It offers training programs, as well as a lot of free resources on its web page, and has a proven track record of offering techniques to not just help individuals but also contribute to cultural change and social justice efforts.

FEDUP Collective (https://fedupcollective.org) is an organization focused on providing services to, and advocating for, trans+, intersex, and gender-diverse people with eating disorders. This population has been found to be at high risk of developing eating disorders, yet often does not receive support and treatment that adequately addresses the intersection between gender identity and eating disorders. FEDUP's web page includes a wealth of information about eating disorders, as well as providers including therapists and registered dietitians that it has vetted. They even have information about support groups that take place both online and in person.

ANAD (https://anad.org), which stands for Anorexia Nervosa and Associated Disorders, is an organization in the USA that provides free support to people struggling with an eating disorder. It offers recovery mentors, support groups (for example, for teens, adults, and parents), and a helpline. ANAD's webpage contains a ton of information, including guides for how to seek treatment and support for eating disorders and a directory of eating disorder providers. They also offer a lot of volunteer opportunities for people interested in helping others who are struggling with an eating disorder.

STRIPED (www.hsph.harvard.edu/striped), which stands for Strategic Training Initiative for the Prevention of Eating Disorders, was founded at the Harvard T.H. Chan School of Public Health and Boston's Children's Hospital in 2009. STRIPED provides training to professionals interested in eating disorders prevention, but I came to learn about its advocacy work first. For example, STRIPED director Bryn Austin has been a part of its team working toward legislation that would protect youth from nonprescription diet pills and supplements that are currently poorly regulated and potentially unsafe for developing bodies (and minds!). Its web page contains resources and information addressing beauty ideals, body image, eating disorders, colorism, weight stigma, supplement use, and the importance of advocacy about all of these issues.

The **Centre for Appearance Research** (CAR; www.uwe.ac.uk/car) at the University of the West of England, Bristol, UK, is the world's largest research group focused on appearance and body-image issues. However, CAR is not just a research center but also a hub of activity and innovation concerning body image. CAR's members produce The Appearance Matters podcast, and its web page includes videos and other resources. They've even developed a board game for children to teach them about a variety of appearance-related issues.

With All (https://withall.org/) is an organization that aims to empower adults with the tools they need to help children and young people foster a positive body image and relationship with food. They also provide grants for those with financial need who also need intensive treatment to recover from an eating disorder. With All hopes to change cultural perspectives on health related to body and food, and provides valuable resources on their web page.

You'll notice that most of these organizations were developed relatively recently, and I seem to hear about other, similar organizations and opportunities for support and treatment all the time.

There are also body-positive influencers on social media. There are podcasts about body positivity and rejecting diet culture, and there are web pages that contain helpful resources for people looking to improve their body image. Not everyone knows about all of these resources, but hopefully more and more people will benefit from this body-positive content.

I really do feel that there are reasons for hope.

EXPERT ADVICE

Dr. Meghan Gillen, Professor of Psychology and body image expert, The Pennsylvania State University

"We need a cultural shift away from scrutinizing, fixing, and 'working on' our bodies. Instead, think about what you love, value, respect, and appreciate about your body. Human bodies are amazing. They allow us to dance, walk, hang out with friends, play sports, make jewelry, draw, and write messages to our friends. Our bodies give us the opportunity to pursue our hobbies and pleasures."

Journal: how will you change the world?

At the beginning of this book, I asked you to reflect on your own body image goals. I hope reading this book has offered you the opportunity to think about your attitudes, habits, and goals when it comes to your body and your health in general. Now it is time to set some new goals, but these goals should be less about you and more about other people in your life. How can you help other people to improve their body image? Can you change how you communicate with others (for example, by not talking about body size)? Can you provide resources to someone who is struggling? Can you unfollow social media accounts that are not body positive and support those that are? How will you change the world even in just one, very small way?

Be the change

Cultural change can be slow. The things that people in any society value and expect from each other – to look or act a certain way – don't change overnight. But cultural change is possible. In fact, people have not always valued thinness or the fashions that we value today. If you look at pictures depicting people from 100 years ago – or even 20 years ago! – people looked different. There were different hairstyles and clothing, and people presented themselves to the world differently.

There will always be trends in terms of what our culture suggests we do to make our bodies look attractive. Some of the trends may be relatively harmless (for example, certain hairstyles), but some may be relatively risky (for example, some forms of cosmetic surgery). We don't have to agree with these trends or follow them. When something seems unhealthy or even just uncomfortable, we can go our own way. If we reject certain trends, others may feel empowered to as well. If consumers don't buy certain products, companies will stop producing them. If we stop following certain influencers on social media, they may become less popular and less powerful.

As individuals, we can contribute to cultural change. We can work to improve our own positive body images and we can become part of a movement where other people do as well. We can do our part to create a world where it is normal for girls and women to appreciate their bodies and not be dissatisfied with them.

**What exactly would that world look like?
Why don't we try to find out?**

Sky Iris, 19 years old, she/her, UK

When I was an early teenager, I was much more aware of how my body looked and had more concerns about it. I went to a school that required us to wear uniforms, and I think that made me notice that the uniforms fit us all differently. I knew some of us looked better than others in the uniform. But then I think I outgrew these worries, and I don't spend a lot of time thinking about my body these days. I actually think that people – society in general – wants me to care about how my body looks more than I do!

When I was younger, I also felt like I should dress to impress boys. But I came to realize that getting attention for showing off your body is not necessarily the kind of attention you want to get. I didn't gain anything by dressing for other people. Then the pandemic and lockdown started, and I spent about 2 years of my mid- to later teens mostly at home. I didn't wear make-up, and I didn't spend much time on my appearance. It saved so much time! And I survived without male attention.

Now, at college, I like to go out and meet people, but I am not necessarily looking for a relationship. If someone comes into my life and adds something meaningful to it, then I could see being in a relationship with that person. But otherwise, I am not sure that it's really important to my happiness. I have good friends and I'm busy with school.

I think one of the most significant influences on my body image has been my sister. We are close in age but look very different. She's relatively tall, lean, and blond, and I am relatively short, curvy and have brown hair. We hardly even look related. She gets a lot of attention for her model-like appearance, but I know that part of why she looks the way she does is due to an anxiety disorder that affects her ability to enjoy food. I know that I am physically fit, I eat nutritious and varied meals, and I am able to really enjoy food. Still, people make all sorts of assumptions about our behaviors based on how we look. Knowing how absurd others' comparisons of us is has allowed me to ignore most of what people say and to do what is best for myself.

Story continues …

I like to think about a road as an analogy to our bodies. Roads get you from here to there, even though they are discolored, full of potholes and bumps, and far from perfect. But how would we get anywhere without them? Our bodies are the same in that they aren't perfect, but they provide us with so many opportunities. They allow us to keep driving along through life.

If I could offer younger girls some advice, I'd tell them to remember to focus on their own path and not worry about others' paths. I'd tell them to not torture themselves worrying so much about how they look but to focus on taking care of themselves. I also know that when you feel good about yourself, you are better able to bring support and authenticity to your relationships with others. It can be hard to appreciate yourself for all of the qualities you have to offer the world, but the more you attend to those other qualities, the easier it gets.

SUMMING UP #ChangetheWorld 

- There are many reasons why it's important to develop a positive body image, one of which is that by exhibiting a positive body image you have the power to start to change how other girls think about their bodies.
- Current beauty ideals and the cultural focus on our appearance can make it difficult to feel good about your body, but it's important that you resist these ideals and don't stigmatize other people who don't conform to them.
- Thinking about issues that are more important than how you look and being engaged with issues that are meaningful to you can help you develop as a well-rounded, confident person. By choosing to foster your positive body image, you set an example for those around you and help to lead our society closer to understanding how important it is for all of us to be accepting and positive about who we are.

FIND OUT MORE:

✦ If you love this book, there are other books that are somewhat similar. Check out *Every Body* by Molly Forbes (2024, published by Puffin/Penguin Random House).

✦ *Live Nourished: Make Peace with Food, Banish Body Shame, and Reclaim Joy* by Shana Minei Spence (2024, published by Simon and Schuster) discusses a healthy way to think about food but also describes the importance of body image and the social forces that make it difficult to have a positive body image.

✦ If you want more in-depth information about the topics in this chapter and in this book, read my book *Adultish: The Body Image Book for Life*, which was written with teens and young adults in mind (2024, published by Cambridge University Press).

✦ For more scholarly articles and web pages with information about body image and the importance of nurturing a positive body image and promoting cultural change, see the companion website for this book: www.TheBodyImageBook.com.

Here's a bit more information about the experts who provided insight, advice, and comments for this book.

Jo-Ann Finkelstein, PhD, clinical psychologist, author of *Sexism & Sensibility: Raising Empowered, Resilient Girls in the Modern World* (2024, published by Harmony Books): www.joannfinkelstein.com

Rachael Flatt, PhD, Olympic figure skater, clinical psychologist: https://en.wikipedia.org/wiki/Rachael_Flatt

Meghan Gillen, PhD, Professor of Psychology and body image expert, The Pennsylvania State University, co-editor of *Body Positive* (2020, published by Cambridge University Press): www.abington.psu.edu/meghan-gillen-ph-d

Robyn Goldberg, RDN, CEDS-C, nutrition therapist, author of *The Eating Disorder Trap* (2020, published by the author): https://askaboutfood.com

Oona Hanson, MA, MA, eating disorder educator and advocate, founder of Parenting without Diet Culture: www.oonahanson.com

Christy Harrison, MPH, RD, registered dietitian, journalist, author of *Anti-Diet* (2019, published by Yellow Kite) and *The Wellness Trap* (2023, published by Little, Brown Spark): https://christyharrison.com

Mary Himmelstein, PhD, Associate Professor of Psychology, body image expert, Kent State University: www.kent.edu/psychology/mary-himmelstein

Aubrey Hoffer, PhD, body image expert, Postdoctoral Fellow in the EAT Lab at the University of Louisville: www.louisvilleeatlab.com/people.html

Lindsay Kite, PhD and **Lexie Kite, PhD**, body image advocates, authors of *More Than a Body* (2020, published by Houghton Mifflin Harcourt): www.morethanabody.org/about-us

Cheri A. Levinson, PhD, Associate Professor at the University of Louisville, founder and Clinical Director, Louisville Center for Eating Disorders: https://louisville.edu/psychology/levinson

Lisa L. Lewis, MS, journalist, speaker, author of *The Sleep-Deprived Teen* (2022, published by Mango Publishing): www.lisallewis.com

Yaffi Lvova, RDN, registered dietitian nutritionist, founder of *Baby Bloom Nutrition*: https://babybloomnutrition.com

Anna Lutz, MPH, RD, CEDS-S, founder of *Sunny Side Up Nutrition*: https://sunnysideupnutrition.com

Traci Mann, PhD, Professor of Psychology at the University of Minnesota and author of *Secrets from the Eating Lab* (2015, published by Harper): https //mannlab.psych.umn.edu/secrets-eat ng-lab/book

Dena Moes, RN, CNM, author of *It's Your Body* (2024, published by Countryman Press): www.santafeobgyn.com/welcome/meet-dena-moes-cnm

Brian Pollack, CLSW, founder and director of Hilltop Behavioral Health in Summit, New Jersey: https://hilltopbehavioralhealth.com/

Diane Rosenbaum, PhD, Professor, body image researcher, clinical psychologist: www.abington.psu.edu/person/diane-rosenbaum

Gemma Sharp, PhD, Professor of Neuroscience, Monash University, Australia: https://psychology.uq.edu.au/profile/15048/gemma-sharp

Amelia Sherry, MPH, RD, clinical nutritionist, author of *Diet-Proof Your Daughter* (2023, published by AS Nutrition Publishing): www.ameliasherry.com

Jaclyn Siegel, PhD, body image researcher: www.jaclynasiegel.com

Zachary Souillard, PhD, Assistant Professor of Psychology at Miami University and Director of the Body Image and Stigma among Queer Populations (BISQue) Lab: https://miamioh.edu/profiles/cas/zachary-soulliard.html

Alli Spotts-De Lazzer, MA, MFT, LPCC, CEDS, therapist specializing in eating disorders and author of *MeaningFull: 23 Life-Changing Stories of Conquering Dieting, Weight, and Body Image Issues* (2021, published by Unsolicited Press): https://therapyhelps.us

Tracy Tylka, PhD, body image expert, Professor at Ohio State University, editor of the journal *Body Image*: https://psychology.osu.edu/people/tylka.2

Jennifer B. Webb, PhD, Associate Professor and body image scientist, University of North Carolina at Charlotte: https://healthpsych.charlotte.edu/people/jennifer-b-webb-phd/

Jenna Werner, RD, owner of *Happy Strong Healthy*, podcast host of *What the Actual Fork?*: www.happystronghealthyrd.com

Jason Wood, speaker and author of *Starving for Survival* (2022, published by Orthorexia Bites), Director of Community Engagement at ANAD (Association for Anorexia Nervosa and Associated Disorders): https://anad.org/about/board-and-staff

GLOSSARY

Acceptance (see also self-acceptance): Approving of something without wanting to change anything about it.

Acne (pimples, spots, breaking out): A skin condition where pores become clogged with oil, bacteria, or dead skin cells; results in an inflamed eruption of the skin.

Activists (activism): People who participate, get involved in, campaign for, or bring awareness to a certain situation and act on it to make a change.

Adaptive appearance investment: Regularly engaging in appearance-related self-care, such as grooming behaviors that protect an individual's sense of style and personality; usually includes enhancing one's natural features via nonharmful methods.

ADHD (attention-deficit/hyperactivity disorder): A condition characterized by persistent patterns of inattention, hyperactivity, and impulsivity that interfere with daily functioning and development.

Adolescence: The stage of physical and mental development that occurs between childhood and adulthood; this stage is often marked by the onset of puberty.

Advertising (advertisement): A form of communication that markets or promotes a message in order to sell something.

ANAD (Anorexia Nervosa and Associated Disorders): An organization in the USA that offers eating-disorder information, resources, and support.

Anorexia nervosa: A kind of eating disorder characterized by a fear of gaining weight or by significant weight loss; those with anorexia try to become or remain underweight by depriving themselves of food or by exercising excessively.

Anti-anxiety medication: Medication to treat anxiety disorders; medication that alters the chemicals in a person's brain and can make a person feel calmer and happier.

Antidepressant medication: Medication to treat depression; medication that alters the chemicals in a person's brain to alleviate symptoms of depression.

Anti-fat bias: The negative attitudes, stereotypes, and discrimination directed at individuals based on their body weight or size, often rooted in societal beliefs that equate fatness with undesirable traits.

Anxiety disorder: Constant feelings of worry, anxiety, or fear that interfere with a person's daily life.

Appearance culture: The societal focus on physical appearance, where beauty standards and the way individuals look are often prioritized and valued.

Atkins diet: A low-carb diet; foods like pasta, bread, soft drinks, and sweets cannot be eaten according to this diet.

Autism (autism spectrum disorder): A condition characterized by differences in social communication, behavior, and sensory processing, often accompanied by repetitive patterns of activities or interests.

Avoidance goals: Goals focused on preventing negative outcomes or avoiding undesirable situations, rather than pursuing positive achievements, often linked to stress or fear of failure. These goals can sometimes lead to reduced motivation and feelings of inadequacy.

Benign: Mild, not harmful.

Benzoyl peroxide: A medicine used to treat acne and other skin conditions.

Be Real: A nonprofit organization in the USA that provides educational curriculum content to support positive body image and adaptive eating behaviors.

Binge(ing): A brief period of time in which a person will indulge excessively in a substance, usually consuming a lot of food or alcohol quickly.

Binge eating disorder: An eating disorder that involves binging (at least once a week for at least 3 months) without purging. Binges are described as excessive in terms of how much is eaten and are experienced as uncontrollable.

Blood cholesterol (see cholesterol): When the body has too much cholesterol and it gets stuck in the blood vessels, it can contribute to heart disease.

Body dysmorphic disorder (BDD): A body image disorder. People with BDD focus on their body's flaws and are preoccupied with trying to fix flaws that are usually not noticeably to other people.

Body image: How you think or feel about your body; how you view your physical self on a day-to-day basis.

Body mass index (BMI): A person's weight in kilograms divided by the square of his or her height in meters.

Body neutrality: Similar to body positivity, with more emphasis on accepting and respecting the body for its function and capabilities rather than focusing on its appearance.

Body odor: The different scents the human body gives off; can become unpleasant (or stinky) when sweat mixes with bacteria that are found naturally on the skin.

Body positivity: accepting and appreciating all body types, no matter their size, shape, color, or ability; challenging unrealistic beauty standards with an inclusive view toward all bodies.

Body shaming: Putting another person down because of how their body looks.

Body surveillance: The habitual monitoring and scrutiny of one's own physical appearance.

Botox (botulinum toxin): A drug made from the toxin of Clostridium botulinum bacteria. This toxin is what causes botulism, but it can also have many medical and cosmetic uses such as improving the appearance of wrinkles.

Breast budding: The initial stage of breast development during puberty, marked by the formation of small, firm lumps (breast buds) beneath the nipple area.

Breathing exercises: Exercises that include breath control and deep breathing as a way to calm oneself or practice mindfulness.

Bulimia nervosa: An eating disorder that involves binging and then purging food.

Calorie(s): A unit of measurement to assess the amount of energy in a certain food; a unit of measurement used to describe the energy potential of a substance.

Cami: Short for camisole; a sleeveless undershirt; a spaghetti-strapped tank top that's often wore under shirts and sometimes has a built-in bra.

Cancer: A disease that's caused by an uncontrolled growth of abnormal cells in a part of the body.

Carb loading: Often done by athletes when they have a big race or game – they eat meals with a lot of carbohydrates in them, like bread and pasta, to give the body energy quickly.

Carbohydrates (carbs): An organic compound that's an easy source of energy; carbs can help improve athletic performance.

Cardiac: Relating to the heart, referring to its structure, function, or conditions affecting it.

Cellulite: The appearance of lumps and dimples on the surface of the skin, usually present on the thighs, bottom, hips, and stomach; it can have an "orange peel" or "cottage cheese"-like texture.

Centered: To feel balanced or in tune with one's body.

Centre for Appearance Research (CAR): A center at the University of the West of England, Bristol, UK, is the world's largest research group focused on appearance and body image issues.

Centers for Disease Control and Prevention (CDC): A national public health agency and institution in the USA.

Chocoholic: How a person who feels as though they're "addicted" to chocolate may describe themselves.

Cholesterol: A fatty substance that's carried around the body in the blood. There is "good" (high-density) and "bad" (low-density) cholesterol.

Cisgender: Refers to a person whose gender identity matches the sex they were assigned at birth.

Clean foods: An unofficial term that typically refers to minimally processed whole foods that are free from artificial additives, preservatives, and refined ingredients.

Clitoris: A small, fleshy, erectile organ of the female reproductive system, found at the front end of the human vulva; the primary source of female sexual pleasure.

Cognitive: The mental activities involved in acquiring knowledge and understanding.

Commitment strategy: A strategy developed to help one stick with a goal; for example, telling people about your goals and asking for help in achieving them.

Compassion(ate) (see also self-compassion): To show caring, understanding, and kindness to a person and/or the issues a person is dealing with.

Compulsive exercise: When exercising feels like an obligation, not something enjoyed; exercise that a person feels is necessary, maybe more than once per day.

Consent: The voluntary, informed, and explicit agreement to participate in an activity or allow something to happen. Often used in describing sexual activities as being engaged in willingly.

Constipation: Irregular or infrequent movement and emptying of the bowels; less than regular passage of stool/feces.

Cosmetics: Relating to a person's appearance or products for a person's appearance (for example, make-up).

Cosmetic surgery: A type of surgery performed to change and enhance a person's physical appearance.

Culprit: The cause of something negative.

Cynical: A mindset characterized by distrust of others' motives.

Dense (density): Compacted closely, usually in terms of substance; something that's thick.

Depression (depressed, depressing): a feeling a person gets where they simply cannot become happy; they remain in a sad 'funk' or mood. Depression is also a mental health disorder when it's a lasting negative mood and/or outlook on life.

Dermatologist: A doctor who specializes in skin care.

Despair: To feel hopeless, distressed.

Diabetes: A condition where a person's body doesn't make any or makes too little of a certain sugar (insulin) (type 1 diabetes), or the person's body can't process a certain kind of sugar (type 2 diabetes).

Diet: How or what a person eats; a specific plan of foods to be eaten either to lose weight or for medical reasons.

Dietician (see also nutritionist): An expert who studies food and nutrition. Dieticians teach people what to eat in order to have a healthy lifestyle and/or manage health problems related to illness and disease. Formal schooling, training, and certification is required to be considered a dietician.

Disordered eating: A range of irregular eating behaviors that may include maladaptive dieting, overeating, or food restriction; these behaviors may not meet the clinical criteria for an eating disorder but tend to stem from and cause distress.

Eating disorders: a category of conditions/illnesses that involve troublesome eating habits that can lead to serious problems and even death.

Embodiment: The sense of "being in touch with" or "happily living in" your body.

Empower (empowering): To encourage, support, or make a person feel more confident in themselves and their abilities.

Energy: The strength and activity you're able to experience; derived from the number of calories consumed.

Enhance (enhancements): to increase or upgrade something; improvements.

Evaluate: To judge or analyze something.

Evidence-based information: Information that comes from research that uses a scientific method; information based on scientific evidence.

Exercise: A particular type of physical activity that's usually planned and purposeful.

Fad: Something (like a diet, fashion, or make-up trend) that becomes widely popular, but the hype goes away quickly; short-lived popularity.

Fallopian tubes: A pair of tubes that extend from the ovaries to the uterus to carry eggs (only found in females).

Fashionable: Popular or stylish.

Fast (fasting): Not eating or drinking all or some kinds of foods and drinks, sometimes for a religious observance or for weight loss.

Fat(s): A type of nutrient that the body uses for "fuel" and to store energy.

Fat talk: Negative discussion about the body that typically occurs with peers (for example, "I'm so fat!").

F.E.A.S.T. (Families Empowered and Supporting Treatment for Eating Disorders): An organization dedicated to helping families and caregivers who have a loved one affected by an eating disorder.

FEDUP Collective: An organization focused on providing services to and advocating for trans+, intersex, and gender-diverse people with eating disorders.

Fiber: Food that isn't digested or absorbed by the body.

Filter: A technique that changes the look of an image, usually to refine and improve certain aspects of the image.

Fitness: Relating to exercise and being physically activity; the condition of how healthy or strong someone is.

Fitspiration (fitspo): Words, images, and videos that are intended to serve as motivation or inspiration to improve their health and fitness.

Flatter(ing): Something (for example, a piece of clothing or a new hairstyle) that makes you appear more attractive; to compliment.

Food addiction: A food habit that a person may rely on but that doesn't involve a chemical dependency (alcohol and drug addictions typically involve a chemical dependency). Food addiction isn't considered an eating disorder by psychologists.

Food restriction: To cut out a significant portion of food (or food groups), usually for weight loss or for a health concern (such as diabetes).

Functionality: The ability to perform and serve a specific purpose (for example, legs serve the purpose or function of walking, running, etc.).

Gender dysphoria: The distress or discomfort a person experiences when their gender identity does not align with their sex assigned at birth

Gender identity: A person's internal sense of their own gender, which may or may not align with the sex they were assigned at birth.

Genes (genetics): Biological components that determine the traits and functions of living organisms, passed from parents to offspring; genetics is the science of genes.

Genetically modified organisms (GMOs): Organisms that have been genetically modified using different (biological) engineering techniques.

Genitals: Male and female reproductive body parts (for men, the penis; for women, the vagina).

Groom(ing): To clean up or make neat.

Gynecologist: A doctor who takes care of girls' and women's reproductive health.

Hangry: When hunger and anger are experienced at the same time, usually because hunger leads a person to be in a bad mood.

Harassment (see also sexual harassment): Any type of behavior that can be seen as offensive, inappropriate, and hurtful to another person.

Health at Every Size movement (HAES): An anti-diet, body positivity, diversity acceptance movement.

Healthy: Physical, mental and emotional wellness; free from illness or disease.

Heart disease: A heart condition where a passageway into the heart can be blocked, or something is wrong with the heart's muscles.

High fructose corn syrup: A sweetener frequently used in commercially produced foods and drinks that is made from cornstarch as a cheaper alternative to sucrose (other sugar products).

Highlight reel: A slang term used to describe a quick summary of the most relevant high points of someone's life.

Hormones: Chemicals the body produces that alter and control bodily functions. For example, there are hormones that alter feelings of hunger, sleepiness, and even happiness.

Hormone replacement therapy (HRT): A medical treatment that involves supplementing or replacing hormones; may be done to alleviate symptoms caused by hormonal imbalances or deficiencies; may be used during gender transition.

Hygiene: Cleanliness; practicing cleanliness for health and proper body care.

Influencers (social media influencers): Popular and influential social media users; people who are used to promote certain items to persuade others to buy products.

Insecure (insecurities): To feel unconfident, doubtful or unsure of oneself.

Instincts: Natural tendencies, something a person may do without realizing it.

Intermittent fasting: To limit the food eaten overall by reducing what's eaten during certain periods of time in a day or week. For example, a person may eat regularly for 5 days a week and then eat relatively little for a couple of days a week, or a person may eat within a select window of time each day.

Internalize (internalizing): To take information that's outside of you and make it your own; to believe a thought, attitude, or behavior of others and make it yours – usually without realizing it.

International Society for Aesthetic Plastic Surgery: An international group of surgeons with expertise in plastic and cosmetic surgery. The group promotes the sharing of information among medical professionals and the public.

Interoceptive awareness: The ability to recognize, interpret, and respond to internal bodily sensations, such as hunger, heartbeat, or breathing.

Intimate (intimacy): A close, personal, and deeply connected relationship, often involving emotional or physical closeness.

Intuitive eating: The process of listening to the body's signals of hunger and fullness, and eating what's appealing, satisfying, and healthy.

Investing (invest, investment): to put time, money, or effort into something in order to gain something new in return.

Ironic processing: A term that describes trying to clear your mind of something, which then has the opposite effect. For example, if you tell someone to not think about chocolate, they may end up thinking about it more than they would have if you hadn't told them that.

Juice concentrate: Juice from fruit that is processed or filtered to remove water.

Juicing: Extracting liquid from fruits and vegetables to create a nutrient-rich drink.

Ketogenic (diet): A high-fat and low-carbohydrate (carb) diet. This sort of diet typically allows you to eat foods such as vegetables that grow above ground, eggs, seafood, unprocessed meats, high-fat dairy products and berries.

Labia majora: The outer folding of the vulva, part of female genitals.

Labia minora: The inner folding of the vulva, part of female genitals.

Lifestyle: The way in which a person or group of people live; this can include career, culture, social class, and interests. For example, the lifestyle of a celebrity and a school teacher may be very different.

Literacy (literate): The ability to read and write; the knowledge and understanding of a particular topic, subject, or field of study.

Macrobiotic: An approach to eating that includes whole, unprocessed foods, particularly grains, vegetables, and legumes; thought by some to promote health.

Maladaptive: not helpful; may be harmful or may make something worse.

Manipulate: To control or influence something, especially in order deceive or mislead someone.

Mayo Clinic: A world-famous, nonprofit, medical academic and research hospital, originally in Minnesota but with other locations as well, which also has an online database containing information about certain diseases and illnesses.

Media: Any form of mass communication, which includes broadcasting (such as cable television, streaming), the Internet (such as social media), and publications like newspapers (such as *The New York Times*).

Media literacy (media literate): Knowledge and understanding of the media, how and why it functions the way it does, or how to interpret information available in the media.

Meditation: A variety of different techniques aimed to train the mind to be calm.

Meme: A funny, popular image or video that's widely spread and shared online – especially on social media.

Menstrual blood: The blood and tissue of the uterine lining that passes out of the vagina during menstruation.

Menstruation (menstrual cycle, menstrual period, period, menses): The process of expelling blood and tissue of the uterine lining from the vagina; first occurs for girls during puberty and ends after menopause. Menstruation pauses temporarily when women are pregnant and loss of menses can be a signal that a pregnancy has occurred.

Mental health: Relating to a person's mental and emotional health and well-being.

Metabolism: The chemical processes that take place within the body that are essential to keep us alive.

Micronutrients: Vitamins and minerals that are needed to keep the body healthy; usually found in food.

Mindfulness: A practice of being aware of oneself and one's thoughts, feelings, physical body, and physical surroundings.

Minerals: Solid substances that occur in nature.

Misbeliefs: Misconceptions; wrong beliefs or misunderstandings, based on an error in thinking or judgment.

Motivate (motivation, motivating): To encourage someone to do something; to feel inspired or eager to do something.

Myths: Stories or explanations that are sometimes passed around by communities to explain things that are not well understood.

National Alliance for Eating Disorders: A nonprofit organization providing education, referrals, and support for people with eating disorders, as well as for their loved ones.

National Eating Disorder Association: An American nonprofit organization focused on eating-disorder prevention and treatment, as well as education regarding eating disorders, weight, and body image.

Natural supplements: A type of dietary supplement that contains one or more plant-based products. Supplements can affect health but are not regulated by the Food and Drug Administration (FDA) in the USA.

Nipple: The colored part of the middle of the breast, often pink, tan, brown, or black, where milk comes out of to feed babies following a pregnancy.

Nonprofit organization: An organization that has a goal to provide aid and services, and contribute to an important cause. These organizations don't aim to make money, and any money that they obtain through donations or fundraising is used to further their organization's goals.

Normalized: The process of making something standard, typical, or accepted within a particular context.

Nourish(ment): Food and other substances necessary for health and development.

Nutrition: The process by which our bodies get the essential components of food that are needed to support health.

Nutritional value: Related to the amount of nutrients in a particular food.

Nutritionist: A professional who studies food and nutrition and teaches people what to eat in order to have a healthy lifestyle and/or manage health problems related to illness and disease. A legal certification is not required to be considered a nutritionist.

Nutritious: Describes types of foods that are good for the body and likely to improve health.

Objectified: The act of treating a person as an object or thing, reducing them to their physical appearance or specific traits.

Obligatory: Required or compulsory, often due to rules, laws, or moral expectations.

Obsessive–compulsive disorder (OCD): A mental health condition characterized by recurring, unwanted thoughts, ideas, or sensations (obsessions) that drive a person to engage in repetitive behaviors or mental acts (compulsions) in an attempt to reduce anxiety or prevent a feared event.

Offender(s): An individual who commits a crime or breaks a law or rule.

Opioid use disorder: A problematic pattern of opioid use, leading to significant impairment or distress, such as cravings, withdrawal symptoms, and continued use despite harmful consequences.

Organic foods: Foods that are grown without the use of pesticides or other artificial substances.

Orgasm: The intense physical and emotional release that occurs at the peak of sexual arousal.

Orthorexia: An overconcern with healthy eating that can be psychologically damaging. Although it is not a clinical diagnosis, orthorexia is often described as an eating disorder.

Overweight: Above what is considered normal weight for a person's height by the medical community.

Pad (menstrual pad): An absorbent product worn inside underwear to absorb menstrual blood during a girl's or woman's period.

Paleo diet: Sometimes referred to as the caveman diet; a type of diet that's based on foods similar to what might have been eaten during the Paleolithic era (approximately 2.5 million to 10,000 years ago). A paleo diet typically includes fruits, vegetables, lean meats, fish, nuts, and seeds.

Paradox: A statement or situation that seems contradictory; two things that don't seem to go together or make sense.

Pecs (pectoral muscles): The large, flat muscles located on the chest that play a key role in upper body strength.

Pediatrician: A doctor who deals with the health and wellness of children who are ages 17 and below.

Performance goals: Goals focused on achieving a specific outcome, often measured by external standards or comparisons (for example, winning a competition).

Period: Another term for menstruation.

Period underwear: Specially designed underwear that absorbs menstrual flow; used instead of other sanitary products like pads and tampons.

Personality: The sum of traits that makes up a person's character; a person's nonphysical identity.

Pescatarian: A person who doesn't eat meat but eats fish; a type of vegetarian.

Pesticides: Chemicals used for killing bugs and other organisms that can be harmful to plants (typically plants grown for food).

Photoshop: A type of software used to alter photographs; to digitally change an image using a program such as Adobe Photoshop.

Physical activity: Any kind of movement of the body.

Physical dependency: When the body depends on a substance to continue to function, such as a drug that creates a dependency whereby discontinuing use of it would result in serious and unpleasant withdrawal symptoms.

Pornography (porn): Printed or digital imagery or text containing sexually explicit content.

Portray (portrayal): To represent or show something/someone in a specific way.

Positive body image: Favorable opinions about the body, body acceptance, respect for the body, taking care of the body, and rejecting unrealistic standards of physical beauty.

Potassium: A type of mineral found in foods that's good for the body; it helps with normal muscle growth and helps maintain water in the body.

Presentation (see also self-presentation): How a person shows themselves to the world.

Preservative: Something put into food to make it last longer and not spoil as quickly as a natural or unpreserved food.

Primping: To lightly groom or tidy up, usually the fixing of a person's hair or make-up.

Processed food: Food that's altered before people eat it. Processed foods usually have a lot of sugar, salt, and possibly fats added to them to improve their taste.

Process goals: Goals focused on the actions or behaviors needed to reach an outcome, focusing on effort, learning, or personal growth (for example, improving skills).

Project HEAL: An organization that supports people with eating disorders, especially those who are often left out of treatment (such as some minority groups).

Proportions (body proportions): How something is measured or balanced in parts, in comparison to other parts or the whole of something (for example, proportions of the eyes in comparison to the lips or the whole face).

Proprietary: Owned or controlled by a specific individual or organization; may be protected by trademarks or copyrights.

Protective filtering: Filtering out negative influences on mental health to protect oneself.

Protein: An important nutrient needed to help and protect various parts of the body including bones, muscles, cartilage, and skin.

Psychological disorders: A wide range of mental health conditions that affect mood, thinking, and behavior. Psychological disorders include eating disorders, depression, and anxiety.

Psychologist: A scientist who studies the human mind, including how people think, feel, and behave. Some psychologists provide therapy to help people talk through their problems or mental health disorders.

Puberty: The physical and hormonal changes that lead a child's body to grow into an adult body; this process is marked by the development of secondary sex characteristics (such as breasts, pubic hair, facial hair) and the ability to sexually reproduce (have babies).

Pubic hair: Body hair that appears on the genitals or in the genital regions during puberty.

Purging: Any means of ridding the body of food eaten; it can include taking medication that leads one to vomit or get diarrhea, or exercising extensively.

Quoits: A game similar to horseshoes, in which players throw metal discs at a stake or target.

Realistic (see also unrealistic): Considered to be truthful, attainable, or reasonable.

Regimen: A kind of plan that may involve a medical treatment, diet, or a general lifestyle change.

Reproductive health: Refers to physical, mental, and social well-being in all matters relating to the reproductive system, the systems that enable people to have children.

Research scientist (researcher, scientist): A person who has experience in, is considered an expert in, and studies a specific topic related to science.

Respect: To hold in high esteem or deep admiration.

Revealing: Showing more of something than usual. For example, revealing clothes show more of a person's body or a part of the body than usual.

Salicylic acid: An anti-inflammatory medication that treats acne and other skin conditions.

Salt: Also known as sodium chloride, it's used to preserve foods and make foods taste better.

Safe sex: Sexual practices that reduce the risk of transmitting sexually transmitted infections (STIs) and prevent unintended pregnancies.

Saturated fat(s): A type of fat; a less healthy fat than unsaturated fats; found in most dairy and meat products.

Science (scientific evidence): The study of the world learned by observations and experiments, usually by trained professionals (scientists).

Screen time: The amount of time spent using an electronic device, such as a phone, tablet, computer, or television.

Self-acceptance: The attitude of being comfortable with yourself – the good and the bad – without wanting to change for others' approval.

Self-care: Taking care of yourself physically, emotionally, and mentally, especially during stressful times.

Self-compassion: To be understanding, patient, and kind to yourself, especially when feeling dissatisfied with your appearance, thoughts, or behaviors.

Self-conscious(ness) (see also insecure): To feel uncomfortable about yourself; nervous, tense or shy.

Self-criticism: A person's negative view of themselves.

Self-presentation: How people present themselves to others to create a certain narrative about themselves, and how they want other people to view them.

Sexting (sext): The act of sending sexually suggestive/explicit photos or text messages to another person.

Sexual harassment: An inappropriate sexual contact that is rude and hurtful. Sexual harassment may include unwanted physical contact and assault.

Sexually transmitted infection: An infection spread through sexual contact, including vaginal, anal, or oral sex.

Shaming: To embarrass or put someone down; to make someone feel bad about a characteristic that they possess (or perhaps that they lack).

Sleep hygiene: A set of habits that promote consistent, restful sleep, such as maintaining a regular sleep schedule.

Social circle: A group of people socially connected in one form or another. For example, a small group of friends within a big friends group would both be considered social circles.

Social comparison: When a person compares themselves to other people to determine their worth in some feature, or as a way to see how they measure up against them.

Social media: A group of social websites and electronic applications (apps) that allow people to socialize, create, and share content with others within a digital, social network.

Society: A large group of people living together within a community.

Software: The digital programs and operations within an electronic device (such as cell phone, computer, or game console).

Stigmatize (stigmatizing): Judging someone as lesser because they have a particular quality or due to a circumstance; to regard someone with disapproval due to a feature such as their body size, gender, race, or religion.

Stress: A state of physical, mental, or emotional strain usually caused by struggling to deal with a difficult situation.

Stressed: To be in a state of stress.

Stretch marks: Marks on the body that typically develop due to quick gains or losses in weight; most women and men have some stretch marks.

STRIPED (Strategic Training Initiative for the Prevention of Eating Disorders): An organization at the Harvard T.H. Chan School of Public Health and Boston's Children's Hospital. STRIPED provides training to professionals interested in eating disorders prevention,

Stylist: A person who dresses or does someone's make-up and hair in a stylish, professional manner.

Sugar: A sweet-tasting nutrient that's often desired and added to a lot of different foods to improve their taste.

Suicidal (suicide, suicidal ideation): Thoughts, feelings, or behaviors related to taking one's own life, often stemming from intense emotional distress or mental health struggles.

Superfoods: Nutrient-dense foods that are considered particularly beneficial for health and well-being; some foods are regarded as "super" even though there may not be anything especially beneficial about them.

Superficial: Shallow or surface level, not deep or meaningful.

Tampons: Absorbent menstrual products inserted into the vagina to absorb menstrual flow during a woman's period.

The Body Positive: An organization that trains educators, student leaders, and mental health providers worldwide to help others develop a positive body image.

Toiletries: Products used to clean the body (hygiene products) such as soap, toothpaste, washcloths, etc.

Tummy tuck: Also known as abdominoplasty, it's a procedure that removes fat and skin from the abdomen (stomach), and repairs the abdominal muscles to create a firm, flat look to the abdomen.

US Food and Drug Administration (FDA): A national federal agency that's responsible for the safety of food, medical drugs, and cosmetic products that humans and pets consume and/or use. The USDA doesn't monitor or control products such as vitamins and supplements.

Underweight: Below normal weight for a person's height and age.

Unhygienic (see also hygiene): unclean (not clean); not taking care of your body in a proper way.

Unprocessed foods: Whole foods, foods that aren't changed before they're eaten, such as grains, fruits, and vegetables

Unrealistic: Unreasonable; very difficult or impossible to do or obtain.

Unsaturated fats: A particular kind of fat (for example, fat found in some fish) that is considered healthier than saturated fats.

Unspecified feeding or eating disorder: Eating habits that can disrupt a person's life, and can lead to drastic weight gain or weight loss. A clinical eating disorder diagnosis that applies to individuals who aren't considered to have anorexia, bulimia, or binge eating disorder.

Upward social comparison: The process of evaluating oneself in relation to others who are perceived as better off or more successful, often leading to feelings of inadequacy.

Uterus: An internal female sex organ, which is the growth site for fetuses (babies)

before they're born; contains the uterine lining that's expelled during menstruation.

Vagina (vaginal): The inner canal of the female genitals, leads to the uterus; internal organ of the female genitals.

Vegan: A person who eats a specific diet that doesn't include any meat or dairy products.

Vegetarian: A person who eats a specific diet that doesn't include meat and products made with meat (chicken, pork, fish, beef).

Vitamins: Important elements found in foods that contribute to health and are sometimes taken in pill form.

Vulnerable: Feeling unsafe, unprotected, or overly exposed.

Vulva: External organs of the female genitalia; includes the labia minora, labia majora, clitoris, and other glands and tissue.

Water retention: When fluid builds up inside the body. A common symptom is swelling in the hands and feet. Sometimes called fluid retention or edema.

Waxing: Getting rid of unwanted hair by using hot wax (usually on a person's legs, underarms, face, or pubic area).

Wegovy: A prescription medication containing semaglutide, used to help with weight loss (similar medications go by brand names including Ozempic and Mounjaro).

Weight cycling: The repeated process of losing and regaining weight, often as a result of dieting.

Weight stigma (weight bias/weight-based discrimination): When a person is viewed unfavorably or mistreated because she is overweight. For example, a person may be assumed to be lazy or addicted to junk food, just because she has a larger body.

Well-being: A person's state of comfort and health.

With All (https://withall.org/): A nonprofit organization that aims to empower adults with the tools they need to help children and young people foster a positive body image and relationship with food.

Withdrawal: Unpleasant and potentially dangerous physical and mental symptoms that occur when stopping or reducing intake of a drug when a dependency has developed for it.

World Health Organization (WHO): An organization that's focused on international public health.

Yoga: A practice that includes breath control, meditation, and performing specific bodily postures; widely practiced for health and relaxation.

Yo-yo dieting: When a person loses weight, then gains weight, and then loses weight again, usually from extreme, or inconsistent dieting.

ACKNOWLEDGEMENTS

It has been such a pleasure to revise *The Body Image Book for Girls.* I am humbled knowing that thousands of girls held the first edition of this book in their hands. This second edition is my attempt to get the most recent and best information to as many girls as I can.

I am eternally grateful to my editor, Sarah Marsh, for her support with all of the Body Image books. I had no idea, when we were first connected by colleagues, how much we would be able to accomplish together and that I would value and appreciate our relationship as much as I do. Thank you also to Lori Handelman, who edited the first edition and was essential to all the books that followed.

The support of so many people at Cambridge has been life-changing for me (and, I hope, some of the readers of these books!). I am grateful for Tim Oliver, our amazing illustrator, who helped to bring this book to life. I know that many girls will open this book to see his drawings and only then decide to read a bit. Zoe Naylor provided another fabulous cover design and artistic vision for this book. I am grateful to Anya Agha, who offered a beautiful, updated author illustration.

I am indebted to my colleagues and friends who have indulged my never-ending desire to discuss the issues I've written about in this book, proofread chapters, and repeatedly asked their children which cover design they liked best. I am especially grateful to Kristin August, Laurie Bernstein, Meghan Gillen, Oona Hanson, Jamie Dunaev Price, Jennifer Rappaport,

Amy Sepinwall, Karen Shore, Lorie Sousa, Alli Spotts-De Lazzer, and Michelle Williams for being such wonderful friends.

I am thankful for my graduate and undergraduate students and research assistants who have been an invaluable source of help and encouragement while I work on The Body Image Books. I am especially appreciative of the students who worked with me while I was revising this book: Lily Beck, Saheed Bello, Sofia Bonsignore, Lauren Judit, Clare Lindgren, Dua Malik, Stephanie Malove, Hemali Patel, Alexis Richeson, Ivelise Rodriguez-Ruiz, Swetha Samuel, Violett Springate, and Devon Teschner.

Of course, this book is for and about girls, and I am grateful to all of the girls and young women who allowed me to interview them and who offered ideas and feedback regarding book content, including Anya Agha, Charlotte Davey, Angelina Guarducci, Rhys Hals, Ahmen Hamdiyyah, Megan Hynds, Lauren Judit, Clare Lindgren, Harriet Reeves, Leah Silva, Kayla Staino, Robyn Stringer, Giulia Torcivia, Mae Waits, and Belle Zou.

And, finally, my family: my mom, my stepfather, my sisters, and the many others whom I am fortunate to regard as family; I am grateful for your support. My husband, Dan Hart, has always understood my desire to work on these books and decided to call these books The Body Image Book series before anyone else did (now if his prediction of a movie deal would come through!). I am especially thankful for my children, Charlie and Grace, who make me proud every day.

INDEX